Sheffield Hallam University
Learning and IT Services
Adsetts Centre City Campus
Sheffield S1 1WS

101 943 064 8

Sheffield Hallam University
Learning and Information Services
WITHDRAWN FROM STOCK

Sheffield Hallam University
Learning and Information Services
WITHDRAWN FROM STOCK

The Experiences of Film Location Tourists

ONE·WEEK LOAN

Mixed Sources
Product group from well-managed
forests and other controlled sources
www.fsc.org Cert no. TT-COC-2082
© 1996 Forest Stewardship Council
FSC

D0528053

ASPECTS OF TOURISM

Series Editors: Chris Cooper (*Nottingham University Business School, UK*), **C. Michael Hall** (*University of Canterbury, New Zealand*) and **Dallen J. Timothy** (*Arizona State University, USA*)

Aspects of Tourism is an innovative, multifaceted series, which comprises authoritative reference handbooks on global tourism regions, research volumes, texts and monographs. It is designed to provide readers with the latest thinking on tourism worldwide and push back the frontiers of tourism knowledge. The volumes are authoritative, readable and user-friendly, providing accessible sources for further research. Books in the series are commissioned to probe the relationship between tourism and cognate subject areas such as strategy, development, retailing, sport and environmental studies.

Full details of all the books in this series and of all our other publications can be found on http://www.channelviewpublications.com, or by writing to Channel View Publications, St Nicholas House, 31-34 High Street, Bristol BS1 2AW, UK.

ASPECTS OF TOURISM
Series Editors: Chris Cooper *(Oxford Brookes University, UK),* C. Michael Hall *(University of Canterbury, New Zealand)* and Dallen J. Timothy *(Arizona State University, USA)*

The Experiences of Film Location Tourists

Stefan Roesch

CHANNEL VIEW PUBLICATIONS
Bristol • Buffalo • Toronto

For Pennie

Library of Congress Cataloging in Publication Data
A catalog record for this book is available from the Library of Congress.
Roesch, Stefan.
The Experiences of Film Location Tourists/Stefan Roesch.
Aspects of Tourism: 42
Includes bibliographical references.
1. Tourism. 2. Motion pictures–Social aspects. I. Title.
G155.A1R583 2010
338.4'791–dc22 2009033597

British Library Cataloguing in Publication Data
A catalogue entry for this book is available from the British Library.

ISBN-13: 978-1-84541-121-3 (hbk)
ISBN-13: 978-1-84541-120-6 (pbk)

Channel View Publications
UK: St Nicholas House, 31-34 High Street, Bristol BS1 2AW, UK.
USA: UTP, 2250 Military Road, Tonawanda, NY 14150, USA.
Canada: UTP, 5201 Dufferin Street, North York, Ontario M3H 5T8, Canada.

Copyright © 2009 Stefan Roesch.

All rights reserved. No part of this work may be reproduced in any form or by any means
without permission in writing from the publisher.

The policy of Multilingual Matters/Channel View Publications is to use papers that are natural,
renewable and recyclable products, made from wood grown in sustainable forests. In the
manufacturing process of our books, and to further support our policy, preference is given to
printers that have FSC and PEFC Chain of Custody certification. The FSC and/or PEFC logos
will appear on those books where full certification has been granted to the printer concerned.

Typeset by Datapage International Ltd.
Printed and bound in Great Britain by the Cromwell Press Group.

Contents

List of Tables ix
List of Figures xi
Abbreviations xv
Acknowledgements xvii
Foreword xix
Introduction xxi

Part 1: Film Tourism – An Overview
1   Introduction 3
    Setting the Scene 4
    Tone of the Book 5
    Describing and Defining Film Tourism 6
    History of Film Tourism 8
    Forms of Film Tourism 10
    The Case Studies 12
    The Main Research Locations 14
    Industry Relevance 14

2   Destination Marketing through Film 21
    Imaging Touristic Places 21
    Branding Touristic Places 23
    Imaging Touristic Places through the Media 24
    Media Effects of Fictional Film Productions 28
    Fictional Film Productions as an Unofficial Place
    Marketing Tool 30
    Active Tourism Marketing of Film Locations 33
    Demarketing Strategies 38
    Product Development in Film Tourism 40
    Primary Tourism Effects of Film Productions 49
    Postproduction Tourism Effects 50
    Film Tourism and the Host Community 52
    Sustainability of Film Tourism 54

3   Film Locations as Touristic Places 57
    A Sense of Place 57
    The Commodification and Consumption of Places 59
    The Construction and Commodification of Touristic
    Space and Place 61

Space and Place in Film 63
The Physical Setting of Film Locations 65
Filmic Icons. 68
Film Location Nuclei. 70
Fantasy Lands, Disguised Places, Real Places 75
The Spatial Configuration of Film Locations 77
Location Access. 78
Film Locations as Temporal Constructs. 80
The Links between Film and Location: Core Precursors 86
Becoming a Classic or Cult 95
Literary Precursors 97

4   Profiling Film Location Tourists 101
    Intercepting the Film Location Tourist. 101
    Motivations of Film Location Tourists 102
    Potential Experiences of Film Location Tourists. 104
    Profiling Film Location Tourists 106
    Pre-location Visit Elements 116

Part 2: The Experiences of Film Location Tourists
5   The Spiritual Location Encounter 129
    Spectatorial and Collective Gazing 129
    Romantic Gazing. 133
    Capturing the Filmic Gaze 135
    Mental Visions. 141
    Mental Simulations 144
    Second Gazing 148
    Spatial Location Discrepancies. 151
    Temporal Location Discrepancies 157

6   The Physical Location Encounter. 159
    Shot Re-creations. 159
    Filmic Re-enactments 162
    Interaction with Site Markers 165
    Handling of Film-related Items 170
    Miniature Positioning 173
    Souvenir Collection. 174

7   The Social Location Encounter 181
    Group Interactions 181
    Guide–Participant Interactions 185
    Interactions with Outsiders 190

Part 3: Conclusion

8   Characteristics of the Film Location Encounter 197
       Preconditions for Film Location Tourism. 197
       Characteristics of Film Location Tourists 200
       The Existential Attractiveness of Film Locations 202
       The Location Encounter. 209
       Experiential Benefits of Visiting Film Locations. 212
       A Sense of a Film-imagined Place 216

9   Implications and Future Directions 220
       Implications for Tour Operators 222
       Implications for Destination Marketing Organisations. 224
       Implications for Film Commissions 228
       Further Research Opportunities. 229
       Final Remarks 231

References 234

List of Tables

1.1   The main research locations 15

2.1   Film tourism marketing guidelines 37

2.2   Economic effects of the television series *Der Bergdoktor* for the wider filming area 49

3.1   The different attraction statuses of film locations 65

3.2   *De facto* genres and textual core properties of tourism-inducing feature films 89

3.3   Box office successes of tourism-inducing feature films 93

3.4   Tourism-inducing feature films and their literary precursors 98

4.1   Number of visits to Salzburg by general *The Sound of Music* tour participants 115

4.2   Primary purpose of Salzburg visit for general *The Sound of Music* tour participants 115

4.3   Time, place and method of *The Lord of the Rings* and *The Sound of Music* location tour bookings. 124

List of Figures

2.1   VisitBritain's Online Movie Map for the feature film
      Elizabeth: The Golden Age 35

2.2   Gollum at the Weta Cave, Wellington, New Zealand. 45

3.1   Configuration of the sense of place 59

3.2   Monument Valley – a film location landscape. 66

3.3   Re-created Samurai hut from *The Last Samurai*,
      Taranaki, New Zealand 68

3.4   An example for a potential, secondary film location
      attraction nucleus – Eilean Donan Castle, Scotland,
      featured in the movie *Highlander* 73

3.5   The spatial configuration of film locations 78

3.6   The issue-attention cycle after Downs (1972). 81

3.7   Articles featuring the film production of *The Last
      Samurai* in Taranaki, North Island, New Zealand
      (in chronological order) and the application of
      Down's (1972) issue-attention cycle. 83

3.8   The film location issue-attention cycle. 85

4.1   *The Lord of the Rings* tour participants: country of
      origin ($n = 37 = 100\%$). 106

4.2   *The Lord of the Rings* tour participants: age groups
      ($n = 37 = 100\%$) 107

4.3   *The Lord of the Rings* tour participants: travel company
      (absolute numbers) 107

4.4   *The Lord of the Rings* tour participants: gender
      ($n = 37 = 100\%$) 108

4.5   *Star Wars* tour participants (2003 and 2005): country
      of origin (absolute numbers; $n = 28$) 110

4.6   *Star Wars* tour participants (2003 and 2005): age
      groups (absolute numbers; $n = 28$) 111

4.7   *Star Wars* tour participants (2003 and 2005): travel
        company (absolute numbers; $n = 28$). 112

4.8   *Star Wars* tour participants (2001, 2003, 2005):
        gender (absolute numbers; $n = 38$) 112

4.9   General *The Sound of Music* tour participants:
        country of origin. 113

4.10   General *The Sound of Music* tour participants:
        age groups 114

4.11   General *The Sound of Music* tour participants:
        gender. 114

5.1   Setting the scene for formal posing at the Gazebo. 132

5.2   Guided sight directing 136

5.3   Unguided sight recording 137

5.4   *Star Wars* tour participant engaging in a mental
        simulation. 146

6.1   Shot re-creation of Darth Maul at his lookout 162

6.2   Filmic re-enactment of Obi Wan Kenobi 164

6.3   Directional signpost on Deer Park Heights,
        Queenstown, New Zealand. 165

6.4   Photo board at the *The Last Samurai* location of the
        Samurai village in Taranaki. 167

6.5   Formal posing in front of a name connotation marker:
        'Welcome to the Hobbiton movie set' 168

6.6   Costumed posing with Sting and elven cloak at a
        Lord of the Rings film location 172

6.7   Miniature positioning in front of the Dome
        (*Star Wars* location). 174

6.8   Packing sand at a *Star Wars* film location 177

6.9   *Star Wars* souvenir obtained from locals 178

6.10   *Star Wars* film location trophies. 180

7.1   A *Lord of the Rings* guide engaged in first-hand
        interpretation 187

7.2   Outsiders at the Mos Espa film set 191

7.3   Locals selling Krayt Dragon bone fragments to the
        Star Wars tour participants 193

8.1   Elements defining the existential attractiveness of
        film locations 211

8.2   Configuration of the sense of a fictional media-
        imagined place 217

8.3   Configuration of the sense of a film-imagined place 218

9.1   Developing a film tourism strategy and
        management plan 227

Abbreviations

LOTR	*The Lord of the Rings*
LOTR I	*The Lord of the Rings – The Fellowship of the Ring*
LOTR II	*The Lord of the Rings – The Two Towers*
LOTR III	*The Lord of the Rings – The Return of the King*
SoM	*The Sound of Music*
SW	*Star Wars*
SW I	*Star Wars Episode I – The Phantom Menace*
SW II	*Star Wars Episode II – Attack of the Clones*
SW III	*Star Wars Episode III – Revenge of the Sith*
SW IV	*Star Wars Episode IV – A New Hope*
SW V	*Star Wars Episode V – The Empire Strikes Back*
SW VI	*Star Wars Episode VI – Return of the Jedi*

Acknowledgements

This book would not have come into fruition without the help of so many people that it seems almost impossible to name them all. Nevertheless, I will try my best.

Professor C. Michael Hall and Associate Professor David Duval are the two people that initially encouraged me to embark on the process of writing this book. I'd like to thank them for their input into this project and their support.

The following people played an important part in realising this book: Melissa Heath from Southern Lakes Sightseeing (formerly Wanaka Sightseeing); my dear friends John Wellington and Julie Jones, Wanaka; Seren Welch, VisitBritain; Mark, *Star Wars* tour guide, and the Pioneers Damien, Jeroen, Cristian, Samuel, Christian, Melanie, Colin, Daniel, Joeri, Uschi, Eric, Rick, Andrea, Pat, Jan, Thys and Michel; Stefan and Daniel Herzl, Salzburg Panorama Tours; Sue Radcliffe, Samurai Village Tours; Peter Tennent, Mayor of New Plymouth; Peter Avery, Film Venture Taranaki; Carol Connolly, Samurai Village Tours Guide; Dr Dominic Moran, Tourism Venture Taranaki; Henry Horne, Rings Scenic Tours; Michael Harvey, Te Papa Tongarewa; Alex Snodgrass, for taking me through *The Lord of the Rings* Weathertop location; Susan Ord, Film New Zealand for *The Lord of the Rings* film location maps; Ian Brodie, author; Adrienne Molloy, the University of Otago House in Auckland; Bruce Hopkins, aka *Gamling*, for insights into the filming of *The Lord of the Rings* from an actor's perspective; Ri Streeter, Weta Workshop Ltd. A big cheers to all of you!

Johannes Koeck from the Tyrolean Film Commission 'Cine Tirol' was essential in helping me to get my business off the ground and he gave me valuable insights into the work of an international Film Commissioner. Having his introductory lines in the book means a lot to me. I am also honoured that Richard Taylor from Weta Workshop wrote the foreword for this book. Not only is he one of the world's leading creators of filmic worlds, he also understands the needs of the fans to connect with those worlds.

I would also like to express my gratitude to Mike Grover and Elinor Robertson from Channel View Publications for enabling me to publish my research in the form of this book.

Two more people need to be especially acknowledged: my parents. They've always supported me and continue to do so. Thank you so much for everything, Gerti and Erich.

There is one person I want to thank above all others: my wife Pennie. Without her constant support, professional advice and all the hard work she put into editing this book, it would never have been realised. You are just the most wonderful person!

Foreword

It's hard to imagine that any career opportunity could be more fulfilling than that which we experienced during the making of *The Lord of the Rings*. From the challenge of the project, the creative inspiration of the literature, the wonderful actors and crew we got to work with and, ultimately, the amazing fans that have stayed in contact due to their love of the films and their desire to visit Middle Earth, have been some of the most special experiences of our career.

This book looks at why people go to places where there is nothing to see of the filming, apart from the bare landscape itself. Most interestingly, it demonstrates many parallels between *Lord of the Rings* enthusiasts and fans of other movies. They all seek out film locations in order to experience something that brings them closer to the fictional world of their beloved film. In a sense, their quest is not unlike that of those of us who work in the film industry. We also have to go on a journey in order to create those fantastical worlds.

Whether it is the snow-capped mountains of Austria as seen in *The Sound of Music*, the Tunisian desert portrayed as the planet 'Tatooine' in *Star Wars* or the transformation of the New Zealand landscape into 'Middle Earth', all these movies have one significant parallel: they all breathe with the passion of their makers and each creates a visual story that is, for their viewers, truly believable.

We certainly never anticipated the kind of following that *The Lord of the Rings* films have generated. We are, nevertheless, thrilled that they showcase New Zealand in a way that has brought so many visitors to our country and allowed them the opportunity to experience some of the magic that these lands offer and that Peter Jackson captured so beautifully in the movies.

Richard Taylor
Creative Director, Weta Workshop, New Zealand

Introduction

We are travellers. The longing for other countries, the curiosity for other cultures and the interest in other people are the impulses that drive us to explore; leaving behind the familiar in order to discover the unknown. We may travel in reality or in our thoughts and dreams, through books and, of course, through films, which lead us to the ends of the earth and beyond.

For more than 100 years, it is film, more than any other medium, which has taken us on journeys and through which the adventures and impressions we see on screen can be experienced with all the senses when we venture 'on location'. As a result, the creative and consistent link between the fields of film and tourism is, above all, an exciting, surprising and promising path, one which will have immense benefits for visitors and investors in the future.

In the author of this book, I've come to know a man who handles this topic not only with comprehensive and scientific accuracy, but also with immense personal dedication. His impressive 'experiences and wanderings' in connection with the effects of film tourism in many countries around the world, provides us with very important and valuable findings. His recommendations for the tourism industry are extremely helpful and practical suggestions, which can be further implemented.

Tirol is not only a very popular and oft visited holiday destination, it is also a much treasured film destination. Since the founding of Cine Tirol as the region's film commission, numerous film productions from Europe, the Americas and Asia have been carried out in Tirol. These moving, exciting and surprising stories have presented Tirol to a large international audience. In this way, many people have been made aware of our region or reminded to return to this 'Land in the Mountains' in order to rest and recover, or enjoy their free time and holidays – thereby bringing the circle of film tourism to a close here in the Heart of the Alps.

In this sense, Stefan Roesch invites his reader on a very interesting, informative and inspirational journey, following the trail of film productions. I urge you to take this invitation with an open and curious heart. You're bound to be amazed.

German translation:

Wir sind Reisende – die Sehnsucht nach anderen Ländern, die Neugier an anderen Kulturen, das Interesse an anderen Menschen lassen uns immer wieder aufbrechen, um das Vertraute zu verlassen und das Unbekannte zu entdecken. Wir tun es tatsächlich oder scheinbar – in unseren Gedanken und Träumen, in Büchern und vor allem in Filmen, die uns bis an die Enden der Welt führen und dabei staunen lassen.

Seit mehr als hundert Jahren sind es Filme, die wie kein anderes Medium in der Lage sind, unsere Reisen beginnen zu lassen – so können wir all die Abenteuer, Erlebnisse und Eindrücke, die wir zuvor auf der Leinwand oder auf dem Bildschirm gesehen haben, vor Ort und 'on location' mit allen Sinnen wahrnehmen.

Die kreative und konsequente Verknüpfung von Film und Tourismus ist ein überaus spannender, überraschender und Erfolg versprechender Weg, nachhaltigen Nutzen für viele Menschen und Unternehmungen zu stiften.

Im Autor dieses Buches habe ich einen Mann kennen gelernt, der dieses Thema nicht nur mit umfassender, wissenschaftlicher Genauigkeit, sondern auch mit großer, persönlicher Hingabe behandelt – seine beeindruckenden 'Erfahrungen und Erwanderungen' im Zusammenhang mit filmtouristischen Maßnahmen bzw. deren Wirkungen in vielen Ländern rund um den Erdball sind sehr wichtige und wertvolle Erkenntnisse, seine Handlungsempfehlungen sind sehr hilfreiche und machbare Vorschläge zur weiteren Umsetzung.

Tirol ist nicht nur ein sehr beliebtes und viel besuchtes Urlaubsland, sondern auch ein sehr geschätztes Filmland: seit der Gründung von Cine Tirol als regionale Filmförderung konnten zahlreiche Filmproduktionen aus Europa, Amerika und Asien nach Tirol geführt werden, die einem großen Publikum im In- und Ausland spannende, berührende, überraschende und unterhaltsame Geschichten inmitten der Tiroler Bergwelt erzählen. Viele Menschen werden auf diese Weise auf Tirol aufmerksam oder daran erinnert, in dieses 'Land im Gebirg' zurückzukehren um erholsame und/oder erlebnisreiche 'Freizeiten' zu verleben – so schließt sich ein filmtouristischer Kreis im 'Herz der Alpen'!

In diesem Sinn bin ich sicher, dass Stefan Rösch mit seinem Buch zu einer sehr interessanten, informativen und inspirierenden Reise auf den Spuren von Filmproduktionen einlädt – nehmen Sie diese Einladung mit einem freudigen und neugierigen Herzen an: Sie werden staunen!

Johannes Koeck
Cine Tirol

Part 1
Film Tourism – An Overview

Chapter 1
Introduction

I was first introduced to the lengths that film tourists are willing to go when, in 2003, I came across a news item on the internet that reported an increasing number of movie fans who were trying to access *The Lord of the Rings* (LOTR) locations in New Zealand. During the world premiere of *The Return of the King* in December 2003 in Wellington, New Zealand, around 120,000 fans lined the city's streets to catch a glimpse of the film's cast and crew. Many of those fans were overseas visitors who had travelled to New Zealand to experience something of the magic of the movie. Many of them also used this opportunity to travel up and down the country to visit the film locations and yet there was not much to be seen, as the film crew had left few traces of the filming itself.

When I started doing research on the topic, I realised that not much attention had been paid to the phenomenon of film tourism by tourism researchers, nor by the tourism industry itself. It also became clear that film tourism had its beginnings long before the success of LOTR. The fact that film productions can attract tourists to film locations had already been acknowledged in academia in the 1990s (Aden *et al.*, 1995; Riley & Van Doren, 1992; Riley, 1994; Riley *et al.*, 1998). Anecdotal media reports on tourism-inducing film events, such as *Crocodile Dundee* (1986) in Australia and *Braveheart* (1995) in Scotland, supported the researchers' arguments. In 1996, the British Tourism Association – today's VisitBritain – was the first tourism organisation that tried to capitalise on film tourism through the publication of a movie map featuring locations from various films shot in Great Britain.

Over the last 10 years, film tourism has come increasingly to the fore, both in academia and in the tourism industry. The LOTR movies have made a significant contribution to this development. Nevertheless, many aspects of this tourism niche had only been examined anecdotally, in particular aspects concerned with the actual location encounter. There is ample evidence that watching films can create strong emotional connections to the places represented on the silver screen. It is the purpose of this book to invite you to accompany film location tourists on some of their journeys in order to understand the impacts films can have on our lives.

Setting the Scene

This book is first and foremost based on my personal research and case study fieldwork conducted over a period of three years. Additional material is derived from other sources, in particular from consulting projects, personal networking and from international conferences and seminars I have participated in over the last five years.

The main aim of the book is not to be overly theoretical, but to provide practical insights into the nature of film tourism and into the behaviour and experiences of its consumers – the film location tourists themselves. Therefore, it intends to address academia as well as industry stakeholders. For a better overview, the book is divided into three parts: general aspects of film tourism, the experiences of film locations tourists, which contains the fieldwork results, and conclusion.

Chapters 1–4 are intended to introduce the reader to the realm of film-induced tourism and to provide an overview for this fascinating area of tourism. Chapter 2 deals with some of the general aspects of film tourism, including destination marketing, product development opportunities, the sustainability of film tourism and community impacts. Chapter 3 examines film locations from a geographical point of view and analyses their potential as tourist attractions. Chapter 4 attempts to profile film location tourists by drawing on fieldwork research as well as secondary sources.

Chapters 5–8 are entirely based on concrete on-site field research with film location tourists. Due to the global nature of popular media (Morley, 2000) – of which feature films are a major segment – I concentrated my fieldwork research on three global case studies that subsequently inform Chapters 5–8. These three case studies are based on research undertaken at the LOTR locations around Wanaka, New Zealand, at *Star Wars* (SW) locations in Tunisia and at *The Sound of Music* (SoM) locations in and around Salzburg, Austria. Participant observation and image-based data were utilised in order to record behavioural issues (Collier & Collier, 2004; Feighey, 2003; MacCannell, 1992; McIntosh, 1998; Palmer, 2001), while interviews were used to identify experiential aspects (Denscombe, 1998; Jordan & Gibson, 2004; Seidman, 1998). Chapters 5–7 contain the three components of the actual film location encounter, which are its spiritual, physical and social components.

Chapter 8 results in an analysis of the film location encounter with all its different facets, including the preconditions for film location tourism, characteristics of film location tourists, the existential attractiveness of film locations and how a sense of a film-imagined place is generated. The final chapter, Chapter 9, provides practical applications for the tourism industry, in particular in terms of marketing and product development opportunities.

Tone of the Book

As relationships between media, society and individuals cannot be studied in a theoretical vacuum, the implementation of an underlying paradigm is essential to ground any fieldwork (DeFleur & Ball-Rokeach, 1989). Guba (1990: 17) circumscribes a paradigm as a 'basic set of beliefs that guide action'. Movie watching is a very emotional activity (Morkham & Staiff, 2002). Therefore, it did not seem suitable to approach this research from a supposedly 'objective' positivist stance. This conviction is echoed by Beeton's (2005: 243) statement that 'quantitative data is rarely sufficient to illuminate [the film location tourists'] expectations and subsequent experiences'. As the fieldwork research informing this book explores the on-site behaviour and experiences of film location tourists, a qualitative approach has been adopted. Such an approach aims to learn 'how individuals experience and interact with their social world, [and] the meaning it has for them [...]' (Merriam, 2002: 4).

The applied disciplinary viewpoint is that of a cultural geographer. Geography is the study of places (Cresswell, 2004), or more precisely, it is concerned with 'the combination of factors that makes each individual place on the face of the earth somehow unique' (Hudman & Jackson, 1999: 1). It can therefore be said that the core of human geography deals with place construction and representation – the search for a sense of place and self in the world (Aitken & Zonn, 1994). Film and tourism are arguably placed within temporal and spatial contexts and the construction of place and meaning. In addition, geographers have undertaken research in the areas of tourism and recreation for several decades (Hall & Page, 1999). The tourism geographer sees tourism within a spatial context, observing, analysing and explaining the relationships of leisure activities and facilities in particular areas or regions (Ritchie & Goeldner, 1994). Pearce (1999: 77) notes a significant lack in tourism geography studies concentrating on a localised scale, especially tackling questions of how 'tourism is arranged in space'.

The last consideration is that the geographical research of film is a relatively new field in geography. Although cultural geographers began to research film in the mid-1980s (Burgess & Gold, 1985), as late as the mid-1990s, Aitken and Zonn (1994: 5) describe the analysis of film from a geographer's perspective as an 'embryonic research area'. Since then, a number of studies on the geography of film have been published (Cresswell & Dixon, 2002; Le Héron, 2004; Kennedy & Lukinbeal, 1997; Peckham, 2004; Rose, 1994). Cresswell and Dixon (2002) confirm that film as a medium is a distinct geographic object worthy of academic inquiry. Kennedy and Lukinbeal (1997: 47) choose to adopt a holistic approach to geographic research on film, which they refer to as transactionalism with regard to the fact that 'geographic research on film should not seek one unifying theory, but rather move into a multiplicity of scales and combine different theoretical frameworks in creative ways'. Kennedy and Lukinbeal (1997: 38) conclude that '[r]esearch on film tourism could provide real-world examples with which to examine the validity of theoretical discussions about the relationship between film images and the effects of those images, through audience behaviour, on actual places'. This statement nicely summarises the intention of this book, namely to provide both academia and tourism stakeholders with real-world examples of film tourism in order to understand the complex relationship between film and tourism.

Describing and Defining Film Tourism

Two forms of fictional screen-based media types

The two forms of fictional screen-based media types – cinema and television broadcast – are distinct in their method of representation. This can be concluded from four main points of difference. First, cinema advertises a feature film as a public event. In contrast to cinema screenings, television productions are watched in a private, more casual atmosphere. The second distinction is the differing combination of image and sound. Whilst cinema concentrates on a highly developed image to draw the audience's attention, television has to rely heavily on the medium of sound due to the relatively small nature of the screen compared to that of the cinema.

The cinematic narrative develops around a specific problem that has to be resolved at the end of the movie. Television, on the contrary, prefers the open-ended serial that is configured through a series of interconnected episodes. Consequently, the viewer has more time to develop empathy with the characters as opposed to a one-off feature film. Lastly, both types of media have different demands on the audience. While feature films address an inquisitive audience that seeks to connect with the narrative and its meaning, the television spectator, on the contrary, is a person who has passed over the responsibility to the television broadcaster: he or she glances at a world outside but is at the same time separated from the complexity of the real world (Ellis, 1992). In this book the term 'film' stands for 'feature film' as well as for television productions such as TV movies, documentaries and serials. The terms 'feature film' and 'movie' are used as equivalents.

Definitions

'Film tourism' is a specific pattern of tourism that drives visitors to see screened places during or after the production of a feature film or a television production. According to Scotland's national tourism organisation, film tourism is 'the business of attracting visitors through the portrayal of the place or a place's storylines in film, video and television' (Scottish Tourist Board, 1997: 1). For Riley *et al.* (1998: 920), 'film tourism' develops when 'people are seeking sights/sites seen on the silver screen'. In academia, the terms film tourism or film-induced tourism are used as equivalents. Tooke and Baker (1996:87) take their definition a step further. For them, film tourism is 'the effect of both cinema film and of television film on the numbers of visitors coming to the place where the filming is believed to have taken place'. Tooke and Baker's (1996) assumption that visitors to film locations do not know for sure where the filming has taken place is contested in this book. Rather, research for this book uncovered that most of these visitors are generally well informed about the filming process and the involved locations.

A further point of critique is that the above-mentioned definitions fail to address the necessity for further refinement. Both of the terms 'film tourism' and 'film-induced tourism' refer to tourists who decide to travel to a place that they have previously seen on screen. This does not necessarily imply that these tourists actually intend to seek out the precise shooting locations from the movie. If they have been influenced in their travel decision through a movie as an organic image source (Gartner, 1993) and are inspired to experience, for instance, Florence due to its exposure in *A Room with a View* (1985), then they are film tourists. On the other hand, if the film tourist to Florence intends to visit the precise locations used for shooting scenes from the movie, he or she is a 'film location tourist'. Hence, there is a clear distinction to be made between the influence of a film production to attract visitors to a portrayed place such as Florence in general, and the intention to see the precise locations used for on-location shooting. In order to clarify things, the term 'film tourism' is used as a general, generic term in this book that also encompasses the notion of 'film location tourism'.

Film locations are highly place-specific as they have specific spatial interrelationships, including distance and direction. In this book, the term 'film location' is used for '[a]ny place other than the studio where a film is in part or completely shot' (Konigsberg, 1997: 220). In other words, it refers to a place where a film or film scenes were produced in a real physical setting other than a studio (Beaver, 1994). Konigsberg continues (1997: 220): 'Sections might be added to already existing buildings, entire structures constructed, or parts of the natural terrain changed, but the film would still be considered as shot on location'.

At this point, a clear distinction has to be made between on-locations and off-locations. While on-locations are locations found in the environment, off-locations are artificial locations in film studios, film parks or other such locales. It is not within the scope of this book to deal with off-locations, a topic that is dealt with extensively in Sue Beeton's (2005) book *Film-induced Tourism*. Therefore, when using the terms 'location' and 'film location' in this book, these terms always refer to on-locations.

In all of the cited literature concerned with film tourism, the visitors seeking the portrayed places are referred to as either film-induced tourists or film tourists. It can be misleading to use these terms in such a simplified manner, as they imply that there is no distinction necessary between a person visiting a place portrayed in a film or associated with it, and a person visiting the precise location where on-location shooting took place. Hence, the term film location tourist is applied only to the latter type of visitor. The film location tourist is a person who actively seeks to visit an on-location from a feature film. In this book, the precise definition of the film location tourist is: a film location tourist, whether pre-planned or by coincidence, is a person who actively visits a precise on-location that has been used for shooting a scene or scenes that were portrayed on the cinema or television screen.

History of Film Tourism

The Mutiny on the Bounty (1935) was one of the first feature films to cause major tourism influxes to a film location (Bee, 1999). After the release of the film, Tahiti turned into a major tourist destination. The actual emergence of the phenomenon occurred over a decade later with the release of films such as *The Third Man* (1949), *Niagara* (1953), *To Catch a Thief* (1955), *Bridge on the River Kwai* (1958), *Lawrence of Arabia* (1962) and *The Sound of Music* (1965). For over 55 years, visitors have travelled to Vienna to experience the original sites from *The Third Man* (1949) (Bly, 2004). The city of Salzburg, location of the movie *The Sound of Music* (1965), still profits from around 300,000 film tourists per year. Of these, 70% state that the movie is the main reason for their visit (www.drehpunktkultur.at/txt07-11/1011.html, accessed 31 July 2008).

The evolution of mass tourism in the 1970s and 1980s, along with the emergence of blockbuster film productions, augmented the development of film tourism. Grihault (2003) argues that film tourism did not significantly take off until the release of the Hollywood blockbuster *Jaws* (1975), which served to redefine the status of the Hollywood feature film as a marketable commodity and cultural phenomenon and steer it toward 'an era of high-cost, high-tech, high-speed thrillers' (Schatz, 2003: 24). Morley and Robins (1995) dubbed this period as 'the development of a new media order', which is defined by the formation of multi-national media concerns such as Time Warner, Disney and Bertelsmann. The biggest mergers occurred in the USA when Viacom acquired the CBS Corporation for US$37.3 billion in 1999 and America Online took over Time Warner for US$165 billion (Bettig & Hall, 2003). This process of conglomeration was accompanied by significant inter-industry developments between cable television, internet and even telephone provider companies (Lewis, 2001). The consequence, especially within the movie industry, was an expanding consumer market aimed towards globalised marketing and promotion strategies. The box office successes of a number of big budget movies such as *Star Wars* (1977, 1980, 1983, 1999, 2002, 2005) and *Titanic* (1997) and television series like Dallas (1978–1991) indicated a surmounting of cultural boundaries the world over, through the generation of globally accepted images. For example, the US-American production *Godzilla* (1998), despite a very negative critical response and a poor domestic box office return of US$136 million, generated an additional US$248 million internationally, making it the fourth-biggest box office hit of all time in 1998 (Bettig & Hall, 2003). As Bettig and Hall (2003: 56) argue '[t]he simplistic dialogue and intensive use of extravagant special effects make the action-adventure movie a genre that easily transcends cultural and linguistic boundaries'.

Between the 1980s and the 1990s, the advertising budget per film rose from US$6.6 million to US$16 million, the average amount of money spent per film on production climbed from US$14.4 million in 1984 to US$29.9 million in 1994. For *Jurassic Park* (1993), the producers spent US$68 million on advertising, but this risk was rewarded when the film set a new box office record (Puttnam, 1997). Seven years later, the average production cost of a feature film rose further to US$54.8 million, with additional marketing expenditures of US$27.3 million, resulting in a total production cost of US$82.1 million per feature film (Bettig & Hall, 2003). Nowadays, six major film studios produce the lion share of all US film releases: Warner Bros. Pictures, Walt Disney Pictures, 20th Century Fox, Paramount Pictures, Universal Pictures and Columbia Pictures. All these developments have contributed to the fact that people not only 'travel further and further for leisure [but also] that these processes are mediated by a whole series of different factors', including the consumption of film (Jancovich *et al.*, 2003: 31).

Without doubt, the most well-known example of a tourism-inducing film production is the fantasy trilogy *The Lord of the Rings*, filmed in New Zealand and accompanied by an enormous media blitz. The national tourism organisation, Tourism New Zealand, estimated the combined press promotion value of LOTR I and II for New Zealand tourism at around US$41 million (Yeabsley & Duncan, 2002), thanks to the media coverage generated through the trilogy, which reached a worldwide audience of 600 million people (Tourism New Zealand, 2003b). A report estimated that the media exposure of the world premiere of the third instalment in Wellington was worth NZ$25 million in free advertising (STUFF, 2004). In the aftermath of the on-location filming, the New Zealand government and its affiliated tourism bodies branded the country as 'The Home of Middle Earth' (Piggott et al., 2004). Between 2001 and 2002, the New Zealand Government invested NZ$9 million in order to maximise the leverage effects initiated by the movie trilogy (Clark, 2001). It is not possible to quantify the influx of film tourists generated by the LOTR movies, but a few examples highlight their impact on many travel decisions. In Wellington, the exhibition *The Lord of the Rings* Motion Picture Trilogy at Te Papa Tongarewa Museum was so successful that it was toured around the world. Between 19 December 2002 and 21 April 2003, the exhibition attracted 219,539 visitors to Te Papa Tongarewa, the highest number ever achieved by a temporary exhibit hosted in the museum (Harvey, 2003). Interest in LOTR film locations still continues, with around a dozen tour operators offering location tours, ranging from half-day tours to 10-day-long itineraries. In spite of the tension between the mystification of the country as a pre-historical 'Middle Earth' and its claim to be a modern and world-leading nation of creativity in many areas (Jones & Smith, 2005), film tourism has brought millions of dollars into the country and has exposed New Zealand to the world in a fashion that can only be described as priceless.

Forms of Film Tourism

Film tourism can take on many different forms. For some it may be the sole purpose of their travels, for others it may involve the participation in an organised location tour, or the visitation of a very specific focal point from a particular scene. The different characteristics of film tourism are also defined by the type of location portrayed in the film. While some locations have long been on the tourism circuit and were well known before filming commenced, other locations are turned into attractions in their own right solely because of their exposure in the film. This is particularly the case where film crews have left sets behind at the conclusion of filming. As a consequence, what used to be an unimportant piece of land suddenly turns into a tourist attraction in its own right. This was the case with the LOTR Hobbiton film set in Matamata, New Zealand, where visitor numbers climbed from 11,500 in 2003 – when it was opened for the public – to 29,200 in 2004 and as high as 46,800 in mid-2005 (Tenbrock, 2005). Another example is the SW locations in Tunisia, where some of the film sets are the main attractions for the local jeep tour operators.

In the case of big blockbusters such as LOTR and SW, film tourism can be the sole or main travel purpose. I interviewed film location tourists who stated that they had travelled to Tunisia with the sole intention of visiting the SW film locations. Similarly, during the first few years of LOTR film location tourism, a high percentage of hard-core fans visited New Zealand solely to travel around the different film sites from the trilogy (M. Heath, 2005, personal interview). The latter example also proves that the degree of fandom of the film location tourists can alter over time. In the initial phase after a film's release, film locations are likely to attract a considerable percentage of location visitors with a very high degree of fandom. Typically, this percentage then shifts increasingly towards film location tourists with a lesser degree of fandom and to 'coincidental' location visitors. These two types of film location tourists often include their film location visit into a main holiday or general itinerary. Again, such a visit can be pre-planned or coincidental.

It is probably fair to say that most people have encountered film locations on their travels in one form or another. A tour guide might point out the fact that the travelled area or landscape features in a film; a holiday in Scotland might include a pre-planned visit to the Highlander castle (i.e. Eilean Donan Castle); a trip to New York presents us with dozens of film sites known from various films; a road trip through Iowa, USA, might lead a tourist past a sign saying 'Field of Dreams movie site'.

Some films generate so much tourism that it is profitable for private operators to create film-related products and packages. For instance, a SoM fan visiting Salzburg can book a movie package consisting of a location tour, a themed dining experience and a visit to the original von Trapp villa, nowadays a hotel and museum. In a similar fashion, a LOTR film fan travelling to Wellington can participate in an organised location tour and then go on to see the Weta Workshop museum 'Weta Cave', which exhibits original movie props and has film-related souvenirs on sale.

Film locations can be consumed in a way that only a specific focal point attracts any interest. Such a focal point can be a set piece, a plaque, a signpost or a specific view. These focal points – referred to as (visual) icons (Riley *et al.*, 1998) or markers (MacCannell, 1976) – are the centrepiece for destination marketing strategies, as their importance in the image-building process of a place or destination is paramount. The Devil's Tower Monument in Wyoming, site of the movie *Close Encounters of the Third Kind* (1977), is a focal point par excellence. It captures the very essence of the movie through its otherworldly form, it signifies the visited location as a movie site through its high recognition value and its compact form enables visitors to capture it in photographs and on video cameras.

Film location tourists may even visit locations that have nothing to do with the actual filming. For instance, the movie *Seven Years in Tibet* (1997) tells the real story of the Austrian climber Heinrich Harrer, who enters Tibet during WWII and meets the Dalai Lama. Filmed in the Andes and Tyrol, the movie portrays Tibetan landscapes that do not exist. Nevertheless, the movie sparked interest to visit Tibet (Mercille, 2005). On the other hand, for many travellers, knowing that a landscape has been the site of a film production is simply part of the romance of travelling through the area. They consume the desert of Egypt as the film site of *The English Patient* (1996) without having to see the exact camera locations. It is the experience of 'being there' that enables visitors to simulate the feel and atmosphere of the film in connection with the landscape.

Lastly, film tourism can also take place off-location. Off-location film tourism encompasses a wide variety of different film-related attractions and events, such as film studio tours, film studio theme parks, film premieres and film festivals (Beeton, 2005). Film studio tours are themed, film-related tourism packages designed for tourists willing to visit existing sets, mainly from television serials. During some of these tours, participants are given the opportunity to watch the actual filming process of the serials, such as during the Bavaria Film Town Tour in Munich, where visitors are guided around film sets in action. Film studio theme parks, on the other hand, constitute purpose-built tourist attractions. They require the use of highly developed rides, animatronics, computer animations and virtual reality and are often based around a film studio. All major studios operate such theme parks, including Warner Brothers (Movie World Gold Coast, Movie World Florida, Movie World Germany), Universal (Universal Studios Hollywood, Universal Studios Florida) and Fox (Fox Studios Sydney). Film festivals and film premieres, defined as one-off events (Beeton, 2005), also cause an off-location visitor influx. Film festivals can be global, national or regional. Global film festivals can be differentiated into three types: festivals with business agendas (Cannes, Sundance and ShoWest), festivals with geopolitical agendas (FESPACO, Havana, Sarajevo, Midnight Sun) and festivals with aesthetic agendas (Pordenone, Lone Pine and Telluride) (Turan, 2002). These events attract celebrities, the press, film buffs and, of course, thousands of fans.

The Case Studies

The empirical part of this book (Chapters 5–8) is informed by case study research on the topic of the on-site behaviour and experiences of film location tourists. A holistic, multiple and comparative case study design (Eisenhardt, 1989; Bouma, 1996; Yin, 2003) was selected as a suitable approach to the research in order to draw generalisations. The three cases on which this comparative case study design is based are as follows: the participation in a 12-day-long LOTR location tour in New Zealand, the participation in a week-long SW location tour through Tunisia and the participation in eight half-day SoM location tours in Salzburg, Austria.

The selected LOTR research tour was a full-day van tour organised by Southern Lakes Sightseeing. The company is based in Queenstown in the central South Island of New Zealand. Southern Lakes Sightseeing started as a small sightseeing tour operation in April 2001. The company director saw the potential to include a LOTR location tour in late 2002 as the area around Wanaka and Queenstown features around 15 major LOTR locations (Brodie, 2002). Between 2002 and 2005, the demand for the tour increased between 200 and 240% each year (Tenbrock, 2005). The trip lasts from 9am in the morning until 6pm in the evening and participants are transported in a van that seats eight passengers. According to the company's website, the main assets of the tour are that participants have the opportunity to visit a large number of locations, get to handle LOTR weapon replicas, have the chance to meet the author of the LOTR location guidebook, are provided with a gourmet lunch and that the tour is limited to a maximum of eight people.

The main SW locations are clustered in the USA and Tunisia, with single locations in Norway, Italy, Spain and Guatemala (Reeves, 2001). The locations in the USA are scattered throughout the state of California, with major scenes shot in Death Valley, the Buttercup Valley and Redwood State Park on the Oregon border (Reeves, 2001). In Tunisia, all the locations lie comparatively close together in the Southern half of the country (Ham & Hole, 2004). In spite of an extensive search in popular literature and on the internet, it was not possible to identify any existing, commercially organised tours to SW locations. This finding was backed up by the Tunisian Tourist Board (Tunisian National Tourist Office, 2005, via email) and a similar response was received from Gus Lopez (2005, via email), who has scouted-out and mapped many SW locations in Tunisia. The only attempt to instigate an inbound SW location tour was undertaken by UK-based Tatooine Tours, but was never realised due to a lack of demand (Beckett, 2005, via email). Because of the lack of commercial SW film location tours in Tunisia, I took part in a trip organised by a group of *Star Wars* fans in 2005. The group travelled in three four-wheel drive vehicles and had recruited local drivers. The trip took one week and included visits to around eleven major locations.

The selected SoM tour operator for this project was Salzburg Panorama Tours, based in the heart of the city of Salzburg at Mirabell Square. During the on-location shooting of the movie in 1964, the tour operator already existed, though under the name 'Kleinbusse Mirabell-platz'. The company was contracted by the SoM film producers to transport cast and crew to and from the locations and throughout the city. From 1966, the first US-American tourists wanted to see the SoM locations and Kleinbusse Mirabellplatz consequently started to conduct specialised SoM tours at the beginning of the 1970s. Since then, the tour sequence has remained unchanged, apart from some minor detours around some of the locations due to traffic restrictions (S. Herzl, 2005, personal interview). Today, the company uses busses that seat up

65 passengers and during the main summer season, two busses run two tours in the morning, departing at 9am and in the afternoon, departing at 2pm. All SoM tour guides have to complete a special training programme before conducting the tours and follow a relatively strict script that is English speaking only. Three major locations are visited along the route.

The complete fieldwork took place over a period of approximately half a year. The research methods applied were participant observation and image-based data (while participating in the actual tours) and a semi-structured interview was conducted with one informant after the conclusion of each tour.

The Main Research Locations

The large number of individual locations involved in the underlying fieldwork research for this book has made it necessary to provide the reader with an overview of these locations (Table 1.1). Whenever precise fieldwork locations are mentioned in the text, they always refer to the locations enumerated and named in this list. The list contains first the location label, the two further rows provide a description of the key scene(s) filmed at the relevant location as well as its key physical attributes. As with the LOTR and the SW locations, the abbreviations in brackets in the location label row stand for the precise parts of the LOTR trilogy and, respectively, the SW saga.

Industry Relevance

As previously mentioned, the aim of this book is not only to address academics, but also stakeholders from the film and the tourism industry. As I have worked closely with stakeholders over the last few years to develop film tourism-based products and marketing strategies, some of the insights I have gained should be made available for the reader. Wherever possible, best practice examples and industry-relevant results are incorporated into the individual chapters. The intention is to provide interested stakeholders with practical tools that they can utilise to benefit from film tourism.

In order to profit from film tourism spin-off effects, the groundwork has to be laid down in the pre-production phase. Only when the involved tourism stakeholders and the responsible production company manage to establish a good working relationship from the start, can professional ~~~~eting and product development around a film produc-
hroughout the whole production cycle, this working
be maintained and fostered in order to obtain access
:ial and sites, and in order to grant copyrights to film
ι a possible tourism-inducing effect cannot be deter-
ιtset, if the tourism-inducing measures are in place at

Table 1.1 The main research locations

	Involved scene(s)	Physical location attributes
The Lord of the Rings **locations, New Zealand**		
Flight to the Ford (LOTR I)	Elven princess Arwen Undomiel tries to escape the Ringswraiths on horseback	No site access; man-made structures in full view
Pillars of the Kings = Argonath (LOTR I)	The Fellowship paddles down the river Anduin in elven canoes and passes the mighty statues of the Pillars of the Kings	Statues were studio-made; no direct access to the scene in view; man-made structures in full view; location: River Kawarau, Central Otago
Gladden Fields (LOTR I)	King Isildur returns home with the ring after Sauron's defeat and is ambushed and killed by orcs	Small shallow river with leafy trees on both sides; location: Arrow River, Central Otago
Deer Park Heights locations (small round-shaped mountain overlooking the town of Queenstown)		
Deer Park Heights: The thorn bush (LOTR II)	Frodo, Sam and Gollum hide under the bush from the Ringwraiths in the Dead Marshes	Thorn bush is a real bush that still exists
Deer Park Heights: Éowyn and Merry conversing at the campsite (LOTR III)	Merry and Éowyn have a conversation about friendship, bravery and the upcoming battle against Sauron's armies	Precise shot re-creation possible
Deer Park Heights: Riders of Rohan campsite (LOTR III)	Eomer and two other Rohan riders trot along a tarn (= little mountain lake) and greet King Theoden of Rohan	Scene shot from a camera beam

Table 1.1 (*Continued*)

	Involved scene(s)	Physical location attributes
Deer Park Heights: The Rohan refugees around the tarn (LOTR II)	The people of Rohan on their way to the mountain fortress of Helm's Deep; in this scene they are about to surround a tarn (= small alpine lake)	Extreme camera zoom to enlarge the tarn in the scene; snow on the mountains in the background in the scene
Deer Park Heights: Legolas fires arrows (LOTR II)	Legolas fires two arrows at the oncoming wargs (= werewolf-like creatures)	Precise shot re-creation possible
Deer Park Heights: Legolas spots the wargs (LOTR II)	Legolas spots the oncoming wargs	Flip scene (180 degrees conversed)
Deer Park Heights: Aragorn's cliff (LOTR II)	Aragorn is attacked by a warg and dragged over a cliff	Real cliff is only two metres high; man-made structures in full view
Deer Park Heights: The stew scene (LOTR II)	Éowyn and Aragorn converse over a pot of stew	Possible spatial discrepancies: the colour of the tarn in the background and its water level
Deer Park Heights: The Bay of Belfalas (LOTR III)	The Corsairs of Umbar, the allies of Sauron, pillage their way into the Bay of Belfalas to join Sauron's armies	Summit of Deer Park Heights; town of Queenstown in full view; use of a wide-angle camera lens; digital alterations
Star Wars **locations**		
Obi Wan Kenobi's Hermitage (SW IV)	External shot of Obi Wan Kenobi's home on the planet Tatooine	Small fishermen's hut still in existence; building is deteriorating fast; location: island of Djerba

Table 1.1 (*Continued*)

	Involved scene(s)	*Physical location attributes*
Mos Eisley cantina (SW IV)	External shots at Mos Eisley involving Luke Skywalker, Obi Wan Kenobi and the droids R2-D2 and C-3PO	Small building with a fake entrance; building still exists, but in a very bad state; location: island of Djerba
Stormtrooper checkpoint (SW IV)	Luke Skywalker and Obi Wan Kenobi are questioned by Imperial Stormtroopers while entering the town of Mos Eisley	Area around the location has changed significantly; location is a lived-in neighbourhood on the island of Djerba
Lars Homestead interior (SW II, IV)	Several scenes from SW II and SW IV, including the introduction of Luke Skywalker to the audience in SW IV	Sidi Driss Hotel, Matmata; some of the decors used for SW II scenes were still existent in 2005
Star Wars **Canyon (canyon of Djebel Krefane near the village of Bouhlel)**		
Star Wars Canyon: Jawa Sandcrawler flats (SW IV)	Two scenes: R2-D2 is sucked into the Jawa transport vehicle and Luke Skywalker and Obi-Wan Kenobi burn the bodies of some dead Jawas	Flat sand plain; nothing of the Sandcrawler structure remains, the sight is not identifiable through any specific, physical attributes
Star Wars Canyon: Jawa Rock (SW IV)	R2-D2 is stunned by the Jawas	Precise shot re-creation possible
Star Wars Canyon: Mos Eisley lookout (SW IV)	Obi-Wan Kenobi, Luke Skywalker and the two droids R2-D2 and C-3PO overlook the area towards the spaceport of Mos Eisley	Cliff is difficult to reach and demands a short but steep climb

Table 1.1 (*Continued*)

	Involved scene(s)	Physical location attributes
Lars Homestead exterior or 'The Dome' (SW II, III, IV)	Several scenes from SW II, SW III and SW IV, including the scene where Luke discovers the destruction of his home and the murder of his relatives by Imperial Stormtroopers (SW IV) and the last scene in SW III with foster parents Owen, Beru and the infant Luke staring into the sunset, while being observed by Obi Wan Kenobi	Purpose-built set, badly deteriorated; location: chott (salt plain) between Nefta and the Algerian border
Darth Maul's lookout (SW II)	Sith Darth Maul lands his spaceship on Tatooine in the middle of the night	Contains a flip scene; location: rock feature of Ang Jemal; location was also used for *The English Patient* (1996)
Jedi duel site (SW II)	Light sabre duel between Darth Maul and Qui-Gon Jinn	No identifiable features; location: yardang field near the oasis of Touzeur
Ksar Hadada set (SW II)	Anakin repairs his pod racer on the outskirts of Mos Espa	Purpose-built set, measuring 25 by 25 metres; has meanwhile been buried by a giant sand dune; only a little corner of the roof could be seen in 2005
Mos Espa set (SW II)	Mos Espa street scenes in SW I	Gigantic purpose-built set in the middle of the desert near Touzeur, containing over two dozen buildings; deterioration is now well advanced

Table 1.1 (*Continued*)

	Involved scene(s)	Physical location attributes
Sound of Music locations		
Back view of the von Trapp house	Several scenes including Maria and the children rowing a boat along the lake towards the villa whilst Captain von Trapp, the Baroness and their mutual friend Max Dettweiler lunch on the terrace	Castle grounds are not accessible to the public and the house can only be viewed across the adjacent lake; location: Leopoldskron palace
The Gazebo	Love scenes between Lisa and Rolf and between Maria and Captain von Trapp	Purpose-built movie set piece; has been moved from its original location
Mondsee wedding church	Wedding of Captain von Trapp and Maria	Real church, situated in the small town of Mondsee
Mirabell Gardens	Several scenes within the 'Do-Re-Mi' song sequence, such as Maria and the children dancing around the Pegasus fountain and their famous performance on the steps	Mirabell Gardens; the gardens are a popular public park in the city of Salzburg

the time, film commissions and tourism stakeholders can react relatively quickly to implement them should the opportunities for film tourism arise.

Finally, this book serves as a means to make film and tourism stakeholders around the world aware of the opportunities to profit from film productions that are out there. My experience has shown that despite the increased media attention in this area, many regional film commissioners and tourism managers have not included film tourism in their strategic portfolio. This book provides insights into how this can be achieved.

Chapter 2
Destination Marketing through Film

Imaging Touristic Places

The goal of place marketing or place selling 'is to construct a new image of the place to replace either vague or negative images previously held by current or potential residents, investors and visitors' (Holcomb, 1993: 133). Packaging labels such as 'dreamscapes' illustrate this selling of place, subsequently resulting in the romanticisation of destinations, such as the Scottish Highlands or the Australian outback. Edensor (2002) refers to such product tailoring as staging and equates it to performing a drama on a stage. Such destination stages serve as a perfect vehicle for the re-imagination of particular themes or events. Place marketing and place selling are the key vehicles for this staging. There are several places in the world with a landscape similar to that of the Scottish Highlands, but there is only one such landscape combined with the myth of Loch Ness, whiskey distilleries, the Scottish clans and haunted castles. It is the combination of the landscape and its unique attachments derived from the place's culture that makes it an outstanding tourism product. Thus, the place itself is packaged around real or imagined cultural traditions and representations (Hall, 1997). The accompanying problems with packaging places are issues of authenticity versus inauthenticity (Mac-Cannell, 1973, 2001; Wang, 1999) and the on-going argument whether the place as such actually exists or not.

Destination marketing and destination image issues in tourism have been dealt with in a number of publications (Baloglu & McCleary, 1999; Buhalis, 2000; Beerli & Martín, 2004; Coshall, 2000; Crompton, 1977; Croy, 2001; Echtner & Ritchie, 1991; Fakeye & Crompton, 1991; Faulkner, 1997; Gallarza *et al.*, 2002; Gartner, 1993; Hu & Ritchie, 1993; McWilliams & Crompton, 1997; Morgan & Pritchard, 1998; Murphy *et al.*, 2000; Selby & Morgan, 1996; Sirgy & Su, 2000; Walmsley & Young, 1998). But what exactly stands behind the term 'image' and what does it include? According to Hall (2003: 105), '[i]mage is a very personal, subjective evaluation of a destination, and includes all aspects that make up an individual's knowledge of that place, whether they are true or not'. In other words, image is the discrepancy between the objective nature of the world and the subjective knowledge of it (Boulding, 1969: 423). It is determined by the conception of the individual's sense of a place.

Images can be subdivided into designative images and appraisive or evaluative images (Walmsley & Young, 1998). Designative images stand for the physicality of a place and its tangible components, whereas evaluative images are concerned with the intangible, individual perceptions and feelings of people about such a place. The image of a place itself is derived from three general agents: organic, induced and real. Organic images are generated through life experiences. In tourism, induced images are provided by the destination, whereas real images are formed by personal experience (Fakeye & Crompton, 1991; Gartner, 1993). All three agents play their role within the destination image-formation process. By being autonomous image agents, movies possess a high credibility, a medium to high market penetration and are perceived as indirect means of imaging a tourist destination.

Images serve as powerful tools not only for branding purposes, but also as essential ingredients for destination imaging of which branding is a part. A destination image is based on a trialectic of perceptions formed through 'general images associated with the destination, images specific to the destination, and person-specific travel attributes' (Hall, 2003: 105). Destination imaging is a key tool for place marketers. In times when the uniqueness of place has become somewhat amorphous, bundling the features of a destination with place-specific emotional images is a question of survival in the global market.

The process of place imaging is called image management and forms an integral part of destination marketing. Image or destination managers are responsible for imaging a place in a positive and enticing light. When promoting a destination such as the Pacific Islands, the sand of the beach has to be depicted as whiter than white, the ocean bluer than blue and the sunbathers nothing less than tanned supermodels. Image managers also have to ensure the compatibility between the created expectations and the actual provision of satisfactory experiences on location. They are key figures in making their destination stand out against other competitors 'through all forms of dissemination' (Croy, 2001: 417).

Ryglova and Turcinkova (2004) established a model of the different factors that impact on a destination image. One influential factor is autonomous media, which significantly decrease or increase the similarity of the perceived image to the reality. The advantages of utilising autonomous image agents from the subgroup of popular media, such as documentaries, television programmes or feature films, are threefold; they possess high credibility, high market penetration and they are not perceived as direct sales instruments (Gartner, 1993). Because image managers generally have no influence over autonomous image agents, they have to either maximise or minimise on the derived autonomous images and place them within their own destination marketing strategy. Once the visitor is present at the destination, the cognitive images perceived in the pre-visit stage are combined and compared with the real images on site (Croy, 2004). It is at this point that pre-visit expectations derived from induced, organic and autonomous image agents fuse with the actual visitation experience (Beerli & Martín, 2004).

Branding Touristic Places

Branding is the mechanism by which marketing communications are controlled (Blythe, 2000). It is, therefore, an integral part of the marketing process (Keller, 2002) and has become an essential tool for place marketers (Kotler & Gertner, 2002). To brand a product or a place, there needs to be 'a tangible product or service after which the organisation or owner has incorporated design and quality, and developed appropriate packaging and decided on a suitable brand name' (Bradley, 2003: 111). Following this step, the basic brand is complemented by intangible additions through advertising, which promise the potential customer the purchase of an experience, rather than a mere, tangible object of consumption. The general objectives of branding are as follows (Bradley, 2003: 111):

- to conform to the legal patent protection the inventor may have
- to guarantee quality and homogeneity in markets where buyers and producers cannot meet face to face
- to differentiate products and services in a competitive environment

The last two objectives are especially important when it comes to the branding of tourism products. Naturally, producers and consumers in the tourism market do not always meet in person over the purchase of a product. Furthermore, the increasing competition of tourist destinations on a global scale makes it essential to differentiate the products through development of a unique brand. As such, the definition of the term 'brand' is 'any combination of name, symbol or design which identifies a product or service and differentiates it from competitors' (Bradley, 2003: 112). The advantages of branded products as opposed to unbranded ones are a higher price differentiation as well as a higher product and image differentiation (Blythe, 2000). The latter advantage is mainly due to four different levels of semiotics upon which the branded product is based (Blythe, 2000: 122–123):

(1) A utilitarian sign about the practical aspects of the product, including meanings of reliability, effectiveness, fitness for purpose and so on.
(2) A commercial sign about the exchange values of the product, perhaps conveying meanings about value for money or cost-effectiveness.
(3) A socio-cultural sign about the social effects of buying (or not buying) the product, with meanings about membership of

aspirational groups or about the fitness of the product for filling social roles.

(4) A sign about the mythical values of the product. Myths are heroic stories about the product, many of which have little basis in fact.

With the branding of touristic places, the latter two semiotic signs are most essential, as their use can raise the image differentiation and quality through the improvement of the evaluative images of a destination or place. In the tourism industry, visual brand icons are deployed by logos, corporate or product colours, typefaces, layout and the incorporation of unique natural or cultural features (Moser, 2003). An illustrative example of a tourism branding strategy is that of Tourism New Zealand. Between July 1999 and February 2000, Tourism New Zealand created the brand '100% Pure New Zealand' (Morgan et al., 2002). By using this slogan, together with the brand symbol of the silver fern, the branding of New Zealand as a tourist destination created the necessary image of its uniqueness. Visual aids portraying 'typical' New Zealand tourism products serve to reinforce that image even further. These images reflect the uniqueness of New Zealand through a combination of tangible and intangible assets that the country pos-sesses. The aim of this branding strategy is to position New Zealand 'as a place and an ethos shaped by its inhabitants over time' (Warren & Thompson, 2000: 26), with its 'purified' landscape as its essence. The result of the enormous success of this country branding strategy can be seen in the 2008 Country Brand Index by FutureBrand (2008), in which New Zealand ranks top in the categories of 'authenticity', 'natural beauty', 'friendly locals' and 'desire to visit'.

Imaging Touristic Places through the Media

With the onset of postmodernity, the experience of touristic places has become a media-imagined experience of place (Schofield, 1996). These mediated experiences lead to what Giddens (1991: 5) denotes as a unitary framework of experience in respect to the basic axes of time and space. Gold and Ward (1994) even come to the pessimistic statement that the traditional sense of place is disappearing due to the post-modern promotional practices applied by the media. The deconstruc-tion of place, with its subsequent reconstruction in the destination image, characterises the post-tourism experience. This is especially the case in film tourism through 'eclectic combinations of visually stimulat-ing reconstructions of selected elements from the past and the present' (Schofield, 1996: 333).

Butler (1990) distinguishes the basic forms of oral, literary and visual media, all of which have shaped tourist visitation patterns to particular destinations. According to Butler (1990), the medium of literature mainly addresses the 'elite' tourist, whilst the visual medium appeals both to the elite and the mass tourist – by simultaneously covering the whole continuum between familiar and exotic places, with a slightly larger share within the latter area. A more detailed focus on the influence of oral and literary media as it relates to image formation would exceed the scope of this book, particularly as this phenomenon has been widely covered within the existing literature (Herbert, 2001; Howard, 2003; Ousby, 1990; Morgan & Pritchard, 1998; Robinson, 2002; Robinson & Andersen, 2002; Smith, 2003). Rather, it is the visual medium that is the focus of this book.

The influence of visual media on destination image and tourist patterns has been recognised by several authors (Croy, 2001; Hyounggon & Richardson, 2003; Morgan & Pritchard, 1998; Schofield, 1996). Visual media encompass a variety of different traditions, such as paintings, sketches, posters, postcards, brochures and the moving picture (Butler, 1990). Film-related promotion tools for tourism range from television commercials, travel documentaries on television, video or DVD, commercials before or during the screening of a feature film to fictional moving pictures such as television series, television programmes and feature films. Schofield (1996) agrees with Butler (1990) that the most powerful instrument in creating and shaping images today is arguably the visual medium, in particular television and feature films. This can be partly attributed to the fact that we place more importance on visual information sources than on written ones (Butler, 1990; Morgan & Pritchard, 1998). After all, it is a proven fact that the acquisition of human knowledge is generated through visual perception; some estimates suggest this method is as high as 90% (Dodwell, 1956).

It is thus not surprising that out of all the classic tools used in advertising, television is commonly regarded as one of the most powerful sources. The reach and frequency of television advertisements are higher than any other promotional method (Dominick, 1999). A survey of Japanese tourists revealed that for 70.1% of respondents, film and television programmes featuring the UK were the most important information source about the country, followed by works of literature (64.2%), travel guidebooks (57.7%) and tourism promotional material (47.5%) (Iwashita, 2006). Another advantage of television adverts is their ability to place the product within a realistic scenario, so that the audience is able to see the use of the product in action. Within the last two and a half decades, the tourism industry has established the use of television commercials and television documentaries to promote its products (Hanefors & Mossberg, 2001). Television documentaries influence the organic and induced image of a destination, thus providing the viewer with a pre-visit place image. The desired effect is a decisive push in the audience's travel decision-making process towards the portrayed destination or place. This process has been appropriately dubbed the 'Palin effect' (Barnett, 1005: 68); a consequence of an increase in visitor arrivals reported at some of the places visited by the *Monty Python* star Michael Palin during his journeys to exotic places for his travel documentary series. A similar phenomenon has been reported by the organisation Parks Australia, which manages the Christmas Island National Park. After the screening of a television documentary about the famous march of the island's Red Crab population, Parks Australia received a number of emails from all over the world from potential tourists interested in visiting the island (Nelson, 2005, via email). Similarly, on the isle of Mull in Scotland, the children's television series *Balamory* (2002–2005) sparked an influx of sightseeing families (Connell, 2005a, 2005b).

The portrayal of places through non-tourism-related television productions, such as fictional television films or television series, has sparked a new development in place imaging through television. With series such as *Dallas* (1978–1991), which continues to attract 400,000 visitors a year to Southfork Ranch in Texas (Dettmer, 2005), television introduced a new phenomenon – the attributes of a place could now be globally received and accepted through televised images, which resulted in the creation of a globally accepted sense of these portrayed places (Massey, 1994). The tourism industry has recognised this development and has started promoting places through television and feature film productions with various branding strategies. In some cases, the promoted places have even taken on fictional brand names. The UK leads the way when it comes to utilising film productions in order to maximise the image potential of places. The latest film tourism campaigns included marketing efforts around the film productions of *The Da Vinci Code* (2006), *Elizabeth: The Golden Age* (2007), *The Other Boleyn Girl* (2008) and *James Bond – A Quantum of Solace* (2008).

Media-based destination imaging is achieved by the implementation of two different types of media, namely official and unofficial imaging media (Bordelon & Dimanche, 2003). Official imaging media are all media that are deliberately and actively initiated by tourism marketers to promote destinations. They encompass a wide range of different media types, ranging from the more classic print media such as brochures, flyers, press articles and travel magazines to state-of-the-art homepages, promotional DVDs and television travel documentaries. Official imaging media always guarantee the active involvement of the community in the question of place construction and promotion, so that the preferred images to be transported by these media can be actively selected and packaged by the people they will directly affect. Certainly, there are often arguments within the concerned communities about how their place should be portrayed. Nevertheless, a consensus is usually achieved by the active involvement of all relevant partners within the community in order to prevent the use of negative images.

Unofficial imaging media are all sources of media that are not actively installed by tourism stakeholders to promote a place as they consist of unintended images. Such media can be novels, photographs, television commercials, websites, magazines, television programmes or feature films (Bordelon & Dimanche, 2003). Unlike official imaging media, the responsible bodies in the community usually have no influence over the images transported by these media, which can portray a place in a positive, negative or neutral way. Questions of partnership and community exclusion arise. This can be especially problematic if a place is portrayed in a negative way. In many cases, an intervention is impossible. Another difficulty is that any initiative to reduce the inflicted damage after the unofficial place exposure might already be too late.

Yet, in saying this, unofficial imaging media also have advantages over official imaging media. Unofficial imaging media can be seen as 'free advertising' for the community as it is the media agent who has to invest the money into the distribution of the medium message. In addition, unofficial imaging media are not accompanied by the 'hard-sell' factor of official media campaigns. As it is not the initial intention of an unofficial imaging medium to promote a place for tourism, the audience might be more receptive to unintended place promotion messages. Thirdly, as already mentioned, unofficial media often reach a wider target audience than official media, due to the financial constraints of most tourism bodies. Finally, unofficial media can penetrate the tourist bubble through the use of images that would otherwise be regarded as negative or detrimental. For example, the portrayal of Transylvania in Romania as the home of Dracula with its attached images of eerie castles, vampires and ghostly phenomena does not fit the model of the tourist bubble (Judd, 1999), which is exemplified by the safe, carefree environment created for the modern mass tourist in hotel resorts, leisure parks or cruise ships. Yet Bran Castle in the Carpathian Mountains, although only loosely connected to the story of Dracula, has become a very successful tourist attraction as a representational place of the Count's fictive castle as it was described in Bram Stoker's novel (Muresan & Smith, 1998). Another example can be found in the images that are associated with Scotland, where '[g]hosts, spectres, and every kind of odd entity from fairy-folk to the Loch Ness monster seem to be everywhere' (Inglis & Holmes, 2003: 51). On the Western shore of Loch Ness, the purpose-installed Loch Ness monster museum in Drumnadrochit has become a top attraction in the area by building on this popular myth.

Media Effects of Fictional Film Productions

Mass media are able to influence societies and even provoke action among them. A popular example of this phenomenon is Orson Welles' famous science-fiction radio programme *The War of the Worlds* that aired in 1938. The programme pretended to be a realistic, live coverage of an alien attack on California, which resulted in nationwide panic.

Some scholars argue that the mass media can strengthen our current values (Schramm & Roberts, 1974). Another effect is the acquisition of status through repeated appearances in the media: celebrities or politicians might gain a high social status through this process. The mass media can also cause what is dubbed 'information overload' or 'data smog'. To put this in Shenk's (1997: 11) words: 'Information, once rare and cherished like caviar, is now plentiful and taken for granted like potatoes'. As such, the average individual receives so much information in ever-shorter intervals that it 'may cause us to tune out' (Hiebert & Gibbons, 2000: 131).

In the mid-20th century, research on mass media effects focussed on the assumption that the effects of mass media operate on a personal level. Several theories and models have been developed to address this hypothesis. The agenda-setting theory proposes that the content of a media message is not able to force a public response, but that it establishes an agenda the public has to respond to. According to this theory, the gatekeepers decide on the agenda and the content of the messages. In other words, the media do not force opinions on us, but they dictate what topics we should think about (McCombs & Shaw, 1972). Several studies have found relationships between the topics covered by the media and public attitudes towards these topics (Bryant & Zillmann, 2002). The theory of agenda building suggests a reversed process whereby the members of society themselves, rather than the media, can influence and shape what kinds of messages are regarded as important (Hiebert & Gibbons, 2000). Barack Obama's 2008 Presidential election campaign was mainly driven by his popularity, which ultimately set the agenda for the media of what and how to report.

The uses-and-gratification model is concerned with the needs that people want to satisfy while using media (and non-media) sources. This model has been classified into a fourfold system, comprising the elements of cognition, diversion, social utility and withdrawal (Dominick, 1999). Diversion can be further divided into stimulation, relaxation and release of emotions. The mass media can also be used as social utilities, for instance, when a movie becomes an occasion for a social outing or when we have a conversation with friends about a media message. For some people, the mass media – particularly the visual media – help to overcome loneliness. This phenomenon is referred to as the para-social relationship. The term 'withdrawal' as used by Dominick (1999), stands for the capability of the mass media to create a buffer zone between people.

Under the premise of the uses-and-gratification model, individuals are generally in control of the consulted media (Hiebert & Gibbons, 2000). This model also addresses the problematic nature of pinning down the three objects of analysis – the nature of the influence, the influenced subjects and the results of the influence – into one coherent theory. The variability in the presentation of media messages, the responsiveness of the recipients and the interdependent connection of different forms of communication all prevent one from posing simplistic causalities. '[W]hat is presented by the mass media is highly diverse and undergoing continual alteration' (Blumer, 1969: 185). This complexity has been acknowledged by both media research camps, the pluralist as well as the radical, resulting in a widely accepted intermediate perspective on media influences. However, one major shift within this process 'was a reconceptualization of the audience as an active producer of meaning' (Curran *et al.*, 1996: 263), a revision of the theory that has provided a more satisfying means to explain why despite addressing mass audiences, the reception of messages affects individuals differently.

The applicability of the uses-and-gratification model in regard to visual media is supported by a scientific experiment that exposed a group of volunteers to a movie screening (Hasson *et al.*, 2004). Using magnetic resonance imaging (MRI), the researchers found some significant results. The brains of all subjects revealed similar brain activity patterns while watching the movie, regardless of age or gender. Another finding was that different types of shots activate different brain areas. A close-up shot of an actor showed different brain activity (area of face recognition) than a landscape shot (area of navigation). However, the researchers found regions of the activated cortex that showed no similarities between the different test persons. Their conclusion reveals that these regions might contain intrinsic stimuli that are not related to external stimuli. This result confirms the argument of Morkham and Staiff (2002) that movie watching enables the viewer to take part in an emotional, intellectual and physical experience.

According to uses-and-gratification research on the reading of visual texts for entertainment purposes, several potential pleasures have been identified: genre familiarity (Abercrombie, 1996); empathy and escapism (Dyer, 1992; Papadimitriou, 2000); cognitive satisfactions derived from problem solving, the making of inferences and of predictions about events (Abercrombie, 1996); repetition and difference (Neale, 1980); making moral and emotional judgements on the actions of characters (Knight, 1994); and sharing our experience of a filmic text within an interpretive community (Feuer, 1992). Konigsberg (1987: 144–145) assumes that enduring film genres and therefore specific types of filmic texts reflect 'universal dilemmas' and 'moral conflicts' and respond to deep, intrinsic, psychological needs.

Hyounggon and Richardson (2003) compared the influence of the place exposure of Vienna in the feature film *Before Sunrise* (1995) with a potential interest in visiting the place, with place empathy, place familiarity and with cognitive or affective images. The study results indicate a strong connection between place exposure and an interest in visiting the place, as well as between place empathy and the cognitive or affective images transported. Another conclusion is that involvement with the film characters is not attached to components of destination image or familiarity; nor is there a significant connection between the portrayal of the place and the degree of familiarity with it. The critique of this experiment is that the results are based on a single movie, which is problematic because cinematic '[p]roducts are intrinsically heterogeneous. No two films can be as alike as two hamburgers sold by a large corporation' (Cameron, 2003: 114). As such, generalisations derived from this study are difficult to justify. A further point of critique is that the researchers generated their data under experimental conditions and not in a real-life situation. Thus, the external validity is somewhat flawed. As watching a movie is an emotional action, one should be sceptical about measuring emotional components quantitatively. Nevertheless, Hyounggon and Richardson's (2003) general findings support earlier studies (Aden *et al.*, 1995; Riley & Van Doren, 1992; Riley, 1994; Riley *et al.*, 1998) that the exposure of a place in a feature film can lead to an interest in location visits.

Fictional Film Productions as an Unofficial Place Marketing Tool

Riley and Van Doren (1992) define feature films as non-marketer controlled hallmark events, a concept based on Ritchie (1984). According to Ritchie (1984: 2), hallmark events are '[m]ajor one-time or recurring events of limited duration developed to enhance the awareness, appeal and profitability of a destination in the short and long term. These events rely for their success on uniqueness, status, or timely significance to create interest and attract attention'. Hallmark events can be traditional fairs such as a World Expo, festivals such as the Carnival in Rio de Janeiro, culturally unique events such as the Oktoberfest in Munich, historical commemorations like ANZAC day commemorations at Gallipoli, major socio-political happenings such as papal visits and sporting events such as the football World Cup (Ritchie, 1984). The term 'hallmark' stands for something of an outstanding nature, both in temporal and spatial aspects, and is often combined with the term 'event'.

The term 'event' is defined as 'a one-time event staged for the purpose of celebration; a unique activity' (Sonder, 2004: 5). According to Hall (1992: 1), the primary function of events is 'to provide the host community with an opportunity to secure high prominence in the tourism market place'. In other words, events significantly promote and brand destinations (Dimanche, 2002). Unlike traditional hallmark events, feature films are regarded as non-marketer controlled, in that the tourism bodies have no control over the film production (Riley & Van Doren, 1992; Preston, 2000). Therefore, feature films are an unofficial place-marketing tool, as are novels or television productions. Apart from this distinction, feature films indicate the same attributes of Ritchie's (1984) hallmark concept: the limited duration of viewing time; awareness, appeal and profitability through special effects, famous actors and cinematographic scenery; recurring events due to re-releases on DVD and free-to-air television screenings are all factors that contribute to the so-called film exhibition cycle. Finally, movies possess uniqueness, status and timely significance because of their general, inherent and distinctive nature (Riley *et al.*, 1998).

The advantages of feature films in contrast to traditional hallmark events are numerous. They have a longer period of location exposure. They ensure a deeper identification of the viewer with the location through empathic involvement with the storyline and the characters. They can alter the autonomous images of the location through the use of film sets, props and special effects. They can penetrate different target groups through the universal medium of cinema and finally, feature films have the ability to promote a location without the targeted intention of professional advertising, as they are a passively received medium (Riley, 1994). The final point might contribute to a more emotional involvement with the location and might also send out strong impulses for its active exploration (Riley *et al.*, 1998). Watching films from the secure environment of a person's home may also attribute to the ability of films to create tourism (Riley & Van Doren, 1992).

A number of feature films have caused an influx of visitors to screened places without the support of institutional structures. In these cases, the initial location visitors are 'pioneers' who find the locations through precise research. Followers succeed through word-of-mouth propaganda. For instance, film location tourists flocked to the small bay of Wallilabou on St Vincent, where the set of Port Royal from *Pirates of the Caribbean* (2003) had been built. This influx was initiated by individuals with a high degree of fandom for the movie without any external structural input. Even today, with the set still in place, it lacks any professional promotion, yet it receives film location tourists in significant numbers (Long, via email). The same phenomenon occurred with *Field of Dreams* (1989), where the visitation to the cornfield depicted in the movie was initially purely by word-of-mouth (*The Economist*, 1999). The island of Cephalonia, featured in the movie *Captain Corelli's Mandolin* (2001), had a significant visitor influx due to its exposure in the film production, although it was not promoted as a film location by the responsible destination marketing organisation (Hudson & Ritchie, 2006b). This can also be the case with television series, as examples such as the German series *Der Bergdoktor* (2007–ongoing) have proven, whereby film fans go out of their way to find even the remotest locations (personal on-site observation, May 2008). These and other examples clearly contradict the assumption of Cousins and Andereck (1993), who suggest that in order to attract film location tourists, the promotion of film locations must be run by a professional destination marketer.

Even supposedly negative images can contribute to the attractiveness of a destination. Bordelon and Dimanche (2003) evaluated a sample of 12 feature films of the horror, mystery and thriller genre produced in New Orleans. In spite of the negative associations between some of these images and idealised images of New Orleans as a tourist destination, the authors stress the importance of these unofficial media images, as they contribute to the somewhat mystic and supernatural character of the city and thus to its status as an important attraction. Another example is the novel and subsequent feature film *The Beach* (2000), filmed on location at Maya Bay on the small island of Phi Phi Le in Thailand. Although both the novel and the film portray the negative impact of backpacker culture on the island, turning it from a paradise into a nightmare scenario, Phi Phi Le has, nevertheless, attracted significant numbers of backpackers (Higgins-Desbiolles, 2001). Boat operators still offer tours to the film site, which has long since been mythologized amongst backpackers (Law *et al.*, 2007).

It was in the period of the late 1980s to early 1990s when the tourism industry first began to recognise the ability of feature films to generate tourism. Nowadays, it has become the ultimate goal for tourism marketers to place their product (i.e. destination) within a film, as there are numerous advantages of film destination placement over other means of product placement. These comprise the association of the destination with an emotional component, uninterrupted concentration on the displayed product and the elimination of competition. In addition, destination placements in television serials provide recurrent exposure of the displayed destination or locations and prevent the audience from switching away from this type of product placement, as it is not perceived as a hard-selling advertisement (Vialkowitsch, 2005). Argu-ably, the ultimate type of destination placement is any placement that connects the fictional places with the real names of the displayed locations or destination. The Tyrolean Tourism Organisation even managed to sneak their corporate logo into a lengthy scene in the German television series *Der Bergdoktor* despite the responsible film production company being wary about any corporate placement.

Active Tourism Marketing of Film Locations

Touristic place marketing opportunities are provided throughout the film exhibition cycle with its various windows of exhibition, which normally lasts up to 36 months (Grihault, 2003). In the case of a movie series such as *Star Wars* (SW) or *The Lord of the Rings* (LOTR), this postproduction cycle can last up to six years or more.

The first window of active tourism marketing is the possibility of a joint promotion between the film and the tourism industry. This opportunity occurs during the location filming phase. Suitable tourism promotion tools in this phase are press conferences, press reports about the filming or deliberate statements by cast and crew about the community hosting the on-location shooting.

During the movie premiere, the hosting community can organise after-parties, special press screenings and the distribution of leaflets and brochures. An additional marketing opportunity during this exhibition window and throughout the cinema release is the screening of place promotion commercials before the start of the movie. This was utilised during the screening of *Rob Roy* (1995), where the national Scottish tourism organisation showed an image trailer in participating cinemas, containing typical place images of the Scottish Highlands (Beeton, 2001a). The screening of tourism commercials in the cinema has also been practised with movies when their storyline takes place at an identifiable location, but had in fact been filmed elsewhere. An example would be the movie *Troy* (2004). Filmed in Mexico, Malta and Spain, the Turkish Tourism Ministry screened one-minute-long commercials in European cinemas prior to the film, to promote Turkey and particularly the region around the antique city of Troy as well as its remains (Seibert, 2004).

A third marketing opportunity associated with the actual cinema screening is to insert location information into the end-credit acknowledgments, although this in itself can involve difficult negotiations with the film company, not to mention the fact that the audience usually leaves the cinema without paying particular attention to end-credits. New release windows after the actual movie screening, such as DVD and free-to-air television releases, encourage new place imaging strategies such as the inclusion of location features on the DVD, as well as television travel documentaries and television commercials highlighting the film locations.

Alternative marketing opportunities, which can be implemented at any stage of the film exhibition cycle, are the design of special home-pages or homepage features, the production of movie maps and the publication of location guidebooks. The first official movie map was that of the former British Tourist Authority (BTA), now operating under the name VisitBritain. This map was published in the early 1990s and was followed by two re-prints (Beeton, 2005: 62).

Busby and Klug (2001) conducted a small interception visitor survey in the Notting Hill district of London, where a movie with the same title was produced in the mid-1990s. Their goal was to identify the extent of visitor awareness of one of the BTA movie maps. By using the next-to-pass technique, the researchers conducted 150 face-to-face interviews at Portobello Market in Notting Hill during a market day. The results of the survey indicate that the majority of the respondents (92%) had no knowledge of the movie map before visiting the district of Notting Hill; 7% recognised the map from having seen it in advertisements; 1% did not answer the question; and only 2% of the respondents stated that they had consulted the online version of the movie map. Busby and Klug (2001: 326) conclude that although only a small percentage of the Notting Hill visitors had pre-visit knowledge of the BTA movie map, the movie map campaign raised the awareness for some of the places represented.

Newer movie map instalments have focused on movies such as the *Harry Potter* films: *Harry Potter and the Philosopher's Stone* (2001) and *Harry Potter and the Chamber of Secrets* (2002). The *Harry Potter* movie map displayed eight film locations – including the imaginary Platform $9\frac{3}{4}$ at London's Kings Cross Station, Alnwick Castle, Lacock Abbey, Gloucester Cathedral, which was used for the portrayal of Hogwarts School of Witchcraft and Wizardry, the London Zoo and the village of Goathland, which served as Hogsmeade Station. The map also promoted 32 additional tourist attractions that linked to seven themes around mysti-cism and magic (Grihault, 2003; Tourism New Zealand, 2004). After the release of the second *Harry Potter* film, VisitBritain conducted a visitor survey at the promoted locations (Grihault, 2003). The result was that only some of the locations featured in the movie map reported visitor increases; this particularly affected smaller attractions, which experienced a notice-able boost in new visitor influxes. Established attractions such as the London Zoo and Gloucester Cathedral reported a drop in visitor attendance. Grihault (2003) concludes that VisitBritain's *Harry Potter* movie map campaign was limited in terms of media coverage and other promotion measures. He attributes this problem to the strict copyright laws the production company, Warner Brothers, imposed on VisitBritain. The latest VisitBritain movie map projects were based on the movies *The Da Vinci Code* (2006), *Elizabeth: The Golden Age* (2007) (Figure 2.1) and *The Other Boleyn Girl* (2008), all of which were purely online-based. With their

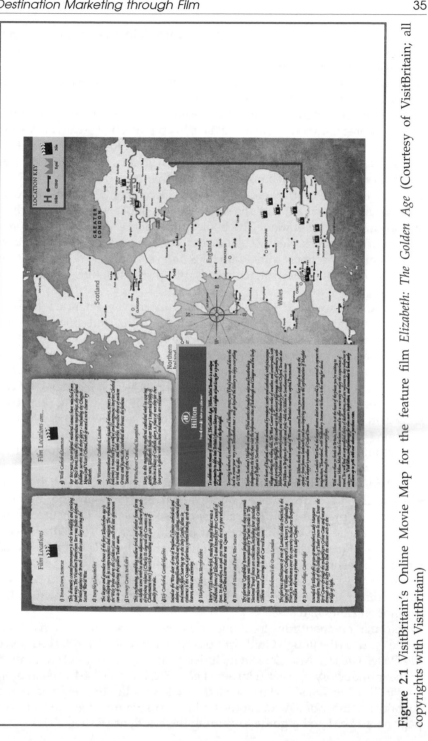

Figure 2.1 VisitBritain's Online Movie Map for the feature film *Elizabeth: The Golden Age* (Courtesy of VisitBritain; all copyrights with VisitBritain)

most recent movie maps instalments, VisitBritain has focused on new means of distribution by placing the maps on a specific film tourism subpage within their website. In addition, they secured extensive copyrights for wider film tourism campaigns of which the movie maps were an important marketing centrepiece.

Location guidebooks are another essential instrument for promoting film locations. Location guidebooks have been published on a wide variety of films, among them *Perfect Strangers* (2003), *Whale Rider* (2002), *Ned Kelly* (2003), *The Sound of Music* (SoM) (1965) and various *James Bond* movies. The LOTR location guidebook is probably the most well known (Brodie, 2002), selling over 290,000 copies between December 2002 and May 2006 (Brodie, 2006, via email) and has since been re-published as a travel diary and as an extended edition. The book guides its readers to the different film locations across New Zealand and contains over 50 film locations with detailed directions, some with GPS data, comments and photos from cast and crew and the contact details of specialised film location tour operators.

In addition to the cited opportunities to convey intended touristic images within the various windows of the film exhibition cycle, the tourism industry can provide film location experiences via infrastructural means. For instance, the instalment of on-location markers such as signposts, information boards and plaques can help tourists identify otherwise unrecognisable or meaningless places as film locations. Private enterprises can start up specialised film location tours, as has been shown in New Zealand where businesses offer a wide variety of LOTR location tours. Table 2.1 summarises the different film tourism marketing opportunities available to marketers during the various windows of the film exhibition cycle.

Besides the implementation of intended touristic images within the film exhibition cycle, independent media attention around the film production, premiere and release can also generate exposure of the screened places. In Australia, the feature films *Mad Max* (1980), *The Man from Snowy River* (1982), *Mad Max II* (1985) and *Crocodile Dundee II* (1988) created an estimated US$50 million of publicity for every advertising dollar in the USA alone (Riley & Van Doren, 1992). This number is of such a dimension that no tourist organisation could afford an equivalent promotion campaign.

Information about film locations has even entered conventional travel guides such as the Rough Guide or Lonely Planet series. The 2004 edition of *The Rough Guide to New Zealand* includes a full page about LOTR locations in the introductory chapter (Harper *et al.*, 2002: ix). The 2004 version of the *Lonely Planet to Tunisia* (Ham & Hole, 2004) was the first ever edition to contain a number of SW locations. Fodor's Austria travel guide features a page about SoM and a guide to finding the locations (Fisher, 2001).

Table 2.1 Film tourism marketing guidelines

Windows of exhibition	*Steps in film tourism marketing*
Before location filming	• Copyright negotiations with the production company about the use of image material for tourism marketing purposes • Access to the script or storyline • Familiarisation with the planned film locations
During location filming	• Take photos of the location shooting • Production of a documentary about the location shooting (= making of) • Press releases about the location shooting • Commentaries from actors/director on the location shooting with a direct connection to the destination • Press conference on set • Web blogs reporting from the film sites
After location filming	• Ongoing press releases • Production of merchandise with a film connection • Distribution of destination marketing material (flyer, press kits, special website features) • Installation of signposts, plaques, etc. at the locations
Cinema release	• Cinema advertisements with a concrete reference to the destination • Competitions featuring on the websites of the involved tourism stakeholders • Mentioning the destination/locations in the end-credit acknowledgments • Display of destination marketing brochures in participating cinemas • Integration of film tourism marketing material in the marketing mix of the film distribution company • Target group-specific destination advertisements in magazines and fanzines • Local film premiere at the destination • Special screenings and previews for the public at the relevant destination • Organisation of a press tour with journalists to the destination
Before the film's release on DVD	• Negotiations with the film distributor regarding the integration of film tourism marketing material (DVD-inlays, competitions, destination features on the DVD)

Table 2.1 (*Continued*)

Windows of exhibition	Steps in film tourism marketing
Before first public television screening	• Special premiere at the destination • Production of a travel show to the destination for television • Organisation of a press tour with journalists to the destination
First public television screening	• Screening of the television travel show about the destination • Television advertisements for the destination/the locations

Despite all these active marketing opportunities for the tourism industry, using movies for place promotion can also be counterproductive: '[I]f the tourism images conflict with other popular images that are more influential, such dissonance will at the very least confuse, if not put off, potential tourists' (Beeton, 2004: 133). The responsible image managers have to ensure that proper demarketing tools are in place in case of counterproductive developments.

Demarketing Strategies

Some places associated with films subtly nurture elements of dark tourism (Bordelon & Dimanche, 2003). The town of Burkittsville in Maryland in which scenes from the cult horror movie *The Blair Witch Project* (1999) were filmed, was overrun with film enthusiasts after the screening. The tourists purchased rocks from residents' backyards and took dirt from the local cemetery (Dishneau, 1999). Places that usually represent sites of atrocity, such as graves, massacre or accident sites, as well as places associated with war or 'dark' movies have been labelled 'black spots' (Rojek, 1993). For instance, a Paris tourist agency designed a tour following the final route of Diana, the Princess of Wales, through the city to the tunnel where she and her party crashed (Lennon & Foley, 2000). Smith (2003: 24) points out that many black spots have been exposed in feature films, including *Schindler's List* (1993), *Saving Private Ryan* (1998) and *The Bridge on the River Kwai* (1957). Evidently, the screening of the movie *Schindler's List* initiated visitations to concentration camps in Germany and Poland (McKercher & du Cros, 2002). River cruise operators in Thailand offer tours to the main attractions from the war movie *The Bridge on the River Kwai* (1957) and participants have the chance to see the Death Railway, the famous bridge itself and Hellfire Pass. For Baudrillard (1994: 59), war films such as Francis Ford Coppola's *Apocalypse Now* (1979) blur reality in an extreme way: 'The war became film, the film becomes war, the two are joined by their common haemorrhage into technology'. Smith (2003) assumes that the film tourists often visit dark spot locations not because of their historic interest in them, but because of their portrayal in movies. In spite of the aforementioned cases, negative filmic images can decrease the touristic value of a place through its representation as part of a negative plotline, through dark images and other perceived deterrents. This can result in a loss of touristic appeal for the portrayed place or destination. Image managers are requested to counteract such a scenario by implementing demarketing strategies.

A different scenario of urgent demarketing unfolds where the local community cannot cope with the influx of film location tourists (Beeton, 2005). This is especially the case in rural communities and areas with insufficient infrastructures in place. A variety of problems are likely to occur in such situations, including an increase in car crime, vandalism, traffic congestion, overcrowding, an abundance of new, tacky souvenir shops, lack of privacy for residents, lack of public toilets, increased property prices and rents, wear and tear and souvenir hunting (Beeton, 2001a, 2001b; Künzler, 1999; Mordue, 1999; O'Connor, 2002; Riley *et al.*, 1998; Sciolino, 2003; Tooke & Baker, 1996; Yeabsley & Duncan, 2002).

Another problematic issue can be the exploitation of the tourists themselves. False expectations can be created through the violation of place authenticity, the selling of fake or overpriced memorabilia, the general neglect of the toured film locations and overpriced tourist facilities. As Beeton (2002) suggests, a combination between pre-visit demarketing strategies and on-site visitor management can be helpful in order to decrease some of the potentially negative effects of film tourism. Beeton (2005) identifies social, economical and environmental demarketing potential through increased security, the training and accreditation of local guides, road restrictions, the creation of external park-and-ride car parks, the creation of film-related experiences and attractions to ensure a high-yield tourist segment, improved signage, spatial visitor restrictions and the provision of basic infrastructure such as toilets and rubbish bins.

Beeton (2002, 2005) applies the identified demarketing possibilities to an integrated model of demarketing and visitor management within a three-stage process. During and after the release of the medium, she proposes a low-key demarketing destination promotion on the part of the responsible tourist manager. Strong demarketing is suggested during the information-gathering phase by potential visitors. Visitor management finally comes into play with the actual site visits. As Garrod *et al.* (2002) show, neither the type nor the severity of a negative impact can be related to a specific type of visitor attraction. For the tourists themselves, visitor management is simply a basic precondition for a properly managed attraction.

There is an evident lack of research on how destination image changes over time (Gallarza *et al.*, 2002). Long-term postproduction effects of image destination via a feature film can occur (Croy & Walker, 2001), but this notion has not yet been modelled. Arguably, a positive destination image plays an essential role in the travel decision process, although its creation can be time consuming and arduous work. On the other hand, once a negative image has been established, it is much more time and labour intensive to turn it back into a positive image.

Product Development in Film Tourism

The following overview of the possibilities of film-related tourism product development is by no means exhaustive. Its intention is simply to provide the reader with a general idea of how film productions can be utilised to establish new attractions within a destination or how already established attractions can be newly invented by emphasising their link to a film.

Basic infrastructure

The most basic means to signify a place as a film location is to install infrastructure such as signposts, plaques or photo boards. The instalment of such signifiers serves as a link between the two spatial constructs – the real place and the fictional place. As one can imagine, taking a photo of a landscape with a signifier in the foreground renders it as authentic to others. The presence of signifiers is particularly important where no identifiable features in the landscape can be used to convince oneself of the authenticity of the place as a film location. Position and content of these signifiers are essential aspects of the film location experience and they need to be accurate and clearly defined. Misplaced signposts, overloaded photo boards or insufficient information certainly do not add to the experience; on the contrary, these signifiers might even have a detrimental effect on the actual location encounter. On the other hand, if the position of the signifier matches with the actual location and its content conveys the emotional component of the place, basic infrastructure such as signposts and photo boards can contribute to the depth of the location experience.

Original film sets and set pieces

In most cases, film production companies remove film sets at the conclusion of location filming. The companies fear copyright breaches by people taking photos of sets before the premiere of the production. In addition, when filming takes place on public land, authorities often issue filming permissions with the condition that in the interest of environmental protection, all set pieces must be removed after the location shooting is finished. Finally, film sets are not built to last and corrode and erode after a relatively short period of time.

There are a few examples around the world where film crews have left entire sets or set pieces behind. One of the most well-known examples is probably the aforementioned LOTR Hobbiton set located at Matamata in the North Island of New Zealand. Built on private farmland, the production company started to dismantle the set when heavy rain stopped them from completing the removal. For some unknown reason, the workers never returned and the set turned into a tourist attraction. This is even more astounding given the fact that all that is left to see is the landscape and a few barren, wooden-clad Hobbit holes. The farmer has been trying for years to redecorate Hobbiton to make it look more like it appears in the movie, but has so far failed to convince the production company to give him the necessary permission.

In Tunisia, the film production company Lucasfilm was persuaded by the Tunisian Tourist Board to leave behind the sets that were used during the location shooting for *The Phantom Menace* (1999), *Attack of the Clones* (2002) and *Revenge of the Sith* (2005) (Tunisian National Tourist Office, 2005, via email). Their intention was to use the sets as future focal points for tourists in order to increase visitation to the general area around the film locations. In spite of these efforts, the Tunisian tourism industry has completely neglected the marketing potential of these sets, which are only visited by a handful of local tour operators offering half-day trips to some of them. Some of the sets are in such a bad state that they will soon disappear under the desert sand.

The world-famous glass pavilion or Gazebo from the film *The Sound of Music* still exists in its original form, although it has been relocated. In 1991, the City Council of Salzburg moved the glass pavilion from its original grounds at Leopoldskron palace to the Hellbrunn palace due to an increasing number of fans trespassing on the property in order to see the pavilion. Nowadays, it is one of the highlights of any SoM location tour.

As long as a few basic rules are observed, the existence of original sets or set pieces on location can significantly contribute to the attractiveness of a film location. It is important for the tourism stakeholders involved to negotiate the rights situation with the film production company from a very early stage. The goal should be to achieve consent to maintain the set with the proviso that it remains inaccessible to the public until the film is screened. It must also be determined from the outset who will be responsible for maintaining the set or set pieces and who will undertake the necessary renovations or even material replacements of the set. Certainly, if we talk about film location tourism on public land, one also has to look at the question of who will profit most from the potential visitations. Film location tourism on public land generates problems, especially in protected nature reserves. The New Zealand Department of Conservation supports location filming even in relatively fragile areas as long as everything is returned to its original state after the wrap-up. For this reason, several LOTR sets had to be torn down despite the protests of fans the world over.

Reconstructed film sets and set pieces

Even after the removal of film sets and set pieces, tourism stake-holders and interested landowners have the opportunity to establish a film tourism product. The reconstruction of film sets or set pieces can be a means of creating such a product by enhancing the attractiveness of a film location. The potential danger is that visitors may be disappointed as reconstructed sets are clearly not the original sets. With this in mind, the film tourism stakeholder has to show a great deal of sensibility towards the issue. An exemplary reconstruction can be seen on New Zealand's North Island near Te Uruti, where parts of the movie *The Last Samurai* (2003) were filmed. A piece of farmland was used to build the Samurai Village set, which contained around a dozen buildings and various set pieces such as a well, a wooden arch and fake trees. After the conclusion of the location filming, the farmer managed to convince the film production company to leave a few set pieces behind, the well and the arch amongst them. Although the buildings themselves were taken down, the farmer re-created one of the village huts in the exact same spot as the original hut. In this case, the mixture between re-created hut and original set pieces is combined to create a formula that enables the visitor to experience the look of the set and the location both through visual signifiers as well as through authenticity.

A very popular example of a reconstructed film location signifier can be found in the Harry Potter movies. At London's King's Cross Station, from which the fictional 'Hogwarts Express' departs platform $9\frac{3}{4}$ in the *Harry Potter* books and films, station authorities put up a sign between platforms 9 and 10 as there was an ever-increasing demand from fans to be able to have 'visual proof' of the fictional platform (Welch, 2008, personal communication). In keeping with the famous movie scenes in which Harry and his friends enter the imaginary platform $9\frac{3}{4}$ through the wall, a station trolley is wedged into the brickwork, as if in the process of disappearing through it. The site has long since become an iconic spot for tourists with both the sign and the trolley being essential signifiers for the authenticity of this place (Iwashita, 2006). One simply has to enter the keyword 'platform $9\frac{3}{4}$' into a web-based image search engine in order to get a sense of the location's popularity.

Established tourist attractions with a film connection

It is the goal of film production companies to find locations that are easily accessible, close to production facilities and require as little physical and digital enhancement as possible. Consequently, many locations contain the necessary features from the outset, whether natural or man-made, which are required for location shooting. These features may already be popular tourist attractions, for example an old castle or a specific natural feature; alternatively, places used for location filming can be turned into new attractions.

The Swiss cable car 'Schilthornbahn' featured in the James Bond movie *On Her Majesty's Secret Service* (1968) after a location scout deemed the cable car, with its high alpine mountain station, the perfect location for the film. An additional asset was that the station was still under construction. Schilthornbahn Ltd gave the film production company the opportunity to design the interior in keeping with the 'look' of the film. Both sides agreed that the film production company would finance the interior construction works and hand over to Schilthornbahn Ltd on completion of filming (www.schilthorn.ch/?uid=49, accessed 12 August 2008). The negotiations turned out to be a significant marketing tool for the film-friendly cable car operator: the movie was a success and the Schilthornbahn experienced a considerable increase in visitation. The operator went as far as adding the fictional name of the mountain station 'Piz Buin' in the Bond film to the corporate logo. The name is also emblazoned on each individual cable car.

The Scottish castle of Eilean Donan, situated on the West coast of Scotland, is a prime example of how long film tourism can last in connection with an established tourist attraction. In 1985, the castle was extensively used as one of the main locations for the movie *Highlander*; it still attracts movie fans today who explicitly ask for stories about the location shooting and look for film memorabilia (Stenson, 2008, via email).

Established attractions with a minor role in the tourism circuit can experience a significant boost in visitors, as the example of the book and subsequent film *The Da Vinci Code* (2006) illustrates. The relatively unknown Rosslyn Chapel in Scotland and the church Église Saint-Sulpice in Paris were overrun by fans after the release of the book, followed by a new surge in visitor numbers after the film's release in 2006 (Bloss, 2007; Olsberg/SPI, 2007).

Film museums

Film museums are generally institutions that deal with the history and technological development of film. There are very few film museums with a specific focus on generating film tourism. Considerable challenges have to be tackled before being able to realise such a museum. Apart from sourcing a suitable exhibition space with all its involved costs, the initiators must get hold of original exhibits and various memorabilia from the film(s), the location shoot and from the involved cast and crew. The Italian town of Brescello has managed to establish such a museum, which is centred on the popular Italian feature films *Don Camillo and Peppone* released in the 1950s and 1960s. The museum is fairly small, yet it displays props, small set pieces and original pictures from the shooting and also contains a souvenir shop. Two statues in front of the museum depict the two films' main characters of *Don Camillo* and *Peppone*.

A non-profit organisation in the city of Salzburg has long since planned to establish a SoM museum in the city centre next to the picturesque Mirabell Gardens, which are a prominent feature in the film. The organisers plan to exhibit objects from both the real von Trapp family as well as from the film and anticipate 130,000 visitors per year (www.drehpunktkultur.at/txt07-11/1011.html, accessed 26 May 2008). The establishment of this museum would be a complement to participation in a film location tour or a visit to the von Trapp villa and could encourage film tourists to stay a little longer in the city.

In 2006, the Swedish town of Ystad opened a combined film museum called 'Cinetek' and a film location tour around the television crime series *Wallander* (2005, 2008), which is based on Henning Mankell's popular book series. According to the museum's curator, the target groups are 'DINKS', 'Wealthy Healthy Older People' and 'Active Families'. Most visitors come from Scandinavian countries and Germany, which are also the main target audiences of the television series. The average age of visitors is between 30 and 45, but there are also families with children who mainly want to visit the museum in order to get a glimpse of how films are made. There is also a walking tour that visits around 20 film locations (Maris, 2009, via email).

Film-specific exhibitions

In 1991, Planet Hollywood was the first commercial venture to base a business concept around the display of film props. Planet Hollywood entered the themed restaurant market using Hollywood stars Arnold Schwarzenegger, Sylvester Stallone, Bruce Willis and Demi Moore as promotional draw cards. The concept behind Planet Hollywood was to combine a dining experience with the exhibition of original props from various Hollywood blockbuster movies. As the quality of the food was less a priority than the creation of a showbiz atmosphere of glitz and glamour, the restaurant chain ran into trouble in the late 1990s (Cooke, 2000). Profitability continually decreased, eventually resulting in the closure of over two thirds of the restaurants between the late 1990s and 2009. From 80 restaurants in its peak phase, only 18 Planet Hollywood restaurants are operating at present (www.planethollywood.com/restaurants.htm, accessed 28 May 2009).

A very successful example of a film-specific exhibition was the '*The Lord of the Rings* Motion Picture Trilogy' touring exhibition, which originated at Te Papa Tongarewa museum in Wellington, New Zealand. The exhibition containing various props from the movie trilogy set a new visitor record for the museum with 219,539 visitors between December 2002 and April 2003 (Harvey, 2003). This enormous success convinced the curators to tour the show. So far, it has travelled to various world cities such as London, Singapore, Boston, Melbourne, Sydney and Berlin. The exhibition proved so popular that it was shown at Te Papa Tongarewa again in 2006. A total of 34% of all adult visitors stated that visiting the LOTR exhibition was the main reason for going to the museum; 58% of the visitors were aged between 20 and 34 years and 64% of the visitors were female (Harvey, 2006). In 2008, some LOTR props found a permanent home back in Wellington where the special effects company Weta Workshop have created the Weta Cave (Figure 2.2), a small memorabilia and exhibition space for film fans, based around some of the most popular movies filmed in New Zealand, such as *The Lord of the Rings* (2001–2003), *King Kong* (2005), *The Lion, the Witch and the Wardrobe* (2005) and *Black Sheep* (2006). According to Weta Workshop

Figure 2.2 Gollum at the Weta Cave, Wellington, New Zealand
Source: Author.

Manager Tim Launder, the idea for Weta Cave was born out of the demand of numerous film fans who wanted to be able to connect with the films at the very site where they had been created (Launder, 2008, personal communication). In 2009, Weta Cave played host to around 400 visitors each weekend, the majority of whom were participants of organised LOTR location tours through the Wellington area (Weta Workshop, 2009).

In 2009, the *James Bond* exhibition 'For Your Eyes Only' was hosted by the Imperial War Museum in London. The exhibition featured original movie items, many shown for the first time, including a selection of annotated Bond manuscripts, the 'blood-splattered' shirt worn by Daniel Craig in *Casino Royale* (2006), Rosa Klebb's flick-knife shoes from the film *From Russia With Love* (1963) and Halle Berry's bikini from *Die Another Day* (2002). Another Bond exhibition was recently staged by the Austrian city of Bregenz in the summer of 2008, when scenes for the Bond movie *Quantum of Solace* (2008) were being filmed in the area. As thousands of onlookers were expected to flock to the set, the city council and its tourism board effectively maximised the spin-off effects generated by the film production by attracting the visitors into the exhibition and, therefore, into the city.

Film location tours

Film location tours are the ideal film tourism product to provide film-interested tourists and film fans alike with an emotional experience around the actual location encounter. Film location tours can either be designed around a feature film, a television series or a television feature, as various successful examples prove. In this book, the term 'film location tour' always refers to a guided tour.

The duration of a film location tour can vary from a few hours to up to ten days or even longer. The majority of the tours last between two hours and a full day, as they are mostly organised by small, local operators. The means of transport can be either on foot, by bike, by van or by helicopter. A professional film location tour has to fulfil various quality standards. Initially, the content of a film location tour has to be researched in as detailed a manner as possible. A mere location stop, without the provision of image material, background stories and insider knowledge of the shooting, results in major disappointment for the film location tourist and can provoke very negative word-of-mouth propaganda (M. Heath, 2005, personal interview). The quality of the locations is also an essential key factor in delivering a location tour of a high standard. In this regard, quality not only refers to the physical attributes of the visited locations and their recognition value, but also to their emotional components. The emotional components refer to the strength of the emotional links between the location, the relevant scene and the importance of that scene within the movie as a whole. The provision of image material such as photographs from the shooting, script excerpts, call sheets and similar items is another important factor in providing a quality product. The tour must convey to its participants that by taking part in the whole experience and being able to make this authentic connection to the film, they are in a privileged position. Last but not least, every location tour relies on the quality of the tour guides. The tour guide is the connecting link between the real place and its imaginary counterpart in the movie. Only when the guide is able to bring the imaginary to life can a satisfying film location experience be achieved.

Generally speaking, there are two means of initiating a new film location tour. The tour operator can either risk setting it up well in advance, before the film product is screened, or alternatively, wait for the feedback from the audience before starting up the tour. Both strategies involve operational risks. On the one hand, the success of film products is not guaranteed from the outset; on the other hand, it might be too late to secure location access rights and image material copyrights after a film production turns out to initiate film location tourism. In summary, it has to be emphasised that even film productions with a very high probability of box office success and potentially attractive locations do not guarantee demand for a film location tour. An illustrative example of how easy it is to misjudge the potential for a film location tour happened with an operator in New Zealand who designed a tour around the Narnia movie *The Lion, the Witch and the Wardrobe*. The operator secured exclusive access rights to some of the most stunning locations possible, organised original film material, researched all available sources for background stories and set up a high-quality film location tour long before the cinema screening. Despite professional marketing and public relations, the demand for the tours was very small and not nearly enough to keep the business running. This example shows that the best strategy for tourism operators is to have all the necessary tools in place in order to get started immediately, once there are indications of visitation demand.

Themed accommodation

After it was used as a central location for the television series *Cheers* (1982–1993), the Boston-based 'Bull and Finch Hotel' turned into a major tourist attraction drawing 500,000 visitors per annum, resulting in food and beverage sales of US$6 million and merchandising sales worth US$7 million a year (Neale, 1994). This and other examples show that accommodation providers can profit from a film connection.

Themed accommodation can either be offered as a complimentary or additional attraction to a film tourism package, or else it can be an attraction in itself. One can distinguish between different types of themed film-related accommodation. For instance, accommodation can be themed in accordance with the underlying film production by giving it specific features. The oversized furniture, round windows and doors of the Barliman's Room at the Minaret Lodge in Wanaka, New Zealand clearly resemble a hobbit hole and cater to LOTR fans who want to experience a night or two as a hobbit (www.minaretlodge.co.nz/ lord_of_the_rings_packages.html).

However, as not all film fans want to go to such extremes, another possibility is to provide accommodation that is somehow linked to the film or the filming. When staying at the Chateau Tongariro hotel in New Zealand, LOTR tour operator Red Carpet Tours always reserves the very rooms for its tour participants that the film cast and crew stayed in during location shooting. The Park Hyatt Hotel in Tokyo, with its now famous rooms and bar that feature in the movie *Lost in Translation* (2003), offers themed overnight packages for film fans who want to experience Tokyo by following in the footsteps of the film's main characters, Charlotte and Bob (www.spiegel.de/spiegel/0,1518,283770,00.html, accessed 9 September 2008).

Yet another concept is represented by the von Trapp villa in Salzburg, which opened as a hotel in 2008 and enables guests to stay in the former rooms of the real von Trapp family. Although the building was never used as a location in the movie, it now contains several rooms and offers 'Sound and Dinner' events for two to 30 people. Weddings can be arranged in the adjacent chapel, which is situated in the villa's surrounding park. The park can be visited by tourists and presents exhibits from the family's history. There is also an exhibition room and a souvenir shop, with von Trapp memorabilia in the villa itself (Villa Trapp GmbH, 2008). Here, the visitor experience is a conglomerate between the real story behind the movie and the imaginary film characters from SoM.

An interesting phenomenon occurs at the Sidi Driss Hotel, situated in the desert town of Matmata, Tunisia. This area is well known for its troglodytes or underground dwellings of which the Sidi Driss hotel is one of the most well known. Whilst the hotel is a cultural icon in its own right and a stopping point for the many coaches that pass through the area, it also plays host to one of the most recognisable of all SW locations: Luke Skywalker's home. The location was re-used in *Attack of the Clones* in 2002 in the scene where Anakin Skywalker meets his new step-father, step-uncle and step-aunt and finds out about the fate of his mother Shmi. For filming purposes, the film crew decorated the hotel with various film props and, to the delight of the fans, left these decorations behind after the location shooting was finished. Parts can still be seen today, in particular door frames and wall decorations. Due to the dual function of the Sidi Driss hotel both as an established cultural tourist attraction as well as an important film location, conflicts arise between the cultural sightseers and the film location tourists. In particular, the film location tourists feel that the cultural sightseers do not show the necessary respect for the place, in that they have no knowledge of its importance in film history. This conflict is a key factor in film location tourism and will be dealt with in more detail in Chapter 7.

Primary Tourism Effects of Film Productions

All direct economic effects generated by a film production are defined as primary value creation effects. These include all expenses spent by the film producers on location, such as location scouting, logistic costs during the location shooting, contract work assigned to local craftspeople, builders, artisans and film crew and, last but not least, transport and accommodation costs for cast and crew. Table 2.2 illustrates which sectors profit from the production of a television series and to what extent. It is based on the calculation of direct spending effects by the film production of the German television series *Der Bergdoktor* (*The Mountain Doctor*), which was filmed in the Tyrolean Alps between 1992 and 1999. The calculation is based on the assumption that the production team, consisting of 40 crew members, filmed for approximately nine months each year. In addition, the amount of

Table 2.2 Economic effects of the television series *Der Bergdoktor* for the wider filming area (90 episodes in six series, filmed over six years)

Accommodation	€2.122.846
Catering	€2.185.998
Direct production spending	€15.001.126
Other costs	€1.040.674
Cumulative primary turnover	€20.350.646
Regional cumulative turnover: multiplier 1.6	€32.561.063
Income effect: factor 0.5	€16.280.531
Employment effect: factor 1.6/cumulative turnover	ca. 717
Fiscal effect 1: factor 34.4% of cumulative turnover (all taxes)	€11.200.991
Fiscal effect 2: factor 4% of cumulative turnover (communal taxes)	€1.302.442

Note. All figures in euro (after tax)
Source: Derived from Gspan (1999: 35–39; translated by the author)

money spent by all the actors – around 960 during the course of seven
years – was taken into account.

Three industry sectors profit in particular from these direct effects: the
transportation sector (transport of personnel and goods), small trade (set
construction, provision of building material) and the tourism industry.
As can be seen from Table 2.2, the amount spent on accommodation and
catering injected over 4 million euros into the local tourism economy.
This goes to show that the accommodation sector profits significantly
from film productions. According to the Montana Film Office, around
17–19% of on-site film production spending goes to accommodation
providers (Köck, 2008, via email). The two film teams working on *Dances
with Wolves* (1992) in the winter of 1993/1994 filled more than 400 hotel
rooms over a period of three months. Economics Research Associates
calculated that each US dollar spent on location shooting generated an
additional US$0.84 within the involved region. As such, it is estimated
that the multiplication effect of location filming is around 3.05 per million
US$ (Köck, 2008, via email). Given these multiplication effects for
regional economies, it is not surprising that more and more regions are
establishing their own film commissions in order to attract film
production investment.

Postproduction Tourism Effects

Postproduction effects, or secondary effects of a film production, are
defined as indirectly induced spending injected by the release of a film
production. Secondary tourism effects can result in increased visitation
numbers to the screened location as well as image and promotional
effects for the destination (Riley & Van Doren, 1992; Tooke & Baker, 1996;
Beeton, 2002; Tenbrock, 2005). Tooke and Baker (1996) examined four
cases of television-induced tourism in the UK: the Cricket St Thomas
Estate in Somerset as featured in *To The Manor Born* (1979–1981); Rocking
Castle in Northamptonshire as featured in *By The Sword Divided* (1983);
the town of Stamford as shown in *Middlemarch* (1994); and the town of
Goathland in the North York moors, made famous by the series *Heartbeat*
(1992–ongoing). All these locations noted an increase of visitors shortly
after the series were released: 37% over a two-year period at the Cricket
Field; 93% over a two-year period to Rocking Castle; 27% to Stamford in
the first year; and an increase of 27% to the town of Goathland.

The 26-part Korean television series *Winter Sonata* (2004) evidently
brought 40.4% more visitors to the featured main location of the
Gangwon province compared to the year prior to its screening (Kim
et al., 2007). The series was very successful in Japan, which ultimately led
the authorities of a small Japanese city to organise a *Winter Sonata* festival
held over the course of one and a half months, attracting more than

700,000 visitors and injecting US$21.7 million into the local economy (Kim *et al.*, 2007).

The aforementioned example of *Der Bergdoktor* has also shown a significant increase in overnight stays (an increase of 8.65%) in the year after the release of the first series (Gspan, 1999). The main location, the Mountain Doctor's medical practice located on the Mieminger Plateau in Tyrol, experienced a considerable increase in day visitors. Some years saw up to 200 coaches pulling up at the house (Gspan, 1999). Research in Goathland, UK (Mordue, 1999, 2001) showed that the visitor increase due to the exposure of the town in the television series *Heartbeat* (1992– ongoing) altered the structure of the town's tourism sector. It changed significantly from its status as a remote tourist area catering to overnight guests into a day visitor attraction – a shift denoted as one from romantic gazers to collective gazers. This resulted in a confrontation between the two place identities: the lived-in space of the community and the tourist space of the collective gazers (Mordue, 1999).

Probably the most cited example of film tourism-related visitor influxes is LOTR and its effects on New Zealand's tourism industry. The 2003 New Zealand Ministry of Tourism International Visitor Survey revealed that of those visitors aware of LOTR and its link with New Zealand, 7% accredited the trilogy as a decisive factor in their travel choice; 1% had visited the country specifically because of the films. The latter visitor group is estimated to have contributed around NZ$24 million in expenditure during their stay (Investment New Zealand, 2004) and a total of 30,000 people admitted to having taken part in a 'Rings experience', whether through an organised trip or independently (New Zealand Herald, 2004). Tenbrock (2005) estimates the overall spending of all LOTR film location tourists between 2004 and 2005 to have amounted to NZ$69,252,320 million. According to Tenbrock's calculation, in 2005 the LOTR film location tourist spent an average of NZ$1,595 on products and services within the country, while the general tourist spent an average of NZ$566.

Although these numbers seem fairly small in comparison, the media hype created around the making of the trilogy definitely put New Zealand on the tourist map (Croy, 2004). This statement is backed up by two Tourism New Zealand visitor surveys conducted in April 2003 (Tourism New Zealand, 2003a). These surveys were concerned with LOTR's ability to attract actual and potential international travellers to the country. One survey was conducted at visitor information sites throughout the country ($n = 775$), the second survey was carried out online on Tourism New Zealand's website (www.purenz.com) ($n = 916$). The main conclusion was that 86% of the actual visitors and 65% of the potential visitors were aware of the fact that LOTR had been filmed in New Zealand. Of the actual visitors, 8% stated that LOTR was a very important reason for coming to

New Zealand. Of the potential visitors, 61% stated that they were more motivated to visit New Zealand due to its exposure in LOTR. For 57% of the potential visitors, LOTR was a significant factor in a potential travel decision. Females were significantly more influenced by LOTR publicity than males. The summary's recommendation identifies under 35s, females and the US-Canadian market as the key audiences for further LOTR promotion (Tourism New Zealand, 2003b: 4). It can be concluded that although film location tourism has always been a niche activity, films are a very powerful draw card for destinations. For instance, it is estimated that in 2006, every tenth international tourist visited the UK due to its exposure on the screen, therefore contributing between 4 and 12% of the value of total international tourism worth around £1.6 billion (Oxford Economics, 2007).

The destination image-enhancing postproduction effects of film productions mentioned so far are particularly sought after by destination marketers, as their cost effectiveness is perceived as highly effective. The UK National Brand Index 2005 found that 40% of international visitors to the UK are very likely to visit places from feature films or television broadcasts. Of these, 52% are female, 52% are over 34 years of age, 88% have children under the age of 18 and 56% finished their education at the age of 21 years or older (VisitBritain, 2008, received via email). Of visitors to Ireland, 56% declare film and television to be their main reason for choice of destination (Bolan *et al.*, 2007). It becomes apparent that film productions can possess enormous promotional reach for destinations. Moreover, the publicity generated through film is literally free promotion for destination marketing destinations.

Film Tourism and the Host Community

The host community perceptions of the benefits and drawbacks of film tourism have been looked at in a number of studies. Beeton (2000, 2001b) conducted research on the popular Australian television series *Sea Change* (1998–2000) and its community impact on the town of Barwon Heads, the main location of the series. Of the interviewed residents, 36% agreed with the statement that the series resulted in economic benefits for some of the local businesses; 18% believed the series had raised the profile and image of the town. On the other hand, 41% of the respondents mentioned the need for careful town planning within this context. An increase in tourism was anticipated by 26% of respondents. The research comes to the conclusion that film productions can significantly change the system of a community, even if it is only through the different attitudes of the residents towards both the positive and negative effects of such a production. Beeton (2000: 9) also mentions the problem that 'the relationship between film and tourism is problematic and in most cases the popularity of a film is unclear until well after it has been released, which can be too late for research into its tourism impacts'. A very positive example is the television production of *Winter Sonata* (2003), a Korean production that was immensely successful in Japan. Research has revealed that for 26% of the Japanese viewers, their image of Korea was positively changed after watching the television series. This, in turn, evidently led to an increased interest in Korean culture (Kim *et al.*, 2007).

There have been cases where the local community refused to support the filming due to fears of negative impacts. The aforementioned example of the town of Goathland, featured in the British television series *Heartbeat*, showed that the film tourism-related visitor influx altered the structure of the town's tourism sector considerably from a remote tourist area into a day visitor attraction. This resulted in negative reactions from some locals who opposed the location shooting (Demetriadi, 1996). In a similar fashion, the residents living near the proposed film location for the television series *Baywatch* (1989–2001) protested against the location shooting, which resulted in the selection of an alternative location in Hawaii (Beeton, 2001b). Wright (2004) found that at some of the LOTR film locations, the involved communities were divided over the question as to whether the films have had a positive impact for them. In areas where the community was more involved in the filming process, the filming had a positive effect on the social identity by creating a sense of local pride. From a financial point of view, only a small number of individuals profited from the increased visitation numbers. These were mainly individuals who had some connection to the filming process, such as landowners or tour operators who provided transport to the cast and the crew at the time.

The case of the British television children's series *Balamory* (2002–2005) illustrates that small tourism businesses can indeed significantly profit from film location tourism. Filmed in the small Scottish fishing village of Tobermory on the Isle of Mull, the local tourism businesses experienced a considerable increase in customers. Out of 101 tourism businesses surveyed on the island, 61.5% stated an increase in business, in particular accommodation providers such as hotels, guest houses and bed and breakfast establishments. In Tobermory itself, accommodation providers reported a visitation increase of families with young children by 77.4% (Connell, 2005a). The opinions of the effects of *Balamory* on tourism varied amongst the tourism businesses. A total of 24.2% expressed their concern that the television series might attract the wrong kind of visitors and 54.3% were worried that the increasing commercialism would have detrimental effects on the island's tourism. On the other hand, 46.9% were of the opinion that *Balamory* would contribute to an extension of the summer tourist season (Connell, 2005a).

Croy and Walker (2001) conducted research in the area of film policy and the intersection between the film and the tourism industry. All local government offices and regional tourism organisations in New Zealand were sent a mail-out/mail-back survey by the authors. The overall idea of this survey was to find out what benefits of film production were perceived and identified by the respondents. A total of 54% of the addressed offices responded; 79% responded that feature films have been produced in their area, but only 45% of the responsible authorities have included film production in their development strategies. When asked about the efficiency of feature films as a promotional tool for tourism, 5% responded that feature films are not a suitable tourism promotional tool, whereas 71% considered the possibility of using feature films to promote tourism as being an interesting option. Twenty-four percent of the respondents gave no answer to this question. The identified benefits of film were economic benefits (89% of the responses), employment benefits (67%), increased visitors arrivals (67%), cultural development (22%) and positive effects on the destination image (4%) (Croy & Walker, 2001: 7). Additional research undertaken by Costley (2002) on the impact of LOTR on the local industry provided similar results: 50% of the respondents agreed that the movies would have an effect on the entire business community. Croy and Walker's study (2001) shows that local authorities and tourism organisations in New Zealand noticed the importance of feature films in boosting the local economy. The problem was that most of the stakeholders lacked specific knowledge of how to optimise the benefits from the film production.

Sustainability of Film Tourism

If all the necessary ingredients are combined accordingly, film tourism can be sustained for a long time. Movies can attract film tourists for decades, as examples such as SoM, *The Third Man* (1949) or *The Bridge on the River Kwai* (1957) illustrate. These movies radiate such an emotional power that they become anchored in our societal perception as iconic sites that perhaps one day we will travel to in order to experience them in person. During the second half of the 20th century, a film's post-production cycle has continually expanded. The windows of a film's exhibition have increased from two windows (film premiere and cinema release) up to seven or eight. This enables tourism stakeholders to repeat intended images during each exhibition window, which can last several years. The LOTR trilogy postproduction cycle spanned around three years, from the premiere of the second instalment in 2001 until the release of the extended DVD version of *The Return of the King* in 2004. With the latest developments around the production of two further movies based on J.R.R. Tolkien's world of Middle Earth in New Zealand, the LOTR postproduction cycle will continue for years to come. It is obvious that within this context the LOTR trilogy will also gain popularity once again. It will be up to the responsible tourism stakeholders in New Zealand to maximise the spin-off effects of this new 'Tolkien wave'.

The tourism stakeholders in Salzburg are already one step ahead of their New Zealand counterparts. Due to SoM, which has maintained its popularity for over 40 years, the tourism industry in the city continues to profit immensely from film tourism. The sustainability of SoM film tourism has been maintained through two factors: easy access to the locations and the establishment of organised film location tours. In the year after its initial screening in 1965, the increase of US-American tourists to the city amounted to 20% of all visitors (Huber, 2000). In 1970, every fifth visitor was a US-American (Huber, 2000). Travellers from all over the world come to see the city and its historic sites partly because of its filmic place exposure. In the year 2000, around 50,000 film location tourists participated in SoM location tours. An additional 300,000 film location tourists visited the locations individually (Herzl, 2000). Several commercial tour operators offer SoM tours either by bus or van. There is also a guided city walk that takes in some of the locations on foot. The majority of the locations are concentrated in the historic city core, whilst the rest are situated in the outskirts of the city and in the surrounding lakes region of the Salzkammergut. Popular movie-related entertainment includes 'The Sound of Music Dinner and Show,' a sing-along event that consists of a live band performing the famous melodies. Its annual attendance is estimated at around 10,000 guests (www.soundofmusic show.com). With the newest developments, the opening of the von Trapp villa as a hotel and the plans for a SoM museum in the heart of the city, film tourism in Salzburg will continue to make a considerable contribution to inbound tourism for years to come.

Even relatively small scale productions such as *The Blair Witch Project* (1999), *The Third Man* (1949), *Life of Brian* (1979), the British television series *Hearbeat* (1992–ongoing) or the German television series *Die Schwarzwaldklinik* (1985–1989) continue to attract film tourists many years after their release. If, at the same time, destination marketing tools are in place, sustainability can be maintained even longer. Arguably, the ever faster turn-over of film productions effects our perceptions of individual films, as we are overloaded with visual information. For this reason, it is even more important for tourism stakeholders to concentrate on film productions that are likely to produce long-lasting emotions. It is also important, as Wright (2004) has shown, to involve the communities in film tourism. By driving film tourism through the involved communities and thereby gaining their acceptance, local support cannot only extend its sustainability, but also enhance its quality. At the same time, the involvement of the local community can ensure that over-commercialisation is avoided and the effects of film tourism are embraced.

Chapter 3
Film Locations as Touristic Places

A Sense of Place

Sense of place differs enormously within different cultures. The Aboriginals of Australia see place as the manifestation of their beliefs, which are tied to particular natural features. Their sense of place is a sense of absoluteness and a sense of 'the Sacred', a concept that attaches deep meanings to the physical environment. In contemporary Western cultures, our sense of place is becoming increasingly affected by the ongoing process of time-space compression and the invasion of globalised concepts of place (Massey, 1995). In the middle of the 19th century, it took months to cross the USA by wagon. One hundred years later, airplane passengers were able to cover the same distance in a matter of hours and over the last two decades, new media technologies such as email, the internet, satellite and cell phones enable us to be virtually present at any place and in real time. Today, messages can reach a global audience within seconds, thereby constantly homogenising identities, cultures and places. As a consequence, places have become fluid, of a highly complex nature where identities are constantly open to question (Hall, 2005). The development of a global sense of place through this process (Massey, 1994) has resulted in a crisis of identity for many places. This crisis has led to the emergence of inauthentic places, a sense of placelessness (Relph, 1976) or non-places (Augé, 1995). Non-places lack a relational component, a historical component or are without any identity, as opposed to places (Augé, 1995). Such non-places, for instance, are constructed for and by the contemporary tourist and include different means of transport, airports, hotel chains, leisure parks and wireless networks. Thus, the space of the traveller is the archetype of a non-place (Augé, 1995), as it involves the movement to places that already possess anticipated images implemented by the tourist structure. Massey (1994) even goes a step further and describes this process as the formation of a new, global sense of place. A local sense of place, in turn, is mainly established through face-to-face interactions. On this level, place is equated with community and perceived as 'the authentic' (Young, 1990).

How do we identify with particular places? First of all, a sense of place is important as it shows the individual where he or she belongs. 'To be human is to live in a world that is filled with significant places: to be human is to have and to know *your* place' (Relph, 1976: 1). In other words: 'To live is to live locally, and to know is first of all to know the place one is in' (Casey, 1996: 18). Such a place can comprise micro-scale entities, for instance a house, a garden or a street; it may also relate to macro-scale formations, for instance a region or a country. Geographers, sociologists and anthropologists widely agree that places gain meaning through human beings. After Lefebvre (1991), our sense of place is constituted through acts of naming and the distinct activities and images associated with particular social spaces. Rose (1995) identifies three factors that configure social meaning and a sense of place: a sense of place is natural; a sense of place is constructed by underlying structures of power; and a sense of place is part of the politics of identity (Rose, 1995). Likewise, Canter (1977) suggests that the three elements that form a sense of place comprise of the physical attributes of a setting, the performed activities on site and the conceptions brought to the setting.

We can derive from Rose (1995) and Canter (1977) that places are constructed through global structures of power, which, in turn, influence and shape the politics of power. This process shapes the individual conceptions and expectations brought to a place. Consequently, these conceptions impact upon the performances on site. At the same time, the actual place encounter feeds back into the pre-conceived place representation and subsequently alters it. We can say that there is a global sense of place that, in turn, is experienced differently by each individual. In saying that, even the natural sense of a place and its physical attributes can be standardised. This is particularly the case in tourism where destination marketers operate with messages that draw on globally accepted, material representations of place: Switzerland is inevitably connected with the Matterhorn, Australia with Uluru and Germany with Neuschwanstein Castle. Nevertheless, many places manage to maintain their unique identity not just through their physical setting, but also through attributes created by their cultural and historical ties, all of which are essential factors in shaping place identities: '[T]he salience and relationship between place and space, inside and outside and image and representation are dependent on the cultural and historical context' (Hirsch, 1995: 23).

In summary, the underlying preconditions for bringing a sense of place into being are the underlying structures of power, the physical setting (i.e. the physical attributes of a place) and one's own identity shaped by the cultural and historical context of self (i.e. self-identity) with its subsequent pre-visit conceptions and on-site experiences of place. Figure 3.1 depicts how the sense of place is constructed by the aforementioned elements.

Adams' (1992) three conceptions of place similarly fit into this context. For Adams, a sense of place comes into being through its underlying, physical processes, by public recognition (societal integration) and by a personal sense of place (construction of meaning). Public recognition of a

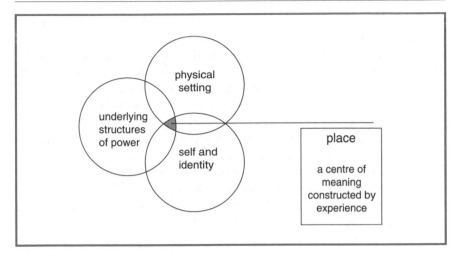

Figure 3.1 Configuration of the sense of place

place depends on a consensus with regard to location and character, while a personal sense of place is attached to individual experiences and sensibilities.

In this book, places are referred to as being tied to a physical location, but other concepts of place are also acknowledged, such as Adams' (1992) concept of television as a (fictional) place of construction and social integration as well as the concept of inner place. The concept of inner place refers to extraordinary experiences, manifest in expressions such as 'I went to a place that I have never been before' when speaking of total physical and mind exhaustion in extreme situations. In a similar fashion, people can travel to inner places when reading a novel or listening to an audio book. The experience of inner place is something very personal, emotional and therefore intrinsic.

The Commodification and Consumption of Places

Over the last two centuries, Western cultures have become 'increasingly self-referential in the sense that [...] sources and horizons of meaning have developed and become generalized, sedimented and then mutated, which are based in hybrid images of machine and organism, especially images based on speed, light and power' (Thrift, 1996: 257). Boniface and Fowler (1993) agree with Thrift (1996) and quote the elements of speed, power and profit as the decisive factors for this development. Thrift (1996) continues that we now live in a world that is almost, or not quite, filled with almost, or not quite subjects, selves, spaces and times. The packaging and commodification methods of the postmodern system are partly responsible for this blurred sense of space, time and place. The result is a symbolic economy of space that consists of two production systems: that of space and that of symbols, the latter one being 'a currency of commercial exchange and a language of social identity' (Zukin, 1995: 23–24). Baudrillard's theory of the simulacrum takes the same line. It proposes that the postmodern world is assimilated to and defined by artificial codes and simulations (Baudrillard, 1983, 1994). Therefore, the postmodern consumer object 'collectively assigns consumers to a code, without however, arousing any collective solidarity (in fact, it does the opposite)' (Baudrillard, 1998: 86). The real has become a hyper-real or simulacrum; the world has been replaced by a copy world. Examples for such simulacra are Disney World, the themed hotels in Las Vegas or even a plastic Christmas tree that looks more 'real' than a real tree ever could. This notion has also been labelled as 'the authentic fake' (Eco, 1986). The situationists denote this shift as a transition into a society of the spectacle. The driving forces behind this transition are the power of the mass media as well as a new angle of the structural apparatus to obscure its power through the mechanisms of consumption, entertainment and leisure (Best, 1989).

As images have become 'the highest form of commodity reification' (Best, 1989: 31), places have become one of the objects of this commodification and therefore objects of consumption. Consumption can be understood 'as a social process that can be traced backwards into the social relations of production and forwards into cycles of use and reuse' (Crang & Jackson, 2001: 328). Such a process is constructed around geographical sites and networks of provisions, as well as the geographical knowledge about these settings. This phenomenon is expressed by the three geographies of consumption comprising the local setting, the global commodity system and the imaginative geographies, the latter encompassing both the global and the local level. Crang and Jackson (2001: 330) see consumption as profoundly contextual, as 'embedded in the particular spaces, times, and social relations that constitute contemporary [...] culture'. Urry (1995: 1–2) argues that contemporary places are places of consumption, involving both the commodification of space and time:

- places are increasingly being restructured as centres for consumption, where goods and services are processed;
- places themselves are in a sense consumed, especially in a visual sense;
- places can be literally consumed; the sense of a place has developed over time;
- localities are able to consume one's identity; therefore, these places become literally all-consuming places.

In regard to the question of how such places are experienced, Peet (1998) proposes six different positions of people in relation to place. 'Existential outsiderness' stands for a notion where all places assume the same meaningless identity. Places acquire meaning, but are still viewed scientifically and passively through 'objective outsiderness'. 'Incidental outsiderness' occurs when places are experienced as backgrounds for activities. 'Vicarious insiderness' denotes the experience of places in a second-hand way, for example when encountering a place on television. 'Behavioural insiderness' demands emotional and empathetic involvement in a place. Lastly, 'existential insiderness' stands for a place relation where places are experienced without deliberate reflection, yet are full of significance.

The Construction and Commodification of Touristic Space and Place

Touristic space can be generally defined as 'any environment which fosters the feeling of being a tourist' (Pearce, 1982: 98). Crouch (1999: 2) redefines this broad assumption as follows: 'Tourism happens in spaces. That space may be material, concrete and surround our own bodies... [but it] may also be metaphorical and even imaginative'. Most touristic spaces are marked by high transient populations, the provision of suitable infrastructure for visitation and an established system of control in order to supervise accessibility issues (Pearce, 1982). Tourist spaces provide the basis for experiences in an environment free from danger and other disturbing elements, exemplified by the concept of the tourist bubble (Judd, 1999).

The initial spark for carving out modern tourist spaces is said to have started with the construction of the British seaside resorts from the late 18th and the early 19th century onwards (Meethan, 2001). These resorts were detached from everyday life, both spatially and temporarily. Only the wealthy could afford the resorts' entrance fees and had sufficient free time at hand. The next evolutionary stage in this process was the construction of high-society resorts along the Côte d'Azur, leaving the middle class free to occupy the original British seaside resorts. The subsequent stages in the construction of touristic spaces saw the ever-increasing development of bungalow camps, hotel resorts and, finally, theme parks in even the most remote corners of the periphery regions. This society-encompassing process has been attributed to 'the differentiation inherent in modernity, of splitting the sphere of work from the sphere of leisure in conceptual, temporal and spatial terms' (Meethan, 2001: 11). The result was an extension of the bourgeois utopia (Harvey, 2000), the suburban privatopias and gated communities, into the sphere of tourism.

The postmodern tourism industry commodifies places by tearing them out of time and space constraints and repackaging them for the consumer (Edensor, 2002). Britton (1991) examines how such places are assimilated into the tourist system through commodification. Places can acquire the status of tourist places through two generic forms of commodification: through inherent attributes or through 'the inclusion of the touristic experience or attributes of the place into a saleable commodity [for example through a film location tour] or symbolic image with recognisable connotations' (Britton, 1991: 462). According to Britton, this commodification is based on two streams: leisure spaces and tourist attractions. Leisure spaces are 'discrete and categorised landscapes that actively maintain and consolidate prevailing production relations' (Britton, 1991: 462). Tourist attractions overlay these spaces as significant places for tourists.

According to MacCannell (1976), tourist attractions gain their status through a five-step process referred to as sight sacralisation. In the first phase – the naming phase – a 'sight is marked off from similar objects as worthy of preservation' (MacCannell, 1976: 44). Especially in the modern world, institutional efforts are required to mark off such a sight; although, sights can also be named without the presence of an external force. An example for this stage would be the erection of churches and chapels around the tombs of holy people and their subsequent naming in medieval times. In the framing or elevation phase, the sight is put on display. The tombs or relics of holy people are displayed, for instance on rostrums, due to an increasing number of pilgrims. This phase can be equated with the installation of an inviolate belt (Gunn, 1988a), with the church or chapel around the tomb serving as a means either to protect or enhance the sight. The two different types of framing that can occur are protection and enhancement (MacCannell, 1976). After a certain period of time, the church or chapel itself can become an attraction nucleus. In this stage, the inviolate zone turns into a new nucleus, now forming a two-clustered tourist precinct comprising the initial tomb and the church or chapel around it (Leiper, 1990). MacCannell denotes this phase as enshrinement. The fourth phase of sight sacralisation is that of mechanical reproduction. It stands for the creation of photographs, prints, postcards and other representational means of the toured object, which subsequently acquire status. It is during this phase of the process that sights become the true objects tourists gaze upon. The fifth and final phase is called social reproduction. Cities, regions and tourism bodies begin to name themselves after famous sights (MacCannell, 1976). In his study of the Norwegian North Cape as a tourist attraction, Jacobsen (1997) draws on the main tenets of MacCannell's semiotic attraction theory of sight sacralisation. He supplements the theory with an additional notion – the concept of the sacred sight. In this case, the sacred sight with a quasi-religious status is the midnight sun when seen from the North-facing plateau of the North Cape.

The commodification of tourism products occurs through the representation of space, that is, through the perception of images implemented by the media. They can also be 'derived from the representational spaces of lived experience, which are organised into more or less coherent narratives at a personalised level' (Meethan, 2001: 86). Everyday experiences – the practice of living and the places grounding that experience – have significantly altered within the transition from modernism to postmodernism. Today, as many geographers agree, everyday experience is heavily influenced by image-formation processes (Aitken & Zonn, 1994). The rapid change in tourist's preferences, values and attitudes over the last two decades (Milman, 2001; Peters & Weiermair, 2000) reflects this mediation of experience. The former, extrinsic reasons for seeking a holiday have given way to intrinsic motivation factors. The tourism industry has long since recognised this trend. Successful contemporary leisure products are heavily themed, individually packaged and staged. An organised coach trip to Morocco might be promoted under a theme such as 'The Secrets of Morocco', where the tourists are supposedly initiated into 'secret' cultures and places where locals stage (in)authentic performances such as trade demonstrations or folklore shows. Only through this emotional integration of the consumer can tourism products stand a chance on the market. This shift has been identified in the wider production process by Pine and Gilmore (1999), who found a clear evolution from manufacturing goods to the provision of services and, finally, the staging of experiences as the primary driving force of capitalism.

According to Britton (1991), places can become tourism products in their own right as they are integrated into the commodification of tourist products in two stages. First, additional meanings of non-commercial goods (i.e. places) are assimilated into tourism products. Second, non-commercially created or non-touristic attractions acquire new meanings that transform them into tourism products. Examples for the latter process would be the commodification of formerly non-touristic places into tourist attractions centred on popular media such as music, literature, television broadcasts or feature films. This meaningful association is achieved by three mechanisms: marketing, imaging and branding.

Space and Place in Film

Aitken and Zonn (1994: 15) define space in film as dynamic, being 'the frame within which a subject is located'. Hopkins (1994) differentiates three notions of cinematic space and geography. The first notion is a 'geography of film'. It stands for the subjective meanings obtained by experiencing a film. 'Geography in film' is the film's representation and interpretation of the environment. Lastly, the 'geography of the theatre' is wholly objective and encompasses the screen and the seating.

It is also important to mention the Greek term 'diegesis', which stands for 'narrated story'. The film's diegesis is the world as portrayed in a filmic narrative and includes both the activities and places of the fictional world, even those not pictured on-screen (Bordwell & Thompson, 1997). As such, place in film stands for the centres of meaning 'in the frame' with which the film characters do, or do not interact. Places do not necessarily have to interact with the characters, as they can purely form the background for the story. There are three different ways of anchoring places and place processes in film (Le Héron, 2004: 61):

- Landscape processes and forces are not important in the story.
- The land dominates relationships.
- The land dominates the action.

With the first notion, landscape shots establish a sense of place, but mostly refrain from direct engagement with the audience or the characters. Thus, places play no significant role in the narrative, which is instead centred around relationships. Where landscapes influence relationships, the opening sequence often begins with landscape shots in order to signal the importance of the land for the narrative (Le Héron, 2004). When places impact on the actions of the characters, landscape plays an active, integral part in the storyline.

As cinema is a kind of virtual reality, it allows the mind to travel to fantastic yet seeming-real places, resulting in the 'suspension of disbelief' (Holmes, 2001). This term describes the alleged willingness of a reader/ viewer to accept as true the premises of a work of fiction, even if it is fantastic, impossible or otherwise contradictory to reality. Suspension of disbelief also refers to the willingness of the audience to overlook the limitations of the medium, so that these do not interfere with the acceptance of those premises.

The seeming-realness of those filmic places is created 'through the incorporation of a set of narrative conventions' (Aitken & Zonn, 1994: 13) around an accepted film genre. For example, a Western movie should be set in the American West and include such iconographic elements as Western style clothing, grand scenic settings and backdrops, hostile elements, both human and natural, and the fight between a male hero and his opponent. The acting, the costumes and make-up, the lighting, the composition of the shots, as well as the sound, all translate these conventions onto the screen and make the cinematic world of the movie believable and thus seeming-real.

Film watching itself is simultaneously romantic, collective and spectatorial. We watch within a community, as the encounter with the filmic world is shared (Hasson *et al.*, 2004). Through the implementation of narrative and cinematic conventions into genres, we also gaze at the familiar. As consumers of spectacle, we collect different signs while consuming different movies. Finally, watching a movie always involves a romantic gaze, as we react to the intrinsic messages of the medium as individuals (Hasson *et al.*, 2004).

The Physical Setting of Film Locations

When planning travel itineraries, people seek out unique experiences, activities and places. To travel is to leave the ordinary and enter the extraordinary. Consequently, physical settings for leisure and tourist activities have to be extraordinary. They have to be imagined as rare, unique, exotic, scenic, exciting and open to interpretation. Such settings usually present outstanding natural features, meaningful (historic) buildings or the location of an important event.

The physical settings of film locations have to be seen from a slightly different angle. They are used for on-location filming because they present features that are essential for the product. Hence, film locations do not necessarily have to be outstandingly beautiful nor do they necessarily have to have a privileged meaning attached to them. Table 3.1 presents the different attraction statuses that film locations can possess. On the other hand, when places are sought out as film locations, they

Table 3.1 The different attraction statuses of film locations

Pre-attraction status	*No pre-attraction status*
Natural features with special meanings =landmarks Example: Devil's Tower Monument, USA *Close Encounters of the Third Kind* (1977)	**Natural features without a special pre-meaning** Example: Mt. Sunday, Canterbury, New Zealand *The Lord of the Rings – The Two Towers* (2002)
Man-made features with special meanings =landmarks Example: Empire State Building, New York *King Kong* (1933)	**Man-made features without a special pre-meaning** Example: Café des Deux Moulins, Paris *Amélie* (2001)
	Film sets and remains Example: Mos Espa set, Tunisia *Star Wars – The Phantom Menace* (1999)

Figure 3.2 Monument Valley – a film location landscape
Source: Author.

may already possess the status of a tourist attraction, whether it is natural or man-made. The Devils Tower National Monument in Wyoming was already established as a significant visitor attraction with around 150,000 visitors a year (Riley & Van Doren, 1992) before Steven Spielberg used it for key scenes in his movie *Close Encounters of the Third Kind* (1977). Visitation to the National Monument grew by 74% after the movie screening the following year. Eleven years after its initial screening, 20% of a surveyed visitor sample attributed their main pre-visit knowledge about the monument to the movie (Riley & Van Doren, 1992). Some landscapes such as Monument Valley in Utah (Figure 3.2) have starred in numerous feature films including *Stagecoach* (1939), *My Darling Clementine* (1946), *The Searchers* (1956) and *How the West Was Won* (1962). Here, the visitor engages not only with the real landscape, but also with a film location landscape as a result of its filmic exposure. The film location tourist engages with this filmic reality and constantly moves between the real and the fictional, imaginary place.

Parallels can be drawn to man-made features that have been used for filming purposes. The Empire State Building has starred in over 100 movies since its construction in 1930 (Empire State Building, 2009). As a landmark of Manhattan, it has received over 110 million visitors (Skillings, 2009). There is certainly a confusion and melioration between the landmark as a tourist attraction as such and its role as a movie history landmark. Most visitors will have seen the Empire State Building on the silver screen before encountering it in reality, but whether it was the silver screen that initiated the desire to visit the building, its exposure through tourism marketing and media, or maybe through a combination of these factors, the fact remains that such questions cannot be answered. Most visitors will simply recall that several movie scenes were shot at the Empire State Building, even if they cannot remember the exact film scenes. The extreme end of the spatial continuum of man-made features represented in movie scenes is formed by an entire cityscape such as San Francisco. Since the 1920s, around 250 feature films have been (partly) shot in the city (San Francisco Film Commission, 2008). Such exposure is certainly not the main factor for the city's status as a major tourist attraction. Yet again, there is a significant melioration between the city and its single attractions with its attached meaning(s) generated through feature films. Visitors wandering through the city certainly recognise many places from popular movies as the city looms large in the popular imagination.

Some places gain attraction status solely due to their representation in feature films. Again these places can be man-made or natural features. Arguably, no tourist would have gone purposely to Mount Sunday, which is just a rocky outcrop in an alpine valley in central Canterbury on New Zealand's South Island. But since it featured in *The Lord of the Rings – The Two Towers* (2002), it has acquired meaning and status for an increasing number of independent film location tourists and a number of tour operators organise film location tours to this place.

Other film locations have turned into tourist attractions due to the remains of film sets or set parts. For example, fans of the movie *Dances with Wolves* (1990) travelled to a remote corner in South Dakota to see the remaining set of Fort Hays. The influx was so significant that the set was moved 13 miles closer to highway 16 near Rapid City, and is now being used as part of a cowboy-themed experience, which includes a show, a dining experience and a film set tour (Rushmore Tours, www.rushmoretours.com, accessed 6 October 2005). The film location has become a schizoid location, as it is no longer connected by place to the movie, yet, regardless, visitors come to experience the film set. Another example is the previously mentioned Port Royal film set from *Pirates of the Caribbean* (2003), situated in a remote bay on St Vincent. Several set constructions have been left behind, amongst them a wooden pier, a building for interior shots and the hotel that features in a lengthy village scene (Long, via email). Similarly in Taranaki, New Zealand, where the Samurai village was constructed for *The Last Samurai* (2003), the property owner has re-created one of the Samurai huts on the exact spot where the original stood (Figure 3.3). The schizoid aspect in this case is that one of the toured objects on-site is the duplication of an original set prop.

The above examples support the fact that film locations do not necessarily have to be places with pre-filming attraction status. On the

Figure 3.3 Re-created Samurai hut from *The Last Samurai*, Taranaki, New Zealand
Source: Author.

contrary, if a place is exposed in a film production, it can turn from a formerly undeveloped tourist place into a new tourist attraction in its own right.

Filmic Icons

Visual consumption through the eye (sightseeing), the photograph or the cinema screen transforms places into attractions (Holmes, 2001; Urry, 1995). Riley *et al.*'s (1998) concept of filmic icons describes the process of cinematic on-site consumption (Riley & Van Doren, 1992; Riley *et al.*, 1998). An icon is a 'sign that looks like the object, or represents it visually in a way that most people would relate to' (Blythe, 2000: 4). Icons can be dynamic and animated, as is the case in films, but they tend to be visual (Barker & Schaik, 2000). Riley *et al.* (1998) distinguish between visual, thematic and physical icons in films that serve as the focal point for film (location) tourists. Visual icons can be heritage attractions such as the Mirabell Gardens from *The Sound of Music*, dark spots such as the railway bridge over the river Kwai from *Bridge on the River Kwai* or natural features such as the Devil's Tower Monument in Wyoming from *Close Encounters of the Third Kind*. An example for a film featuring a physical icon is *Deliverance* (1972), in which four American businessmen go on a weekend white water canoeing trip down the Cahulawassee River in Raeburn County, Georgia. Hoping for a great adventure in the backcountry, things turn horribly wrong when the group runs into a couple of brutal rednecks and the businessmen have to fight both nature and mankind in order to return to civilisation. Due to the physical icon of white water rafting, the movie literally kick-started the region's raft and adventure tourism industry (Riley & Van Doren, 1992). Another example of a tourism-inducing physical icon stems from the movie *The Man from Snowy River* (1982), produced in Australia's Snowy Mountains Region. As a result of the many horse-back-riding scenes, the local horseback sector profited enormously, resulting in an increase of tour operators from 3 to over 30 within just a few years (Beeton, 2001a).

Thematic icons can be found in *Steel Magnolias* (1989), filmed in Natchitoches, Louisiana, which entertains the theme of female bonding, or in *Fried Green Tomatoes* (1991) with its theme of evident self-determination (Riley *et al.*, 1998). Film productions can create more than one icon that people seek to experience. For instance, the movie *Dances with Wolves* (1992) contains the thematic icon of the Wild West as a romantic concept of a historic landscape, while at the same time, some of the locations and sets used for location filming have become visual icons.

For Edensor (2002: 46), iconic sites are 'sacred centres, objects of spiritual and historic pilgrimage' that are provided for individuals by the state. These sites are combined into a specific spatial configuration of reference sites, which, in turn, constitute the attractions of a tourist destination. Such attractions include sites that connote historical events, sites that have heritage status, sites that are symbols of the modernity of a nation or sites that are symbols of official power. Edensor (2002: 49) introduces an additional configuration of spatial tourism attractors – that of 'popular sites of assembly and congregation'. Popular sites are not controlled by the state, but are places where people congregate to participate in communal activities. Parks, stadiums, festival parks, promenades, religious sites and also film locations could be enumerated under this concept. At popular sites, people gather to mingle, to perform, to observe or to sell goods and services. In contrast to iconic sites, popular sites are non-exclusive with regard to social access barriers and therefore seen as authentic (Edensor, 2002).

Because it does not take non-iconic elements such as intrinsic qualities into account, Riley *et al.*'s (1998) icon concept has to be expanded upon. The term icon is defined as a 'pictorial representation of an object; a film image that is taken to represent an object because of its similarity to the object' (Beaver, 1994: 185). As magnetic resonance research has proven (Hasson *et al.*, 2004), visual images activate similar brain patterns, while intrinsic messages provoke individual reactions. Therefore, it would be too simplistic to assume that the mere portrayal of an icon in a film, whether visual, thematic or physical, motivates people to travel to the portrayed locations. The verbal elements within the movie also signify meaning, and human cognition depends on the two basic, independent, but interconnected symbolic systems of the non-verbal and the verbal (Barker & Schaik, 2000). Riley *et al.*'s (1998) notion of icons is not sufficient enough to represent the actual products of consumption. Rather, they combine the non-verbal and verbal textual core properties of a filmic text and, subsequently, visually represent the resulting construct through the additional combination with a physical location. It is this combination that renders a film location as an object worthy to be visited.

Film Location Nuclei

This section integrates film locations into the tourism attraction system. With this in mind, the first question that needs to be asked is what the exact nature of a tourist attraction is. MacCannell (1976) considers a tourist attraction not to be a single unit, but a semiological system assembled by three components: a tourist, a sight and a marker, the latter being particular information about a sight. This concept fits into the notion of the postmodern economy of signs, as it emphasises the fact that tourist attractions' 'significance as markers of meaning and social consumption is far greater than their role as a site of activity' (Richards, 2002: 1049). For MacCannell (1976), successful attractions have to provide two essential components; meaningful experience and sight involvement. The first component decides whether an attraction is recognised as a true object and experienced as such. Sight involvement varies in its degree and refers to the way in which the visitor is connected to the sight and its marker(s). Leiper (1990) argues that MacCannell's definition is only suitable for attraction types that include sightseeing, as some attractions do not necessarily involve sightseeing. Lew (1988) also supports this assumption. For example, many tourists perform sightseeing only on their first visit to the same place, whilst some places have no sights at all that visitors can gaze upon. Some visitors may even consciously abstain from sightseeing, a notion called 'the second gaze' (MacCannell, 2001).

Leiper (1990) also advocates that sights do not necessarily have to have an original marker. Marker-less sights can turn into markers themselves and thus become linked to the region or country that functions as the sight in this case. Nevertheless, a marker has to be separated from its medium. The medium is only the means through which the information is passed on to its receiver. In general, a marker is regarded as information about a specific site or sight. It can be a plaque, a sign, a travel book, stories told by friends or guides. When approaching a tourist attraction, the 'elementary material of first contact recognition is an off-sight marker that is carried to the sight by the sightseer (in his or her hand or head) and a clear view of a substantial sight' (MacCannell, 1976: 121).

Gunn (1988b, 1994) considers attractions to be the most important component of the supply side of tourism and attributes attractions with a magnetic or energizing power. Gunn (1988b) replaces the term 'sight' with that of the term 'nucleus'. This new term stands for the core of the attraction, referring to an attribute of a place. A nucleus can be a person, an object, a sight or an event. For example, the nucleus of a historic gold mining area would be the remains of a stamper battery or a gold miner's hut. Gunn (1988b) developed his nucleus concept into a model that is constructed as a concentric ring model. Outside the nucleus lies the inviolate belt. It provides the wider context of the nucleus in which it is embedded. Every visitor has to penetrate this belt before reaching the nucleus. The purpose of this space is to condition the visitor both physiologically as well as psychologically for the actual encounter of the nucleus. The outermost circle is labelled as the zone of closure. This term stands for the desirable tourism infrastructure around the nucleus and its inviolate belt and includes the elements of transport, services and information.

According to Gunn (1988a), an attraction missing either of these two zones lacks operational professionalism. Pearce (1991) confirms the applicability of Gunn's model, but raises the problematic nature of tourist attractions that possess multiple nuclei and, at the same time, lack a single dominant feature. He suggests instead the definition of such attractions as single nuclei with individual inviolate belts. Drawing on MacCannell's (1976) threefold attraction system and on Gunn's (1988b) concept of the attraction nucleus, Leiper (1990: 371) defines the nature of a tourist attraction as the following: 'A tourist attraction is a system comprising three elements: a tourist or human element, a nucleus or central element, and a marker or informative element. A tourist attraction comes into existence when the three elements are connected'.

The human element – that is the tourist – is defined as a person away from home for the purpose of leisure-related behaviour (Leiper, 1990). Leiper assumes five underlying causes for such behaviour. First, leisure activities are pursued away from one's usual environment in order to find satisfaction in the extraordinary. Second, this quest for leisure concentrates on personal experiences in the nuclear elements of attractions. Third, this whole process is defined by the individual's own needs and wants. Fourth, the markers are a key component in linking the tourist and the nucleus. Finally, the tourist's needs and wants are not always fulfilled.

The second component of Leiper's (1990) model, the nucleus, is appropriated from Gunn's (1988b, 1994) nucleus concept. For Leiper, the term nucleus can represent any feature of a place that is interesting to visit. Important elements of an attraction nucleus are storytelling, dynamic assets, participatory experience, tourist-relevant experience and a focus on quality and authenticity (McKercher & du Cros, 2002). Leiper (1990) also developed an experiential hierarchy of nuclei. According to him, this development was essential in order to do justice to the complex nature of tourists' experiences at attractions. Some tourists might seek only one specific nucleus, whereas others might be involved with a range of nuclei and nuclei elements. Therefore, Leiper introduced the three categories of primary, secondary and tertiary nuclei. They are defined as follows:

> A primary nucleus is an attribute of a place, a potential tourist destination, which is influential in a traveller's decision about where to go. That implies information is available to the traveller about the attribute and is active, pre-visit, in stimulating motivation in the person to travel towards the place where the attribute can be experienced. A secondary nucleus is an attribute known to a person pre-visit, but not significant in decisions about the itinerary. A tertiary nucleus is an attribute unknown pre-visit, but discovered by the individual after arriving in a destination region. (Leiper, 1990: 374)

Film locations can indeed form primary nuclei, as they can be the main reason for a tourist's trip. A particular film location can also form part of a wider travel package and thus result in a secondary nucleus: for example, the Eilean Donan Castle in Scotland (Figure 3.4), where scenes from the film *Highlander* (1986) were shot, continues to attract fans in spite of its relatively isolated position, well off the main tourist routes (Stenson, 2008, via email). Examples of secondary film location nuclei are numerous and obviously depend on the individual knowledge of the traveller, both about the film and where it was (partly) filmed. This complexity is similar to the area of literary tourism where '[l]iterary places may become stopping points along a more general tourism itinerary' (Herbert, 2001: 315). Being either literary places or film locations, some of these nuclei are equivalent to the Eiffel Tower phenomenon: as such a visit to Salzburg has to include a visit to the SoM locations, otherwise this visit would not be complete, just as a sightseeing trip to Paris would not be complete without seeing the Eiffel Tower.

A tertiary attraction nucleus involves active exploration along the travel itinerary. As Leiper (1990: 374) points out, the discovery of such a nucleus may be as satisfying as the experience itself. MacCannell's (2001)

Figure 3.4 An example for a potential, secondary film location attraction nucleus – Eilan Donan Castle, Scotland, featured in the movie *Highlander* *Source*: E. Roesch.

concept of the second gaze may be appropriate to mention at this point, as it involves active exploration 'off the beaten track' and the avoidance or penetration of the pre-determined tourist gaze as implied by the tourism industry. Engaging in the second gaze offers 'a chance to glimpse the real' (MacCannell, 2001: 36).

A tertiary film location nucleus is formed when the tourist discovers the presence of a film location at the destination. This can occur when consulting a travel guide, approaching a signpost along the road or through word-of-mouth. An example of a tertiary nucleus encounter would be apparent in the case of a visitor touring New Zealand who passes through the small town of Matamata, situated in the central North Island of New Zealand, and sees at the town entrance a signpost saying 'Welcome to Hobbiton'. This marker points to the nearby attraction nucleus of the Hobbiton film set from LOTR. Hence, the passing tourist might become interested in booking a tour to the set, although this might not have been part of his or her agenda for the day.

Nuclei are also categorised spatially. They are situated either in tourist destinations as core experiential products, or along transit or travel routes. A further spatial distinction can be made in terms of their spatial distribution within the destination. Some nuclei possess a regional distribution, while others are limited to a zone, city, sight or room. A further widening of this nucleus concept is the symbiosis of several nuclei within a destination, resulting in nuclei clustering. This notion conforms to that of Gunn (1994), who emphasises the importance of attraction clustering as a key factor in the tourism system. With regard to nuclei clustering, Leiper (1990) introduces the concept of the tourist precinct. The tourist precinct is a zone in which tourists move back and forth to experience several different nuclei in a short time, for example the clustered attractions that can be found in a city such as Paris. Film locations can be part of such a tourist precinct when they are distributed over a relatively confined area such as a city. Film locations can also form a tourist precinct in themselves when the actual nucleus is an assemblage of various smaller locations within a geographically major location.

Temporal issues are as relevant to Leiper's nucleus concept as spatial aspects. If the nucleus is an event, then time is the defining criterion. Events can also consist of clustered nuclei; a big sports event, for instance, not only hosts the competition itself, but can offer sub-events such as live concerts, dining experiences, fireworks or laser shows (Leiper, 1990).

The last component of Leiper's (1990) attraction model is that of the marker. Markers link the human element with the nucleus element and therefore act as the catalytic element of an attraction system. Leiper distinguishes between 'detached markers' and 'contiguous markers'. The term 'detached marker' stands for that which provides off-site information about a nucleus, such as travel guides, websites, travel agencies and other readily accessible sources. A further distinction is made between 'generating markers' and 'transit markers'. Generating markers are the various kinds of information people receive before setting off to a tourist destination. Transit markers are placed along a transit or travel route and point directly to the nucleus. Examples of generating markers would be television commercials, press releases or travel stories from friends and relatives. Transit markers are road signs, billboards or brochures found in tourist information centres. They can be either transportable (guide-books) or mobile (tour guides).

Contiguous markers are found at the nucleus itself. They comprise of on-site plaques, information signs or a running commentary provided by a tour guide. In some cases, involvement with the marker may result in higher satisfaction levels than with the location itself (see MacCannell, 1976). This might be the case with locations where the marker signifies more meaning to the place than the actual location. This, in turn, can transform the contiguous marker into an attraction nucleus in its own right.

The role of markers is varied, but essential for establishing a nucleus within an attraction system. They are influential in trip motivation, destination selection, itinerary planning, activity selection, nucleus identification, nucleus discovery, name connotation, the selection of souvenirs and the attachment of meanings to nuclei (Leiper, 1990). Leiper (1990) concludes that there are several ways to utilise his model for further research. Such research could, for instance, be focused on just one of the three components whilst still taking into consideration the other components. Case study approaches, both quantitative and qualitative, could add further contributions to his model. Pearce's (1999: 81) only criticism of Leiper's concept (1990) is his neglect of an examination of the meanings of the different markers and their 'messages conveyed by the information provided'. Dredge (1999), Richards (2002) and Leiper (1997) empirically tested and backed up the market applicability of the model.

In a modified version of Leiper's model film, as the generating marker, sparks interest in visiting a specific nucleus; namely the film location. It follows that this very nucleus is created at the same time through its exposure on the screen. The meanings attached to this new nucleus can signify two things. They can form an entirely new attraction nucleus that did not possess any attraction status prior to its film exposure and they can also generate an additional nucleus within an already existing attraction. Here it is important to add that it is not only the film itself that creates a new nucleus, it may also be formed through its accompanying media coverage, the involved actors, tourism stakeholders and any literary precursors.

Fantasy Lands, Disguised Places, Real Places

'Fantasy lands', 'disguised places' and 'real places' are concepts describing different types of literary places, as put forward by Robinson (2002). Fantasy lands describe 'wholly self-contained places which the reader is invited to' (Robinson, 2002: 51). Disguised places are centred on schizoid locations, for instance, when a writer describes an existing location but situates it in a different geographical setting. Real places are represented in literary works to varying degrees, ranging from pure backdrops for the storyline to their domination of relationships and actions. This is similar to the way in which places and landscapes can be embedded in films.

Robinson's (2002) threefold spatial concept of literary places can be transferred to film locations. The term 'fantasy land' could be used to describe a location that is portrayed as a non-existent, mythical land in the film, such as the fictional continent of Middle Earth in LOTR or the desert planet of Tatooine in the *Star Wars* (SW) movies. The film location tourist is 'invited' into the self-contained place of Middle Earth instead of New Zealand, or to the desert planet of Tatooine instead of Tunisia. The more adventurous film location tourist might even be inspired to 'trace the original sources for such creations' (Robinson,

2002: 51), which can result in visiting remaining film sets in remote areas by following the tracks of the involved cast and crew, or by identifying locals who starred as extras thus turning him or her into a film location tourist.

Disguised film locations come in two forms. One form is created when a location is used for the actual filming, but its geographic position is portrayed differently in the film. For instance, *The Last Samurai* (2003) was partly filmed in the region of Taranaki in New Zealand, though it sought to represent the area around Mount Fujiyama in Japan. The Samurai village used in *The Last Samurai* has been partly rebuilt and a film location tour has been established. The second form comes into being when the location that attracts visitors is based on an existing place, but was in fact filmed elsewhere, as was the case with the production of *Cold Mountain* (2003). The movie was filmed near Rasnov in Romania, although it portrayed the existing mountain with the same name in the North Carolina mountains, Southwest of Ashville. Despite such disguise, film-related packages can be offered for both types of veiled locations. Ashville's hoteliers advertised themed overnight *Cold Mountain* packages and offered guided tours leading up 'the real mountain' (Waggoner, 2005).

Arguably, it is an enormous challenge to conduct research at disguised film locations. While it might be achievable with the first form of disguised places, it is almost impossible with the second form. How would one be able to identify whether the visitors at the real Cold Mountain were attracted because of its exposure on the screen? Apart from this problematic research issue, questions of place authenticity arise. The potential danger is that ill-informed visitors might be disappointed when confronted with disguised places, as they can create false expectations. If the real Cold Mountain does not have any resemblance to the fictional one, dissatisfaction with the location experience is likely to occur. Frost (2006), using the example of the Australian movie *Ned Kelly* (2003), claims that films based on historic events or figures create destination images that are not based on the screened locations but on the places connected to the underlying history. Consequently, film location tourists visit the real historic sites rather than the locations from the film.

The notion of disguised locations is taken even further in the case of *Braveheart* (1995), a fictional film around the historic figure of the Scottish hero William Wallace and starring Mel Gibson. During the first six months of the movie's screening, the long-standing William Wallace historic monument in Stirling reported a threefold visitor increase (Beeton, 2005: 58). The Stirling city council decided to cash in on the sudden popularity and installed a Mel Gibson look-a-like statue at the foot of the monument hill. This new statue has long since become an attraction in its own right. Visitors to the area can now decide whether to gaze upon the real or the reel monument. Here, the toured reel object – the Mel Gibson statue – is not connected to any form of film location. Rather, it possesses a non-place connection to the movie that can be best described as schizoid.

Finally, a real place describes a location where the location portrayed in the film is indeed the location used for the shooting. In this case, on-locations are the real settings for fictional events, whether they are actively or passively involved in the storyline. Preston (2000) assumes that although the reality of the location still differs from the displayed image in the film, to some extent the film location tourist is aware of this difference, although he cannot support his assumptions with empiric data.

The Spatial Configuration of Film Locations

In order to define the spatial configuration of film locations, a summary of their inherent spatial premises and attributes is necessary. First of all, a film location must be geographically separated from other locations and be existent in reality, namely as a physical location. Filming must have taken place at this physical location, involving one or more scenes that make this location identifiable as a distinct setting. The latter aspect ensures that regardless of the difficulty of visibly separating a location from its wider surroundings, the location can be identified by taking on the filmic gaze. The latter term stands for the adoption of the film camera's position as it was set up for shooting the specific location shot(s) or scene(s). This interconnected spatial system will be referred to as a location containing a (filmic) sight.

Arguably, a sight can only be the toured object of the tourist encounter if it involves a significant shot from a significant scene, with its physical location sight consequently identifiable. For instance, the on-location shooting of a battle scene might involve a significant number of shots from various camera positions and angles. These shots might all be recorded within a very confined area of a few dozen metres. In the cutting room, all these shots are edited together into a scene. For the audience, this battle scene becomes a fast sequence of action with perhaps only one or two memorable shots that can be matched on site and consequently toured on location. Figure 3.5 graphically explains the different, spatial location-sight configurations that can occur. A sight can be identical with its location, if the latter contains this very sight (configuration A). However, a location often includes several sights. The different shots were either filmed by a stationary camera that was simply turned in different directions on a revolving base (configuration B) or by using

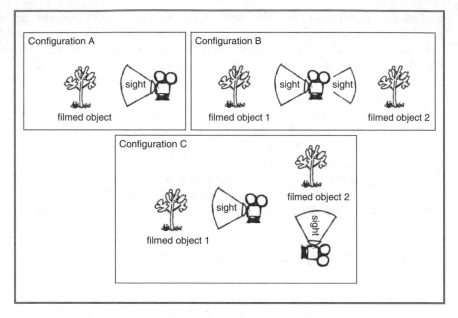

Figure 3.5 The spatial configuration of film locations

different, spatially separated camera positions (configuration C). It can be argued that the resulting, individual sights serve as single nuclei within the attraction nucleus of the location.

One last configuration that needs to be mentioned is when there is no sight at all to gaze upon. This can be the case when access to the actual location is denied or the identification of a distinct sight is not possible.

Location Access

Access issues have been somewhat neglected in tourism research (Hayes & Slater, 2003). It is generally agreed though, that access involves the notion of barriers that hinder access. Dodd and Sandell (1998) identified several access barriers in their study of museums. Access barriers can be physical, financial, emotional, cultural, and also include access hindrance from decision making as well as from information. These barriers can be transferred to all other aspects of tourism. Research has identified that the improvement of access to destinations can result in visitor increases (Hall, 2005).

Access to film locations is an essential factor in film location tourism. Without access, film location tourism is not possible, as the locations and precise sights cannot be toured. Closed-off locations cause disappointment in film location tourists, as Bloss (2007) has shown in the example of *The Da Vinci Code*-induced film location tourism to Paris. Yet, because film producers are goal-oriented and solely focused on producing their film, locations are selected not with future location access in mind, but for their suitability to provide the necessary scenery or background for specific shots and scenes. Certainly, the effort of accessing a location for filming has to be cost effective for the production company but, as many examples illustrate, the necessity of accessing particular places for on-location shooting can result in the inclusion of remote areas. For instance, gravel roads had to be built to access a number of locations for the filming of LOTR and some locations were only accessible via a rough four-wheel drive track (Brodie, 2002). Some of the Tatooine film sets for the SW episodes I and II were constructed amidst the sand dunes of the Tunisian desert near the oasis of Touzeur and were accessible only by four-wheel drive. Arguably, access to film locations within already developed tourist destinations is easier to realise than in undeveloped tourist areas.

Another physical barrier is that of property ownership. Often, film crews shoot on private land in order to minimise property rights issues and claims. In these cases, access to the location has to be negotiated via the landowner, who will probably not want to have people trespassing in increasing numbers. In the instance of LOTR, some landowners have set up organised tours themselves in order to contain the visitation impacts or else they have contracted external tour operators to access their property in an organised and controlled environment.

A major problem with film location accessibility has emerged due to the increase in Hollywood 'runaway' productions, or more precisely internationally mobile films. Many US production companies have shifted their on-location shooting to countries 'off the beaten track'. This can mean a significant effort for some film location tourists in terms of time and cost in order to travel to these places. The film location tourist has to organise the complete travel arrangements, starting with the information-gathering phase through to the booking of all necessary means of transport. Cultural barriers may arise as well, such as communication barriers or unfamiliar customs. In order to locate specific film locations, the hiring of local guides could be inevitable.

Safety is another major access issue. Whether the feelings for potential insecurities are subjective or objective, perceived danger can influence travel decisions to a major extent. Nevertheless, despite the difficulties of accessing film locations, many examples illustrate the devotion of film fans who will travel to even the remotest locations.

Film Locations as Temporal Constructs

The filmic/fictional time(line) and the location time

Every film has its own 'filmic time'. Filmic time is the 'temporal ordering and arrangement of events that exist within the film as opposed to the normal flow of time in the real world' (Konigsberg, 1997: 138). Filmic time can be compressed, extended or slowed down, whereas the 'fictional time(line)' expresses the different streaks of time in which the storyline is set. Fictional time determines the film's historic time period, the seasonal time(s) and the daily time(s) of the fictional events. The cinema audience experiences both filmic and fictional time within the film. Fictional time not only impacts upon the actions of the characters in the film, but also upon the settings. If the historic setting within a film is in the past, as for example in *Braveheart* (1995), then the audience is immersed into a fictional time dating back 700 years. Therefore, the costumes, the set constructions and also the actions of the characters are determined by the fictional time at the turn of the 13th century.

Other streams within fictional time are the portrayed season(s) and the portrayed daytime(s) and their influence over the physical environment. It might be winter in the movie, so the mountains depicted in the film are covered in snow or else the plot might be set in autumn with multi-coloured leaves covering the trees. Other movies include night scenes. One of the most memorable scenes in *Star Wars – A New Hope* (1977) is when Luke Skywalker gazes into the sunset outside his home – presenting the audience with twin suns setting together on the horizon. SW film location tourists might want to experience the location while the sun, in this case only one, sets over the desert of Tunisia.

The major issue with fictional time in a film is the potential generation of experiential, temporal location discrepancies. If the tourist visits a LOTR location in summer, the surrounding mountains will lack the dusting of snow portrayed in some of the film scenes. An additional problem arises through the common procedure of film producers mending or doctoring the temporal condition of the physical location during the shooting. Darkness can be imitated by special camera lenses. Snow can be produced artificially. The Samurai village in the movie *The Last Samurai* (2003), where Tom Cruise's character lives over the period of autumn, winter and spring, sees falling leaves, snowfall and cherry tree blossoms. All of these scenes were shot in one location over a filming period of six to eight weeks in the middle of the New Zealand summer. The production designers simply used fake leaves and cherry tree blossoms on fake trees. For the winter scenes, all the huts as well as the grass around the huts were covered with snow spray, imitation icicles and artificial snow (Radcliffe, 2005, personal communication). Visitors to the Samurai Village location will never be able to experience it in the same autumn or winter conditions as it appears in the movie. It does not snow at the real location and the trees and bushes at the location are native to New Zealand and therefore evergreen.

The film location issue-attention cycle

Another temporal element of a film location is generated by its media exposure throughout the different windows of its film exhibition cycle. Every new window of the cycle is likely to be covered by the media. In particular, before and during location shooting, independent media often hunt down any information snippets available, whether it is about the look of the set decorations or gossip from the set. The media attention can raise public awareness about the opportunity to travel either to the generally portrayed destination or place, or to the particular film locations.

This temporality issue indicates some evident parallels with the notion of the issue-attention cycle, first put forward by Downs (1972). The notion of the issue-attention cycle presumes five different stages, through which public issues are dealt with in an evolutionary transgression within the agenda-setting strategy of the media (Figure 3.6). In the pre-problem stage, an acute problem arises, or an event takes place. Only experts or special interest groups are informed. In the next stage, known as 'alarmed discovery and euphoric enthusiasm', the public becomes more informed about the issue as a result of the media attention it has attracted. At this stage, the public is confident that there will be a solution for the problem presented. In stage three, the public realises the costs connected with the potential solution and, as a consequence, interest in the issue starts to decline with the next stage. Reasons for this decline can be boredom with the topic or else, threat or stress when

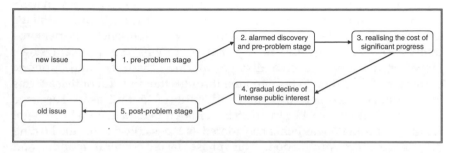

Figure 3.6 The issue-attention cycle after Downs (1972)

concerning oneself with the issue. In the final stage, the public moves on to a new area of interest.

Downs (1972) puts forward three limitations regarding the nature of problems that are likely to enter the cycle. First, the problem has to be existent for a minority within the general population, with the majority not affected by it. Second, the solution for the problem must present benefits for either the majority or an elite minority. Finally, this notion is only valid for problems without 'intrinsically exciting qualities' (Downs, 1972: 41). The issue-attention cycle has been applied within the agenda-setting theory of the mass media and, although initially solely based on subjective observation, has proven to be applicable in real-life situations (Peters & Hogwood, 1985; Neumann, 1990; Hester & Gonzenbach, 1997; Schindlmayr, 2001). In tourism research, Hall (2002) based his examination of the attacks of September 11 and their impact on travel behaviour, as well as the subsequent reactions of the media and tourism policies, on the issue-attention cycle. He identified five distinct stages of how the public and the media dealt with the issue.

The applicability of the issue-attention cycle to film productions and the subsequent follow-on effects of film tourism were tested for this book with the feature film *The Last Samurai* (2003) starring Tom Cruise, of which the majority was shot in the district of Taranaki in the North Island of New Zealand. An electronic content analysis of the database of Taranaki's local newspaper *The Daily News* was conducted in order to find all relevant press reports on the filming. In addition, an analysis of the on-line article database provided by the area's development agency Venture Taranaki (2004a) was undertaken. Included in the list presented in Figure 3.7 are all the articles featuring *The Last Samurai* stories found in both the local newspaper *The Daily News* and in the Venture Taranaki on-line article database.

The filming process for *The Last Samurai* started with an initial reconnaissance in the area by the contracted location scout manager in the middle of 2001. At this point, only a handful of key figures in the district knew about the possibility of hosting a major film production in the area, namely the mayor of New Plymouth, the responsible managers of Venture Taranaki and the landowners of the future Samurai Village location (S. Radcliffe, 2005, personal interview; P. Tennent, 2005, personal interview). This stage can be equated to Downs' pre-problem stage. However, his proposed second stage, 'alarmed discovery and euphoric enthusiasm', has then to be amended through the division of these terms into the stages 'alarmed discovery' and 'euphoric enthusiasm'. The stage of 'alarmed discovery' began on 28 September 2001, when the media got wind that Taranaki was being considered as a possible site for the hosting of a major film production. This phase lasted several months and continued right through the period from 11 to 18 May 2002, when the

> **1. pre-problem stage**
> reconnaissance by location scout
> in the middle of 2001

> **2.1 alarmed discovery**
> first rumours circulate that Taranaki could
> play host to a Hollywood production
> (28/09/01 – 18/05/02)

> **2.2 euphoric enthusiasm**
> Tom Cruise arrives; location filming starts;
> main period of location filming
> (07/01/03 – 08/03/03)

Date	Headline	Coverage international	national	local
2001, 28 September	Taranaki waits in wings for Hollywood decision			√
2002, 11 March	Hollywood eyes Taranaki			√
2002, 19 March	Movie officials on hunt for Cruise digs			√
2002, 22 March	Cruisey Taranaki set for stardom			√
2002, 13 April	Warner Bros check out region as movie location			√
2002, 14 May	Hollywood hotshot comes to Taranaki			√
2002, 14 May	Taranaki tipped for Tom Cruise movie			√
2002, 15 May	Taranaki is first choice for Cruise film		√	
2002, 17 May	NZ to star in Cruise movie		√	
2002, 17 May	Put on your best swansuit – we're going to the movies			√
2002, 18 May	Movie sends buzz throughout Cruise country			√
2002, 18 May	Samurai set for 2003			√
2002, 20 June	Self-promotion paying its way in business confidence			√
2002, 21 June	Film starts here in January			√
2002, 2 August	Taranaki dies off to cinepoium			√
2002, 15 August	Movie magic at work in back-country valley			√
2002, 27 August	Samurai-star rumours slashed			√
2002, 31 August	comedian Connolly to co-star with Cruise			√
2002, 8 September	Tom takes a Samurai vacation		√	
2002, 2 November	When the world comes to town			√
2002, 7 November	Manson base for Cruise			√
2002, 7 November	Film makers deal with weather, plan to shut out public			√
2002, 30 November	Call goes out for extras and that includes you			√
2002, 30 November	Lights, cameras and action in Uruti			√
2002, 7 December	Samurai has rental prices galloping			√
2003, 14 December	Park's cricket ground being prepared for filming			√
2003, 7 January	Cruise and Paltrow set up home in NZ	√		
2003, 7 January	A slice of Samurai scenery in Taranaki			√
2003, 7 January	Cruise makes himself at home			√
2003, 8 January	Japanese village for film almost complete			√
2003, 9 January	Meat firm and movie star talking turkey			√
2003, 9 January	The good oil on chopper sightings			√
2003, 10 January	Tom Cruise to cruise on Oracle	√		
2003, 11 January	A star arrives – and life cruises on beside the surf		√	
2003, 11 January	Claims film set desecrates Maori rites			√
2003, 11 January	Top film viewing spot closed off			√
2003, 11 January	Last Samurai has first scrap			√
2003, 11 January	Cruise to face up to media throng			√
2003, 11 January	Cruise crew set up roger for the summer		√	
2003, 11 January	More screen heavyweights join Cruise		√	
2003, 11 January	Taranaki's Big Break		√	
2003, 12 January	Hunky Tom loo kid in town		√	
2003, 12 January	Rain Man has the golden touch		√	
2003, 12 January	Cruise's lover and children to visit		√	
2003, 12 January	Hongi in Taranaki for Top Gun star Tom, cruising in Taranaki			√
2003, 13 January	Media circus cruises into town		√	
2003, 13 January	Tom does a star turn in Taradise		√	
2003, 13 January	Star gets the picture though words fail for the media			√
2003, 13 January	Taranaki gets star billing from Tom			√
2003, 13 January	Media meeting puts movie makers on Cruise control			√
2003, 14 January	Cruise comment a beauty			√
2003, 15 January	Visiting star gets the whole town talking	√		
2003, 15 January	Port set takes shape	√		
2003, 15 January	The Beast's OK, but Tom wants a cruise cut			√
2003, 16 January	Hip Taranaki popular with Hollywood		√	
2003, 16 January	World media pick up on Taranaki film now			√
2003, 17 January	Samurai cash rolls in to local business till			√
2003, 17 January	Connolly due in Taranaki next month			√
2003, 18 January	Not so Cruisey anymore	√		
2003, 20 January	Tom's private audience	√		
2003, 21 January	City gets set for Samurai invasion			√
2003, 22 January	Film spin-off could last for 18 months		√	
2003, 22 January	No-fly restrictions over Cruise's Oakura hideaway			√
2003, 25 January	The Hollywood hill		√	
2003, 28 January	Visitors check out Samurai movie sets			√
2003, 28 January	Spall arrives for Last Samurai role			√
2003, 31 January	Lake set for Samurai battles			√
2003, 3 February	Samurai crew lets off steam, rubber			√
2003, 6 February	Tom's tastebuds tackle Taranaki takeaways			√
2003, 8 February	Penelope Cruz' in just for a cruise			√
2003, 11 February	Focus on dark side of The Last Samurai			√
2003, 12 February	Toms donation puts school in the shade			√
2003, 13 February	Amazing film set wows Cruise			√
2003, 13 February	Movie bowling along			√
2003, 15 February	Cruise family drops in remote café			√
2003, 18 February	It's Tom Cruise or… bust			√
2003, 18 February	Family's flat moment takes star turn			√
2003, 18 February	Tom thanks kid's class act			√
2003, 20 February	Town turns out to support Samurai crew			√
2003, 21 February	Connolly at his comic best as he wams Taranakiof what's to come			√
2003, 21 February	Billy Connolly gives impromptu performance to Taranakiknala			√
2003, 24 February	Cruisy working dad	√		
2003, 24 February	Mr Connolly I presume. Oh, and welcome…			√
2003, 24 February	Connolly and Spall made to feel welcome			√
2003, 25 February	Filming at the park proves to be a blast			√
2003, 26 February	Oddball of 'Last Samurai'		√	

Figure 3.7 Articles featuring the film production of *The Last Samurai* in Taranaki, North Island, New Zealand (in chronological order) and the application of Down's (1972) issue-attention cycle
Sources: Personal search of the database of Taranaki's local newspaper *The Daily News*; Venture Taranaki, 2004a.

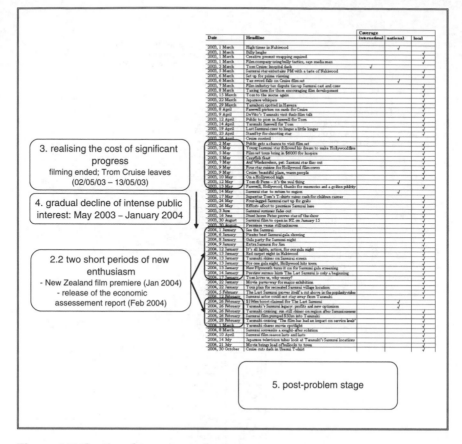

3. realising the cost of significant progress

filming ended; Trom Cruise leaves (02/05/03 – 13/05/03)

4. gradual decline of intense public interest: May 2003 – January 2004

2.2 two short periods of new enthusiasm
- New Zealand film premiere (Jan 2004)
- release of the economic assessement report (Feb 2004)

5. post-problem stage

Date	Headline	Coverage International	national	local
2003, 1 March	High times in Nakiwood		✓	
2003, 1 March	Billy laughs			✓
2003, 1 March	Creative present wrapping required			✓
2003, 1 March	Film company using belly tactics, says media man			✓
2003, 3 March	Tom Cruise: hospital dash			✓
2003, 5 March	Samurai star entertains PM with a taste of Nakiwood	✓		✓
2003, 6 March	Set up for prime viewing			✓
2003, 6 March	Tax sword falls on Cruise film set		✓	
2003, 7 March	Film industry tax dispute ties up Samurai cast and crew			✓
2003, 8 March	Taxing time for those encouraging film development			✓
2003, 15 March	Tom to the movie again			✓
2003, 22 March	Japanese whispers			✓
2003, 29 March	Tamahori spotted in Hawera			✓
2003, 8 April	Farewell picture on cards for Cruise			✓
2003, 9 April	DeVito's Taranaki visit fuels film talk			✓
2003, 12 April	Public to pose in farewell for Tom			✓
2003, 14 April	Taranaki farewell for Tom			✓
2003, 19 April	Last Samurai crew to linger a little longer			✓
2003, 23 April	Stand by for shooting star			✓
2003, 26 April	Cruise control	✓		
2003, 2 May	Public gets a chance to visit film set			✓
2003, 3 May	Young Samurai star followed his dream to make Hollywood films			✓
2003, 5 May	Film set tours bring in $6000 for hospice			✓
2003, 5 May	Crayfish feast			✓
2003, 7 May	Auf Wiedersehen, pet: Samurai star flies out			✓
2003, 9 May	Four star cuisine for Hollywood film crews			✓
2003, 9 May	Cruise: beautiful place, warm people			✓
2003, 10 May	On a Hollywood high			✓
2003, 12 May	Tom & Penz – it's the real thing	✓		✓
2003, 13 May	Farewell, Hollywood, thanks for memories and a golden publicity			✓
2003, 14 May	Samurai star to return to region		✓	
2003, 17 May	Superstar Tom's T-shirts raises cash for children cancer			✓
2003, 24 May	Four-legged Samurai cast up for grabs			✓
2003, 26 May	Efforts afoot to premiere Samurai here			✓
2003, 3 June	Samurai summer fades out			✓
2003, 16 June	Stunt horse Peter proves star of the show			✓
2003, 30 August	Samurai film to open in NZ on January 15			✓
2003, 30 August	Premiere venue still unknown			✓
2004, 1 January	See the Samurai			✓
2004, 6 January	Pirates beat Samurai gala showing			✓
2004, 8 January	Gala party for Samurai night			✓
2004, 9 January	Extra Samurai for Jim			✓
2004, 12 January	It's all lights, action, for our gala night			✓
2004, 13 January	Red carpet night in Nakiwood			✓
2004, 13 January	Taranaki shines on Samurai screen			✓
2004, 13 January	For one gala night, Hollywood hits town			✓
2004, 13 January	New Plymouth turns it on for Samurai gala screening			✓
2004, 14 January	Preview success hints The Last Samurai is only a beginning			✓
2004, 22 January	Tom loves us, why worry?			✓
2004, 22 January	Movie paves way for major exhibition			✓
2004, 22 January	Tour plan for recreated Samurai village location			✓
2004, 5 February	The Last Samurai proves itself a cut above in the popularity stakes			✓
2004, 12 February	Samurai actor could sort stay away from Taranaki			✓
2004, 26 February	$196m boost claimed for The Last Samurai		✓	
2004, 26 February	Taranaki's Samurai legacy: profits and new optimism			✓
2004, 26 February	Taranaki cruising: can still shiner on region after Samurai summer			✓
2004, 26 February	Samurai film pumped $50m into Taranaki			✓
2004, 28 February	Taranaki craving 'The film has had an impact on service levels'			✓
2004, 1 March	Taranaki shares movie spotlight			✓
2004, 8 March	Samurai screenvits a sought-after solution			✓
2004, 10 April	Samurai film season lasts and lasts			✓
2004, 14 April	Japanese television takes look at Taranaki's Samurai locations			✓
2004, 21 July	Movie brings load of bullocks to town			✓
2004, 30 October	Cruise cuts dash in Unami T-shirt			✓

Figure 3.7 *Continued*

final decision to go ahead with the film was made. After 18 May 2002, the media lost interest in this topic, however this changed quickly with Tom Cruises' arrival in Taranaki on 7 January 2003, followed by an international press conference on 13 January. The start of on-location shooting soon afterwards kept the media attention high as locals and visitors alike tried to get glimpses of the sets and of the star, Tom Cruise himself. During this period, the international media attention on the district was significant and this high concentration of interest conforms with Down's stage of 'euphoric enthusiasm'.

Approximately six weeks into the filming, the interest began to decrease until the conclusion of filming and the departure of Tom Cruise from the region on 8 May 2003. This new peak in media attention can be equated to Down's (1972) third stage, as the filming was about to finish and the district of Taranaki would lose the focus of the international media. Interest further declined over the course of 2003.

Another modification to Down's original notion of the issue-attention cycle is a twofold, short flare-up of new enthusiasm. The first phase of new enthusiasm occurred during the movie's New Zealand premiere, which took place on 13 January 2004 in the district's capital city, New Plymouth. The second flare-up of new enthusiasm was initiated on 26 February 2004 as a result of the release of the economic impact assessment study of the postproduction effects of *The Last Samurai* (Venture Taranaki, 2004b). A few media articles followed up on this issue. After this last spark of enthusiasm, the public interest was exhausted and the media rapidly moved on to other issues.

It is important to note that in the aftermath of the filming, the regional tourism industry did not seize the chance to generate any spin-offs from the filming. As the district's tourism agency was in the process of being restructured at the time, no efforts were undertaken to leverage off benefits for the district's tourism industry (P. Avery, 2005, phone interview). Only one private tourism business tried to profit from *The Last Samurai*. The landowner of the farm where the Samurai village had been constructed, re-created one of the huts and established a guided tour around the location.

At this point, the question arises as to exactly what this application of the issue-attention cycle might reveal. First of all, in the case of *The Last Samurai*, the cycle had to be modified slightly, as it was necessary to divide the first stage into the two separate phases of 'alarmed discovery' and 'euphoric enthusiasm' (Figure 3.8). Another modification is the twofold flare-up of euphoric enthusiasm after interest had already declined. Still, this fits somewhat into the notion of the cycle, as Downs (1972) claims that the post-problem stage can still see flare-ups of renewed interest in the issue. In the case of *The Last Samurai*, it was the

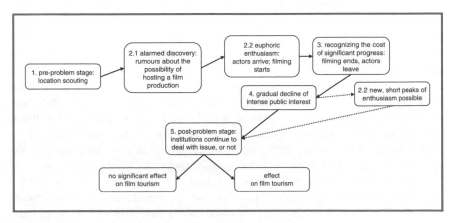

Figure 3.8 The film location issue-attention cycle

thorough and active involvement of the whole community in the filming process (P. Tennent, 2005, personal interview) that sparked the mentioned peaks of new enthusiasm. After the tourism shareholders did not draw on the attention created around the filming, the public interest turned towards new issues. This certainly did not help potential tourism businesses to initiate film location tours or other film-related services. Figure 3.8 displays the modified issue-attention cycle that is adopted to the on-location shooting of a film production with its subsequent effect on film tourism.

Arguably, the intensity of this process and the power of the involved institutions differ enormously from case to case, that is, from film production to film production. When it comes to the process of the on-location shooting of a major film production, at least in Western countries, *The Last Samurai* is certainly no exception. As mentioned previously, only a very small number of film productions can create enough lasting interest in order to have a considerable effect on subsequent film location tourism to the area.

The Links between Film and Location: Core Precursors

In their study of film tourism, Riley *et al.* (1998) conclude that further research should concentrate on the connection between the movie genre and film tourism, the connection between movie icons and film tourism and the correlation between box office success and film tourism. Within the following sections, some of these connectivity issues will be explored further.

Film *de facto* genres and textual core properties

Conventional film genres overlap. They are mixed, hybrid, blurred and often divided into main and subgenres. Stemming from French, the term '(film) genre' indicates a 'type of film and broadcast program either by content or by their specific audience' (Bognár, 1995: 94). Another definition for film genre is a 'term for any group of motion pictures that reveals similar stylistic, thematic, and structural interests' (Beaver, 1994: 171). Notably, film theorists struggle over the difficulty to define distinct film genres; as such a classification cannot be a neutral and objective procedure. 'A genre is ultimately an abstract conception rather than something that exists empirically in the world' (Feuer, 1992: 144). Practitioners and the general public establish their own *de facto* genres apart from those determined by media theorists. This demarcates a problematic relationship between academic and practical taxonomies. Bordwell (1989: 147) argues that 'no set of necessary and sufficient conditions can mark off genres from other sorts of groupings in ways that all experts or ordinary film-goers would find acceptable'. But as genres are 'processes of systematisation' (Neale, 1995: 463), not systems, genres 'only exist in so far as a social group declares and enforces the rules that constitute them' (Hodge & Kress, 1988: 7). Genres provide frameworks within which texts are produced and interpreted. Therefore, target audiences can be addressed more efficiently (Gledhill, 1985) and certain expectations within the audience can be raised (and satisfied) more easily. The instalment of genres provides a suitable framework for the reader to identify, select and interpret texts. It can also enable the reader to assess the reality status of the text.

This book reverts to the *de facto* genres established by the general public that are agreed frameworks for understanding the triangular relationship between the text, its producer and its interpreter. Swales (1990: 54) argues that the 'community's nomenclature for genres is an important source of insight'. The establishment of *de facto* genres in this book also has a very practical reason as the on-line movie database IMDb was consulted for a significant amount of research in the following sections. IMDb provides an exhaustive movie database, detailed information about all referenced feature films and acknowledges the existence of the genre overlap. It draws on genre labels from the generally agreed canon. In addition, its genre nomenclature has also been utilised by other film tourism researchers (Bordelon & Dimanche, 2003).

In order to carve out the necessary genre taxonomy for this book, additional sources were consulted in order to gain knowledge about the generally accepted canon of *de facto* genres. These sources included a thorough search in the internet for recurring *de facto* main genres, the review of two film dictionaries (Beaver, 1994; Konigsberg, 1997) and one film genre reference (Lopez, 1993). The extracted *de facto* genres were further compared with those of two video stores which served as further real-life examples of the community's proposed nomenclature (Swales, 1990).

The general consensus agrees upon roughly 11 main *de facto* genres, plus an additional 10–14 sub or hybrid genres. Out of these, 17 *de facto* genres were derived for this book. These derived genres are: action, adventure, biographical film, comedy, crime, drama, fantasy, historical film, horror, musical, mystery, romance, science fiction, sports film, thriller, war and Western. This nomenclature conforms to that of the IMDb. The classification established for this book assembles the film's generic or textual core properties, which are genre-distinct, into an interpretable nomenclature. The textual core properties of a film include the narrative, the underlying themes, the characters, the iconography, the quality of the acting, the setting, lighting, special effects, sound, camera techniques and editing (Baker, 2003; Campsall, 2002; Corrigan, 1994).

Table 3.2 provides an overview of a number of feature films that have initiated film tourism. The places exposed in the cited movies have either attracted additional visitors in significant numbers or they have become attractions in their own right. The listed feature films are classified into their genres and their textual core properties are also highlighted. The main focus in the textual core property enumeration lies in the under-lying themes, as they may indicate intrinsic key qualities (Hasson *et al.*, 2004). These, in turn, can hint towards a possible connection between the *de facto* genre and its potential to attract film tourists. The list is by no means exhaustive, nevertheless it claims to cite some of the most evident tourism-inducing feature films.

The overview of tourism-inducing feature films presented in Table 3.2 suggests that it is mostly the intrinsic qualities of these movies that initially evoke a sense of longing to experience the portrayed place. The majority of the listed movies possess either the intrinsic qualities of the drama or of the romance genre or even from both classic genres, which have been popular since Antiquity. The textual core properties of these films indicate that it is intrinsic longings and values, centred on an appealing story and shot in attractive locations, which provoke strong reactions from the audience. Interestingly, not one action movie can be found on the list. It seems that this genre does not possess enough intrinsic core properties to initiate film tourism.

Box office numbers and media exposure

Riley *et al.* (1998) assume that tourism-inducing movies have to be box office successes in order to generate sufficient place exposure. A box office success means that a movie has generated more revenue than the film production has cost. Table 3.3 provides box office numbers for the movies listed in Table 3.2, along with their ranking within the 350 highest box office successes worldwide. Where worldwide figures were not available, the US box office numbers are given. It is important to add that the quoted box office numbers are not inflation-adjusted. The latter figures are either not accessible to the general public or simply do not exist. The purpose of this enumeration is to get some indication about the importance of cinema attendance in connection with film tourism.

What becomes clear from the enumeration in Table 3.3 is that box office numbers provide no indication of the ability of a movie to initiate film location tourism, as previously assumed by Cousins and Andereck (1993) and Riley *et al.* (1998). One has to keep in mind that even movies with a significant effect on tourism attract only a relatively small amount

Table 3.2 *De facto* genres and textual core properties of tourism-inducing feature films

Feature film	De facto genres	Textual core properties with the main focus on the underlying themes	Visited location
Amélie (2001)	Comedy/drama/ romance	A young woman's first discovery of love	Café des Deux Moulins, Paris, France
Braveheart (1995)	Action/biography/ drama/war	Life of a historical hero in his battle for freedom	Mel Gibson look-a-like statue, Stirling, Scotland
Bull Durham (1988)	Comedy/drama/ romance/sport	Comical story around a popular type of sport	Durham Athletic Park, USA
Captain Corelli's Mandolin (2001)	Drama/romance/war	Love in times of war on a romantic Greek island	The island of Cephallonia, Greece
Close Encounters of the Third Kind (1977)	Adventure/drama/ science fiction	Alien encounter	Devils Tower Monument, USA
Cold Mountain (2003)	Drama/romance/war	Perilous journey back to a loved one	The 'real' Cold Mountain, USA
Dances with Wolves (1990)	Adventure/drama/ Western	Liberation from personal frontiers; tolerance; the noble savage in harmony with nature	Film set of Fort Hays, USA
Field of Dreams (1989)	Drama/fantasy/sport	Fulfilment of a personal dream	Cornfield in Dyersville, Iowa
Four Weddings and a Funeral (1994)	Comedy/romance/ drama	Romantic notions about love and marriage	Crown Hotel, Amersham, UK
Harry Potter I+II (2001, 2002)	Adventure/fantasy	Addressing everyone's longing to be able to perform magic	Diverse locations around the UK, e.g. Alnwick Castle and Lacock Abbey

Table 3.2 (*Continued*)

Feature film	De facto genres	Textual core properties with the main focus on the underlying themes	Visited location
Highlander (1986)	Action/fantasy	Amelioration of future and past with a place emphasis on the Scottish Highlands; themes: immortality and death duels	Eilean Donan Castle, Scotland
JFK (1991)	Drama/thriller/biography	Biographical story about one of the biggest murder mysteries in history	Book Depository Museum, Dallas, USA
Little Women (1994)	Drama/romance	Romanticising post-war life/family life	Orchard House, MA, USA
Lost in Translation (2003)	Drama/comedy	Finding love to fill an empty life	Bar in the Park Hyatt Tokyo Hotel, Japan
Notting Hill (1994)	Comedy/romance/drama	Romantic love theme between a nobody and a politician	Bookstore from the movie, Notting Hill, London, UK
Pirates of the Caribbean (2003)	Action/adventure/fantasy	Romantic notion of a pirate's life in exotic places	Port Royale film set in Wallilabou bay, St. Vincent
Pride and Prejudice (2005)	Romance/drama	Love story set in the Georgian era	Basildon Park, Lower Basildon, Berkshire; Burghley House, Stamford, Lincolnshire; Chatsworth House, Edensor, Derbyshire; all UK locations
Schindler's List (1993)	Biography/drama/history/war	Life of a contemporary hero, risking his life for the sake of others	Ghetto location in Warsaw, Poland

Table 3.2 (Continued)

Feature film	De facto genres	Textual core properties with the main focus on the underlying themes	Visited location
Star Wars Episodes I, II, IV (1999, 2002, 1977)	Action/adventure/ fantasy/science fiction	A unique, detailed fictional world with characters that have to fight the ultimate battle against the dark side	Set locations around Touzeur, Tunisia
Steel Magnolias (1989)	Drama/comedy/ romance	Life in a small community with all its everyday issues	Town of Natchitoches, USA
The Beach (2000)	Drama/adventure/ thriller	The quest for paradise	Phi Phi Leh Island near Phuket, Thailand
The Blair Witch Project (1999)	Horror/mystery/ thriller	Evil witchcraft; low budget; recorded with hand-held cameras = cult movie	Town of Burkittsville, Maryland
The Bridges of Madison County (1995)	Drama/romance	The bittersweet taste of love	The town of Winterset, USA
The Da Vinci Code (2006)	Drama/mystery/ thriller	Mysterious thriller around a century old secret kept by the Templars	Rosslyn Chapel near Edinburgh, Scotland; Eglise Saint-Sulpice, Paris, France; various other locations
The Fugitive (1993)	Action/adventure/ crime/thriller	Duel between two 'good guys' over the murder of one of the guys wife	Great Smoky Mountain Railroad, USA
The Last of the Mohicans (1992)	Adventure/romance/ war/Western	Love theme in a romanticised time setting	Chimney Rock Park, USA
The Lord of the Rings (2001, 2002, 2003)	Action/adventure/ fantasy/war	Self-empowerment and the fight for the good against superior forces	Circa 50 locations around NZ

Table 3.2 (*Continued*)

Feature film	De facto genres	Textual core properties with the main focus on the underlying themes	Visited location
Thelma and Louise (1991)	Action/adventure/crime/thriller	Women and self-empowerment	Arches N.P., USA
The Man from Snowy River (1982)	Drama/romance/Western	Self-empowerment in a hostile environment	Mansfield district, High Country, Australia
The Sound of Music (1965)	Biography/drama/musical	Family values	Locations in and around the city of Salzburg, Austria
The Third Man (1949)	Mystery/thriller	Hunt for a criminal in a dark yet romanticised version of Vienna	Locations in the city of Vienna, Austria
The Witness (1985)	Drama/romance/thriller	Insight into the life of the 'exotic other' (= Amish)	Amish farm featuring in the movie, USA
Under the Tuscan Sun (2003)	Comedy/drama/romance	Romanticising Italian culture, lifestyle and cuisine	City of Cortona, Italy

Sources: Riley and Van Doren (1992); Cousins and Andereck (1993); Riley *et al.* (1998); Bee (1999); Dishneau (1999); The Economist (1999); Beeton (2001); Busby and Klug (2001); Reeves (2001); Tzanelli (2001); Grihault (2003); Sciolino (2003); Stoddart (2003); Bly (2004); Business and Economy (2005); Pennsylvania Dutch Convention and Visitors Bureau (2005); Long (2005) via email; Waggoner (2005); Eames (2005); Stenson (2005) via email.

Table 3.3 Box office successes of tourism-inducing feature films

Feature film	Box office (in US dollars)	Ranking within the 350 highest box office successes worldwide
Amélie (2001)	33,201,661	—
Braveheart (1995)	204,000,000	350
Bull Durham (1988)	50,888,729 (US)	—
Captain Corelli's Mandolin (2001)	62,112,895	—
Close Encounters of the Third Kind (1977)	300,000,000	191
Cold Mountain (2003)	173,013,509	—
Dances with Wolves (1990)	424,200,000	90
Field of Dreams (1989)	84,431,625	—
Four Weddings and a Funeral (1994)	244,100,000	263
Harry Potter and the Philosopher's Stone (2001)	968,657,891	5
Harry Potter and the Chamber of Secrets (2002)	866,300,000	14
Highlander (1986)	5,900,000 (US)	—
JFK (1991)	205,400,000	348
Little Women (1994)	50,083,616	—
Lost in Translation (2003)	119, 723, 856	—
Notting Hill (1994)	363,000,000	124
Pirates of the Caribbean (2003)	653,200,000	33
Pride and Prejudice (2005)	120,051,592	—
Schindler's List (1993)	321,200,000	170
Star Wars – The Phantom Menace (1999)	922,379,000	8
Star Wars – Attack of the Clones (2002)	648,200,000	34
Star Wars – A New Hope (1977)	797,900,000	20
Steel Magnolias (1989)	95,904,091	—

Table 3.3 (*Continued*)

Feature film	Box office (in US dollars)	Ranking within the 350 highest box office successes worldwide
The Beach (2000)	144,056,873	—
The Blair Witch Project (1999)	240,500,000	269
The Bridges of Madison County (1995)	176,000,000	—
The Da Vinci Code (2006)	757,236,138	26
The Fugitive (1993)	368,700,000	119
Thelma and Louise (1991)	45,360,915	—
The Last of the Mohicans (1992)	75,505,856	—
The Lord of the Rings – The Fellowship of the Ring (2001)	860,700,000	16
The Lord of the Rings – The Two Towers (2002)	921,600,000	9
The Lord of the Rings – The Return of the King (2003)	1,129,219,252	2
The Man from Snowy River (1982)	20,659,423	—
The Sound of Music (1965)	158,000,000	—
The Third Man (1949)	618,173	—
The Witness (1985)	68,706,993 (USA)	—
Under the Tuscan Sun (2003)	60,216,000	—

Source: www.imdb.com/boxoffice/alltimegross?region = world-wide (accessed 5 April 2009).

of visitors compared to their total cinema attendance. In addition, the revenues generated through box office sales hover slightly below 20% of the total receipts of a feature film release (Epstein, 2005), with the rest being gained through television exposure, video and DVD sales and during other windows of exhibition.

The media exposure accompanying the production and the subsequent release of a feature film certainly plays an additional role in generating film locations as new attraction nuclei. One can assume that big budget on-location productions draw significantly more media attention than small or off-location productions. Media coverage of a film production, as can be summarised from the example of *The Last Samurai*, predominantly deals with stories about the stars involved in the filming as well as with the set design. This was also the case during the production of LOTR, when the media attention was mostly focused on the design of the costumes and the sets. In saying that, the connection between a film's tourism-inducing capability and its media exposure has yet to be conclusively examined.

Becoming a Classic or Cult

Anecdotal evidence suggests that so-called 'classic' films have the potential to draw visitors to screened locations long after their premiere (Olsberg/SPI, 2007). Classic films are commonly regarded as productions that are works of cinema having transcended time and trends with an indefinable quality. They appeal universally and continue to captivate their audiences even after repeated re-screenings. Classic films, such as *Gone with the Wind* (1939), *Casablanca* (1942), *The Sound of Music* or *Titanic* (1997), are reference points for their (*de facto*) genre due to innovative craftsmanship and artistic value (Konigsberg, 1997; Lopez, 1993).

Ultimately, it is the public consensus that defines certain films as cinematic classics. The decisive, 'objective' factor behind this notion is the number of re-screenings in the cinema, on broadcast and cable television or on purchased data media such as DVD or video – though of course it would be impossible to provide the average number of re-screenings necessary to turn a film into a classic. However, research related to SoM reveals that 49% of all tour participants of the SoM film-location tour-operator Salzburg Panorama Tours, based in Salzburg, Austria, have watched the movie at least five times before doing the tour (Salzburg Panorama Tours, 2005). It is the anchoring of such a movie in our society, both on a societal as well as on an individual basis that accompanies the social consensus about the quality of a work and establishes it as a classic. This process is continuously paralleled by positive critical acclaim as well as vast numbers of viewers who tend to watch the movie repeatedly over time. The number of movie-dedicated awards might play a minor role in the film's popularity. As the example of SoM illustrates, film location tourists still visit the screened locations 40 years after its release. One reason for this success might be the fact that the movie has been established as a classic. Annual re-screenings are regularly shown in many countries around the world, particularly around Christmas time. The generation that grew up with this film has passed its fondness for it onto the following generations. The result has been a generation-spanning sentimental connection to the movie.

There is no specific time period after which a movie is considered to be a classic. Some enumerations of classic movie lists begin with the 1920s, a starting point for the burgeoning field of film, and end a few decades before the present (www.filmsite.org/classicsfilms.html, accessed 15 October 2008). On the other hand, contemporary time compression demands ever shorter and faster periods of canonisation whether in regard to popular music, famous celebrities or films. An example of the immediate canonisation of a feature film would be LOTR. 'Shot in New Zealand over 18 months, these three films are sure to become instant classics. [. . .] In short, *The Lord of the Rings: The Fellowship of the Ring* is cinematic history' (Clinton, 2001).

In 1998, the American Film Institute presented a list of 'America's 100 Greatest Movies' that were selected by more than 1500 leaders in the country's film community (American Film Institute, 1998). Arguably, such lists are always open to criticism and are purely subjective. 'There are unavoidable pitfalls in trying to compile something like [the American Film Institute list], the most obvious being that you can't exactly promote a face-off between individual statements made by individual human beings living in individual political, social, and business climates as if they came from the same bowl of batter' (Tatara, 1998). Nevertheless, it might be of interest to know that out of the list of tourism-inducing films presented in Tables 3.2 and 3.3, six are included in the American Film Institute's 1998 ranking. These are *Schindler's List* (1993; rank 9), *Star Wars – A New Hope* (1977; 15), *The Sound of Music* (1965; 55), *The Third Man* (1949; 57), *Close Encounters of the Third Kind* (1977; 64) and *Dances with Wolves* (1990; 75). In addition, these movies are included in the *100 Greatest Films* list on www.filmsite.org/afi100 films2.html. All of these examples indicate that there seems to be an overlapping public consensus of about 40–60% regarding the selection of all-time classic movies. It has to be noted that the cited lists reflect a US-American consensus. Nevertheless, as the listed tourism-inducing feature films are mainly US productions, the provided rankings still draw a good picture of the accepted canon.

A feature film might also become a cult movie. This process can occur parallel to the film's transgression into a classic, or else, such a film can become cult without a wide acceptance. A cult film is defined as a 'film without wide popularity but that appeals primarily to a particular group or type of person' (Konigsberg, 1997: 81). Fans of a cult movie tend to watch the medium over and over again, as do fans of a classic. The main difference is that the nature of a cult movie has to be of a 'quirky, often outrageous nature' (Beaver, 1994: 97). Arguably, fans of a cult movie might be more easily stimulated to visit a film location than the average spectator, because such a film is more meaningful to them. 'They [cult films] elicit a fiery and intense passion in devoted fans, and may cause cultists to enthusiastically champion and become devoted to these films, leading to audience participation, fan club membership, and repetitive viewings and showings' (www.filmsite.org/cultfilms.html, accessed 11 October 2008). Most cult films cross genres, with horror and science fiction films regarded as more cult than others (www.filmsite.org, accessed 11 October 2008). Other characteristics are a low budget, the involvement of highly individualistic directors and low-key marketing (www.filmsite.org/cultfilms.html, accessed 11 October 2008). Cult movies may perform relatively poorly at the box office, but achieve cult status over time through word-of-mouth recommendation. In summary, cult, as a product of cinema, is 'largely a matter of the ways in which films are classified in consumption, although it is certainly the case that filmmakers often shared the same "subcultural ideology" as fans and have set out to make self-consciously "cult" materials' (Jancovich, 2003: 1). Again, attempts to classify movies as cult are very subjective and judged by opinion. What is a beloved cult movie for one viewer might hold no meaning for another but, as the example of *The Blair Witch Project* (1999) illustrates, the devotion to cult movies can and does result in location visits.

Literary Precursors

Literature is not only an intensifier of the tourist experience, but can turn a place into a tourist attraction in its own right (Robinson & Andersen, 2002). Literary works can also act as a precursor for a subsequent film production. The institutionalisation of this crossover cycle of production and consumption in the culture industry has been recognised within the social sciences (Bordwell, 1988; McFarlane, 1996; Stam, 1992). The film industry has long since identified the commercial value of adapting successful novels into film scripts. Such adaptations can generally rely on a pre-existing basis of potential filmgoers – the fans of the underlying novel. That is not to say that the filmic product has to meet the expectations of the literary fans: many of them potentially attend the film screening out of pure curiosity, at least, until negative word-of-mouth propaganda has kicked in. This 'pre-guaranteed success' seems to minimise potential economic risks for film production companies. Interestingly, if we look at IMDb's all time box office list (www.imdb.com/boxoffice/alltimegross?region = world-wide, accessed 5 April 2009), nine out of the 20 most successful box office hits are based on a fictional literary work. Another interesting aspect is that many of the tourism-inducing feature films listed in Tables 3.2 and 3.3 are likewise based on a novel. Table 3.4 illustrates this fact.

Table 3.4 Tourism-inducing feature films and their literary precursors

Feature film	Based on a novel	Novel
Amélie (2001)	No	
Braveheart (1995)	No	But loosely based on historic reports about the real William Wallace
Bull Durham (1988)	No	
Captain Corelli's Mandolin (2001)	Yes	*Captain Corelli's Mandolin* (Louis De Bernieres, 1995)
Close Encounters of the Third Kind (1977)	Yes	But turned into a book by Steven Spielberg (1978)
Cold Mountain (2003)	Yes	*Cold Mountain* (Charles Frazier, 1997)
Dances with Wolves (1990)	No	But turned into a book by Michael Blake (2002)
Field of Dreams (1989)	Yes	*Shoeless Joe* (William Kinsella, 1982)
Four Weddings and a Funeral (1994)	No	
Harry Potter and the Philosopher's Stone (2001)	Yes	*Harry Potter and the Philosopher's Stone* (Joanne Rowling, 1997)
Harry Potter and the Chamber of Secrets (2002)	Yes	*Harry Potter and the Chamber of Secrets* (Joanne Rowling, 1998)
Highlander (1986)	No	
JFK (1991)	No	But reliant on a great number of reports about the events; turned into a book by Oliver Stone and Zachary Sklar (1992)
Little Women (1994)	Yes	*Little Women* (Louisa May Alcott, 1947)
Lost in Translation (2003)	No	
Notting Hill (1994)	No	
Pirates of the Caribbean (2003)	No	
Pride and Prejudice	Yes	*Pride and Prejudice* (Jane Austen, 1813)

Table 3.4 (*Continued*)

Feature film	Based on a novel	Novel
Schindler's List (1993)	Yes	Schindler's List (Thomas Keneally, 1982)
Star Wars – The Phantom Menace (1999)	No	But turned into a book by Terry Brooks (1999)
Star Wars – Attack of the Clones (2002)	No	But turned into a book by R.A. Salvatore (2002)
Star Wars – A New Hope (1977)	No	
Steel Magnolias (1989)	No	But script available by Robert Harling (1995)
The Beach (2000)	Yes	The Beach (Alex Garland, 1997)
The Blair Witch Project (1999)	No	
The Bridges of Madison County (1995)	Yes	The Bridges of Madison County (Robert James Waller, 1992)
The Da Vinci Code (2006)	Yes	The Da Vinci Code (Dan Brown, 2003)
The Fugitive (1993)	No	
Thelma and Louise (1991)	No	
The Last of the Mohicans (1992)	Yes	The Last of the Mohicans (James Fenimore Cooper, 1826)
The Lord of the Rings – The Fellowship of the Ring (2001)	Yes	Lord of the Rings – The Fellowship of the Ring (J.R.R. Tolkien, 1954)
The Lord of the Rings – The Two Towers (2002)	Yes	Lord of the Rings – The Two Towers (J.R.R. Tolkien, 1954)
The Lord of the Rings – The Return of the King (2003)	Yes	Lord of the Rings – The Return of the King (J.R.R. Tolkien, 1955)
The Third Man (1949)	No	
The Witness (1985)	No	
Under the Tuscan Sun (2003)	Yes	Under the Tuscan Sun (Frances Mayes, 1996)

As Table 3.4 shows, 42% of the presented feature films are based on novels. It seems that literary precursors can be one of the decisive factors that might turn movies into tourism-inducing events. This assumption is backed by research undertaken on the influence of tourism-inducing film productions based in the UK (Iwashita, 2006). Iwashita found that out of 15 tourism-inducing film productions, the majority are based on literary works. Two additional feature films in Table 3.4, *Braveheart* (1995) and *JFK* (1991), are based on two key historical figures. Furthermore, *The Man from Snowy River* (1982) is based on popular Australian poetry, while *The Sound of Music* (1965) is the film version of an enormously successful Broadway musical. This leaves just 17 films in this list, or 47%, that are solely based on purpose-written movie scripts. Iwashita's (2006) study also found that people with profound knowledge of the film's literary precursors are the most likely motivated travellers to the screened locations. This indicates that literature can have a long-lasting effect on the travel decision-making process of literary-based film location tourists.

Chapter 4
Profiling Film Location Tourists

Intercepting the Film Location Tourist

The complex nature of film location tourism makes it very difficult to identify film location tourists on-site. The first academic researchers on film location tourism concentrated on locations where visitor increases could be easily monitored. For example, Riley and Van Doren (1992) examined reported influxes to the Raeburn Country in Georgia, which featured in *Deliverance* (1972), the set of Fort Hays in Kansas (*Dances with Wolves*, 1990), Devils Tower National Monument in Wyoming (*Close Encounters of the Third Kind*, 1977), Arches National Park in Utah (*Thelma and Louise*, 1987), the *Field of Dreams* corn field in Iowa (*Field of Dreams*, 1989) and the city of Natchitoches in Louisiana (*Steel Magnolias*, 1989). Their key selection aspect was the availability of visitor data before, during and after the filming process. The findings revealed an additional visitor influx to each of the examined locations after the initial movie screening.

In a subsequent paper in 1998, Riley *et al.* widened the number of their cases to twelve in total. They also specified the selection criteria of these cases. First, the film had to be a box office success. Second, the film had to include an icon – visual, thematic or physical – that is identifiable and associated with a particular, existing location. The third criterion concerned whether on-location visitor data were existent and available for analysis. Fourth, this data had to include pre-release figures. With most of Riley *et al.*'s (1998) case study movies, including *The Last of the Mohicans* (1992), *The Fugitive* (1992), *Thelma and Louise* (1991), *Close Encounters of the Third Kind* (1977), *Field of Dreams* (1989) and several others, visitor numbers increased in the years after the film's premiere. For instance, the film *Thelma and Louise* resulted in a visitor increase of 19% to Arches National Park in Utah in the first year after its release in 1991. The average visitation growth before the film's screening amounted to 7% per year. The aggregated increase of all 12 examined films was significant with a 54% increase in the year after the initial screening. Riley *et al.* (1998) also identified a lower increase of visitations to locations situated in public parks (40%) compared to locations situated in private areas (60%). The researchers attribute this phenomenon to the nature of privately operated areas and their more aggressive advertising and marketing strategies.

The problematic nature of identifying film location tourists is best illustrated in the example of Australia's Kakadu National Park and its exposure in the feature film *Crocodile Dundee* (1986). The park's management believes that Kakadu National Park has profited enormously from this exposure by attracting additional visitors (Nelson, 2005, via email). Although the park had already seen a significant increase in visitation before the movie release, the park management has not – until this time – conducted a precise visitor survey to ascertain the movie's impact. It is therefore impossible to make any general statements about the conversion of the park's place exposure into actual film-induced visitations. Furthermore, no information exists about visits to the precise film locations.

As this example shows, it is immensely difficult to track down the precise influx of film location tourists. In order to overcome these problems, a research location has to be a confined place where the identification and consequent interception of film location tourists is possible. In addition, appropriate monitoring tools must be in place in order to analyse the market share of film location tourists in the general sample population.

Motivations of Film Location Tourists

According to Riley *et al.* (1998), film locations can attract a wide range of people: from the tourist on a wider holiday tour, to the hardcore film buff specifically in search for film locations. The pull motivators for film location tourists, according to Macionis (2004), are the three factors of 'place' (location, attributes, landscapes, scenery), 'personality' (cast, characters, celebrity) and 'performance' (plot, theme, genre).

Singh (2003) researched the motivations of visitors to *The Lord of the Rings* (LOTR) film set remains of Hobbiton near Matamata, New Zealand. In his research project, he analyses the initial stimulus that motivated the visitors to travel to the set. His analysis centres on Iso-Ahola's (1982) social-psychological model of tourism motivation, which consists of two motivational dimensions: 'escaping' and 'seeking'. Both dimensions influence the individual simultaneously. Singh (2003) combines these two dimensions with three motivational typologies as applied to tourism (Crompton, 1979; Fodness, 1994; Krippendorf, 1987) and three behavioural motivations as applied to film watching (Dyer, 1992; McQuail *et al.*, 1972; Swanson, 1978). Unfortunately, although having implemented a quantitative methodology design, Singh's sample only aggregates 40 survey participants. The question arises to what extent this sample size can actually provide a valid generalisation. Furthermore, this case study only focuses on one particular movie without making any comparisons to other cases. Another limitation is the fact that Singh (2003) collected the data in New Zealand's international off-season, namely from 23 July until 1 August 2003.

The data resulting from Singh's study are split into four main-motivational drivers and two further motivational drivers. The first main-motivational driver draws upon the icon concept derived from Riley *et al.* (1998). This is further subdivided into the three iconic elements: 'natural scenery of Hobbiton' (named by 17.5% of the participants as the primary motivational driver), the 'Hobbiton movie set' (12.5%) and the 'fantasy theme of LOTR' (10%). The other main motivators were learning (15%), novelty (7.5%) and the comparison of the place in the novel with the film location (7.5%). The two further motivational themes were 'satisfying children's LOTR interest' (17.5%) and the accessibility of Matamata (12.5%). Singh's (2003:70) conclusion reads that the majority of 'respondent motives inclined towards "iconic attractions within LOTR"'. This majority was also seeking to fulfil personal needs.

One has to remain slightly cautious of Singh's (2003) approach. First of all, as the results of this book will reveal, film location tourists are often not able to precisely state what their main motivations are. On the contrary, they will have different motivations that coexist harmoniously without a given preference for one over the other. Second, the motivational drivers 'learning' and 'novelty' are also inherent in Singh's first main-motivational theme. It is not possible to distinguish between the film location tourist's motivation to experience the film set, its surrounding landscape or its function as a fictional place, nor is it possible to distinguish this from the film location tourist's desire to learn about the realities of filming or his or her need to satisfy novelty. This is one combined complex for most film location tourists, except maybe for a small minority that might only be interested in the technical aspect of the filming. Finally, accessibility is not a motivational driver to seek out film locations. It is a precondition in order to attract visitors in significant numbers, as outlined in Chapter 3.

Couldry (1998), in his research project at the set of the British television series *Coronation Street* (1960–ongoing), points out that television off-locations that later became tourist sites have received hardly any academic attention. The project largely concentrates on questions of visitation reasons, authenticity of place, on-site experience and the function of the set as a ritual place. The conclusion of his paper mentions the fictional media's influence on the image of the portrayed places and its function as a pendulum between two worlds: the world of television and the world of the viewer. 'It is this division that the ritual place of Granada Studios Tour and the *Coronation Street* set invert and at the same time reproduce' (Couldry, 1998: 106). Many visitors to the set wished to see cast members, not only to receive autographs, but also to ensure the objective authenticity of the place as the actual film set. Some visitors even suggested putting waxworks of the stars in the background to give the set a stronger sense of objective authenticity. For most fans, the ultimate goal was to be present during the shooting of new scenes. For many fans of the programme, standing on the set was a privilege and the fulfilment of a long-held dream. The set appeals to them as a place with a precise history – a history of filming: 'This is where Vera and Jack got engaged!' Torchin (2002) denotes the television tourist as a mythical tourist who is very naïve and cannot grasp the distinctions between reality and fantasy. It is the 'restless movement' (Torchin, 2002: 264) between the authentic and the imagined location that renders the television destination.

Potential Experiences of Film Location Tourists

The general tourist experience is constituted by the combination of its constructed image, the individual perception of this image and its subsequent on-site consumption and experience. The distinction between the real and the imagined at film locations is blurred and difficult to distinguish. A film location tourist who visits the castle that featured in *Highlander* (1986) experiences both the fictional place that is the main character's home town, as well as the real historic castle of Eilean Donan. McHale (1987: 33) describes this ambivalent zone 'as being in-between, amphibious, neither true nor false, suspended between belief and disbelief'.

According to Sterry (1998), film location tourists experience the visited places not as real places, but as places associated with a particular film, whilst research conducted by Aden *et al.* (1995) paints a different picture. Aden *et al.* identified three sets of paired themes in their on-site research at the cornfield from the movie *Field of Dreams* (1989). These three ambivalent sets are real/unreal, amusement/purpose and community/ isolation. Visitors to the field clearly expressed their awareness about the ambivalence of its function as both a real and an imaginary place. The place is real, because it is a real baseball field they are standing in, yet on the other hand, it is an imaginary site due to its function as a former film location. The second pair of dualities – amusement and purpose – demonstrates that although most visitors encountered the field for amusement, many of these were also doing it for a specific purpose: to escape from the ordinary and to experience something out of the extraordinary, in this case a glimpse of the fictional world of a film. The third pair – community and isolation – indicates that most visitors to the field expressed the need for shared experiences; at the same time, they were seeking solitude when consuming the place. The interaction between the three ambivalent themes is reinforced by the shared fragments of the text. These fragments comprise the history and game of baseball; the film itself as a natural text; and its encounter with different family activities, films and sports. In general, it was the genre and theme of the film that attracted visitors to the location even years after its release (Aden *et al.*, 1995).

The study by Kim *et al.* (2007) on the tourism-inducing impacts of the Korean television series *Winter Sonata* (2003) reveals that younger film location tourists tend to look for active tourism products in order to experience the fictional world of *Winter Sonata*, including concerts, fan meetings and location tours. The researchers suggest that from a destination marketers' point of view, the provision of series-based simulacra is inevitable in order to benefit from the spin-off effects generated by the television production. One such product that would especially appeal to older fans could be the organisation of Korean-style silver wedding events (Kim *et al.* 2007).

In her study on visitor expectations of the half-day LOTR location tour with Nomad Safaris, Queenstown, Carl (2005) found that expectations were met for 58.8% of the respondents. For 35.3% of the respondents, expectations were exceeded and for 5.9%, the generated expectations were far exceeded. In a second survey on visitor satisfaction at Hobbiton, Carl (2005) generated the following data set: 1.1% were very disappointed; 4.4% were disappointed; for 31.9% of visitors, expectations were met; 39.6% described the experience as better than expected; and for 23.1% of respondents, expectations were far exceeded. Carl (2005) attributes the exceeding of expectations to three main factors. First, visitors were surprised about the existence of film set remains at Hobbiton, which they were not aware of prior to the trip. Second, participants of the half-day location tour were thrilled about the high recognition value of some locations that incorporate stunning scenery. Third, satisfied visitors positively commented on the quality of the tour script. Respondents who had collected information before the location encounter were generally aware of the state and nature of the location settings, which resulted in higher satisfaction levels. This argument is also backed by Connell (2008), who discovered that most *Balamory* television tourists with no or little pre-trip research on the film location were more disappointed than informed tourists.

Expectations were not met for tour participants who were surprised by how poorly maintained the Hobbiton film set was. A number of visitors longed for the experience of natural locations instead of a purpose-built, run-down film set. Another factor seen as disappointing was generated by locations that did not match with their screened counterparts, as it was impossible to recognise these locations in their real environment (Carl *et al.*, 2007). According to Carl (2005: 143), the main factors for high visitor satisfaction were the 'quality of the tour and the guides; the landscape of the former film sites and the general area; [and] the experience of visiting a former film set'. The last factor stands for the personal, intrinsic experience of the imaginary. After statistical analysis of her results, Carl (2005) rules out any significant relationship between the frequency of pre-trip film watching and the expectations and on-site satisfaction levels.

Profiling Film Location Tourists

All data displayed in this section have been derived from the three case studies described in Chapter 1. The purpose of the following profiles is not to establish a typology of film location tourists; rather, its aim is to illustrate the heterogeneity evident amongst them.

The Lord of the Rings

The general travel typology of Southern Lakes Sightseeing's clients ranges from the backpacker tourist to the luxury lodge resident and everything in between (LOTR tour guide I, personal interview). As to the clients' country of origin, it is estimated that 25% are British, 25% US-American, 25% Australian and 20% come from other European countries. The remaining 5% seem mainly composed of clients from Canada, Korea and Japan (LOTR guide I, 2005, personal interview). Some basic socio-demographic data of the tour participants encountered on the 10 research tours are highlighted in Figures 4.1–4.4

In Figure 4.1, the two participants from New Zealand were an older couple between 51 and 60 years, who were accompanying a couple from the USA on their holiday tour through New Zealand. The high

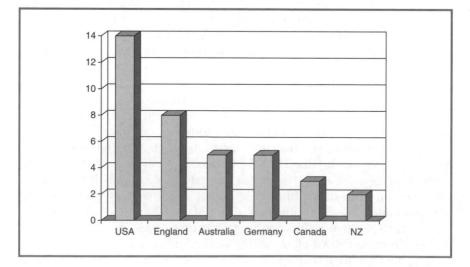

Figure 4.1 *The Lord of the Rings* tour participants: country of origin ($n = 37 =$ 100%)

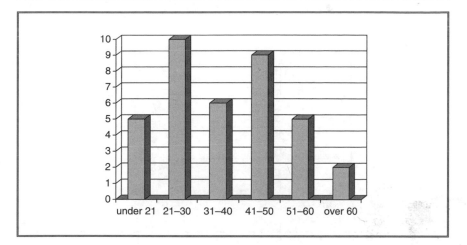

Figure 4.2 *The Lord of the Rings* tour participants: age groups ($n = 37 = 100\%$)

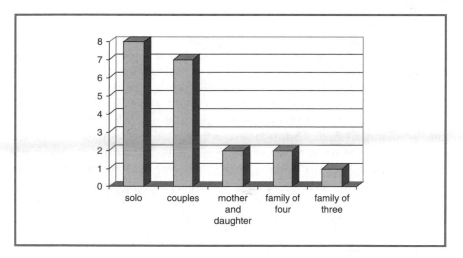

Figure 4.3 *The Lord of the Rings* tour participants: travel company (absolute numbers)

proportion of US-Americans results from two families of four that took part in the tours. Carl (2005), who conducted research with two different LOTR film location tour operators as well as at the film set of Hobbiton, found that US-Americans comprised 28% of tour participants, followed by British (26.5%), Australians (11.4%) and New Zealanders (9.8%). Germans amounted to 3% in total and Canadians to 2.3%. Singh's (2003) research on the Hobbiton set concludes that most tourists originated from the USA (45%) and the UK (25%). By comparing all these figures,

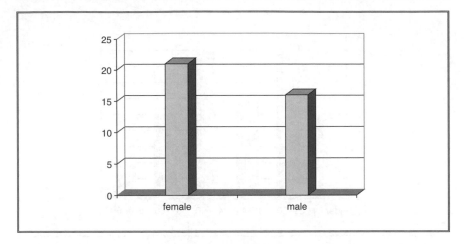

Figure 4.4 *The Lord of the Rings* tour participants: gender ($n = 37 = 100\%$)

one can safely assume that the majority of LOTR location tourists are of US-American, British and Australian origin.

Both Singh (2003) and Carl's (2005) research on LOTR suggests that the majority of LOTR film location tourists are aged between 21 and 50 years. According to Southern Lakes Sightseeing, its LOTR tour appeals across the age spectrum (LOTR tour guide II, 2005, personal interview). The youngest ever tour client was 8 years old, the oldest was 84 years. There is no dominant age group, but three different age clusters can be distinguished. Group one consists of the 'Gappies' – young, independent backpackers who take time off before or after university. These Gappies generally possess a high degree of fandom for the movies. The second group encompasses the 'Revivals', making up the age group of 40–50. Most of Revivals read the novel in the 1970s, when it experienced a popular revival (LOTR guide I, 2005, personal interview). The third group is the 'Initials', over 60 years of age. This group read the novel when it was first published. A fourth group comprises of children between 10 and 15 years, who are accompanied by their parents who do not necessarily have knowledge of the novel or the films (LOTR guide I, 2005, personal interview). These assumptions and observations largely correspond with the data derived from the 10 research tours, as can be seen in Figure 4.2.

With regard to the tour participants' age, the data was derived from field interaction and interviewing. The first group categorised in Figure 4.2 is the group under 21. The Gappies fall into the age group of 21–30 years and the Revivals into the age group of 41–50 years. The two Initials over 60 years of age had neither read the novel nor seen the movies. Another group is the age bracket between 31 and 40 years. People from this group are too young to have been part of the novel's revival in the 1960s, but they may have all read the books from a very young age, perhaps having grown up with the novel that was recommended by their parents.

Solo participants and couples were the dominant types of travellers on the research tours. All solo participants were solo travellers except for one traveller whose girlfriend spent the day elsewhere. As for the couples, they were mainly unmarried and fell into all age brackets above the 10–17 year age bracket. These results correspond to those of Carl's (2005) case study on the similar Safari of the Rings tours. Carl identified 33.3% of tour participants as solo travellers, 27.8% travelled in a group of friends or with one friend and 22.2% of her research participants were travelling with a partner.

The gender distribution of the encountered tour participants seems a little unexpected, given the fact that LOTR is predominantly built on themes appealing to men (Miller, 2003). There were 5% more female than male participants on the research tours. This distribution is similar to that of Carl's (2005) findings: of her 133 surveyed participants, 59.2% were female and 40.8% were male. This distribution also conforms to the findings of Tourism New Zealand's (2003a) LOTR market research summary report that identifies females as a major potential target group of LOTR film location tourism (see Chapter 2). In addition, 55% of the first Te Papa LOTR exhibition visitors were female (Harvey, 2003). Only the research carried out by Singh (2003) shows a slightly different picture, with 52.5% of the Hobbiton visitors being of male and 47.5% of female gender. The female members of the couples on the research tours were indeed participating in the tour out of their own interest, rather than purely accompanying their male counterparts. Of the eight solo travellers on the research tours, five were male and three female.

Apart from one exception (Male, 36, US-American), the length of stay of the informants surveyed during the fieldwork informing this book was between 1.5 and 6 weeks. Informants with more time at hand stayed in backpacker-style accommodation. The modes of transport were equally distributed between public transport, campervan and rental car. The primary information sources consulted were travel guides and word-of-mouth, followed by the internet. The majority of informants had seen each movie between two and five times. Two informants (female, 56, Australia; female, 49, UK) had seen each movie more than 10 times. Five out of 15 informants had not read the novel. Ten out of 15 informants owned the LOTR location guidebook; 12 out of 15 informants owned all three movies on DVD. Two of the remaining informants expressed their interest in purchasing the three movies on DVD after participation in the tour. With regard to the educational background of the informants, 11 out of 15 informants had a university degree. For six of the informants, LOTR was the main reason for coming to New Zealand; for another three informants, LOTR was one of the main reasons; for six informants, LOTR had almost no influence on the travel decision; and two informants based their travel decision solely on LOTR and their desire to see the locations.

Star Wars

The 2005 *Star Wars* (SW) location tour the author participated in was the third tour of this kind after two tours in 2001 and 2003. The first trip in 2001 comprised 11 tour participants; the second in 2003 also had 11 participants, while 17 film location tourists took part in the 2005 tour. Unfortunately, little socio-demographic data exists for the first group of 2001 travellers. The only information available is that the participants were all Belgians and between 20 and 35 years old. Five of them were female and six male. Given the fact that both trips were organised from Belgium, the range of different nationalities on the 2003 and 2005 tours seems surprisingly varied (Figure 4.5). All tour participants originated from Western countries, more precisely, from the triad of North America, Europe and Australasia.

The majority of the 2003 and 2005 SW tour participants were aged between 31 and 40 years (Figure 4.6). Given the fact that SW IV–VI were released between 1977 and 1983, this distribution is not unexpected. Most of the tour participants grew up with the world of SW in their teenage years. They were exposed to SW not only through the filmic texts, but

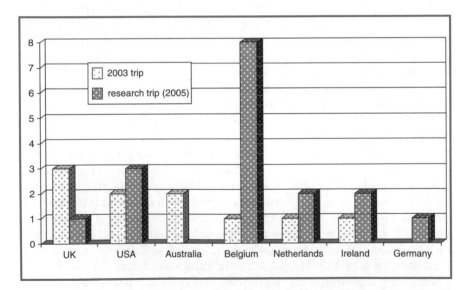

Figure 4.5 *Star Wars* tour participants (2003 and 2005): country of origin (absolute numbers; $n = 28$)
Sources: Personal data collection.

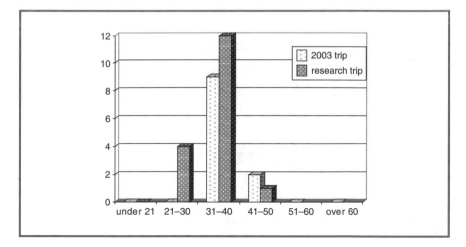

Figure 4.6 *Star Wars* tour participants (2003 and 2005): age groups (absolute numbers; $n = 28$)
Sources: Personal data collection.

also through a massive merchandising scheme. The four participants under 30 years of age on the 2005 research trip explained that they became SW fans in the aftermath of SW VI through regular television releases and the purchase of SW toys.

On both SW location tours in 2003 and 2005, solo travellers predominated (Figure 4.7). The trip in 2001 consisted purely of solo travellers. The female partners of both couples on the 2005 research trip admitted that their main reason for participating in the tour was to spend time with their partners who were the real SW fans.

The predominance of male participants on the three SW tours is evident (Figure 4.8). This result conforms to research conducted on the potential market appeal of *The Phantom Menace* (King & Krzywinska, 2002). As Brooker (2002: 200) notes: 'On the face of it, *Star Wars* would seem to have little to offer a female fan'. Most of the main protagonists in the movies are male and the spin-off merchandise, which includes toys, computer games and trading cards, is aimed at males. As explained above, two of the three 2005 female tour members decided to partake as a favour to their partners. The third female member of the 2005 trip is a big SW fan. No comment can be made regarding the 2001 female tour members and their motives, but it can be assumed that there is a small base of female SW fans.

The nature of the 2005 SW tour made individual bookings of transport and accommodation superfluous. Due to the limited number of places available, bookings were made well in advance, in some cases over a year

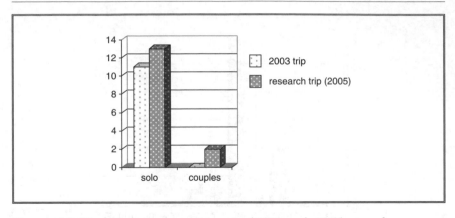

Figure 4.7 *Star Wars* tour participants (2003 and 2005): travel company (absolute numbers; $n = 28$)
Sources: Personal data collection.

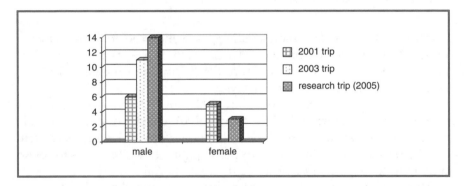

Figure 4.8 *Star Wars* tour participants (2001, 2003, 2005): gender (absolute numbers; $n = 38$)
Sources: Personal data collection.

prior to the trip. Sources of information were the 'Rough Guide Tunisia' and the 'Lonely Planet Tunisia' along with various SW-related materials. In addition, each tour participant was provided with a tour script including travel tips, location information and maps. All informants had watched the different episodes countless times and they all owned the movies on DVD. The SW informants' range of education was more evenly distributed than with the LOTR tour informants: three informants had a high school degree, two a college and three a university degree. Informants' employment also varied and included labourers, managers and those in self-employed roles.

The Sound of Music

Every year, the SOM location tour-operator Salzburg Panorama Tours conducts a participant survey covering the complete tour season with a two-page questionnaire that is handed out during the tour. The data from the 2004 survey ($n = 9702$) as well as data covering the time period of January to July 2005 ($n = 8212$) were made accessible for this book and are interpreted in Figures 4.9–4.11 and Tables 4.1 and 4.2 (Salzburg Panorama Tours, 2005).

What is interesting about this data is the relatively high number of tour participants from Asia. *The Sound of Music* (SoM) seems to have great appeal for some Asian nationalities. On the research tours, the majority of Asian participants were Japanese and South Korean.

The age groups of the general tour participants span the entire age spectrum, with the 21–30 age bracket showing a slight divergence. This seems surprising, as SoM certainly does not fit into the categories of contemporary film genres, such as action, science fiction or fantasy, which one might expect the iPod generation to favour. This distribution reflects the intrinsic quality of SoM and its status as a family classic.

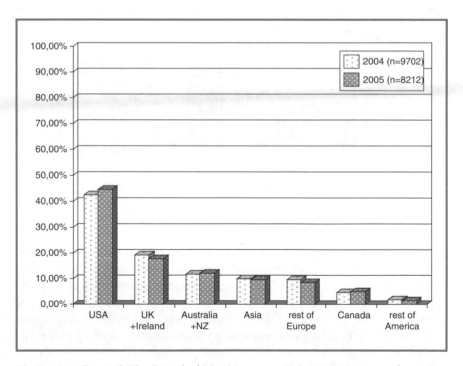

Figure 4.9 General *The Sound of Music* tour participants: country of origin
Source: Adapted from Salzburg Panorama Tours, 2005.

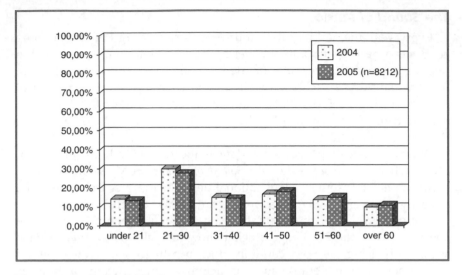

Figure 4.10 General *The Sound of Music* tour participants: age groups
Source: Adapted from Salzburg Panorama Tours, 2005.

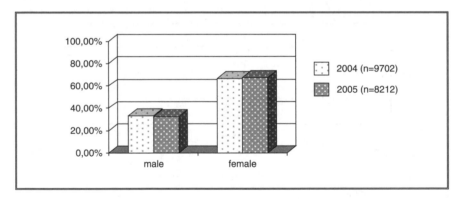

Figure 4.11 General *The Sound of Music* tour participants: gender
Source: Adapted from Salzburg Panorama Tours, 2005.

The fact that female tour participants outweigh their male counter-parts is not surprising when considering the underlying, thematic core elements such as romance, family values, love and marriage. Reports about SoM moviegoers confirm this predominance of female fans, many of whom, over the years, have attended the movie time and again (Strasser, 2000). Personal estimates based on fieldwork conducted for this book suggest that almost all of the male participants, which numbered between 15 and 20%, went on the tour solely to accompany their partners.

Table 4.1 Number of visits to Salzburg by general *The Sound of Music* tour participants

	1 time (%)	2 times (%)	3–4 times (%)	5–10 times (%)	More than 10 times (%)
2004 (*n* = 8212)	83.9	10.9	3.7	0.9	0.6
January–July 2005 (*n* = 9702)	84.7	10.9	3.2	0.7	0.4

Source: Adapted from Salzburg Panorama Tours (2005)

Table 4.2 Primary purpose of Salzburg visit for general *The Sound of Music* tour participants

	Vacation (%)	Conference/ meeting (%)	On the way to primary destination (%)	Visit friends and relatives (%)	Visit Mozart's birthplace (%)	Visit SoM locations (%)	Other (%)
2004 (*n* = 8212)	74.4	0.9	4.1	1.5	1.8	14.7	2.2
January–July 2005 (*n* = 9702)	70.9	1.5	3.5	1.4	3.3	17.2	2.4

Source: Adapted from Salzburg Panorama Tours (2005)

Of all the tour participants surveyed by Salzburg Panorama Tours in 2004, 83.9% were in Salzburg for the first time, while 10.9% had visited the city previously (Table 4.1). In the January to July 2005 survey, the percentages of 'first-timers' and 'repeat visitors' were 84.7% and 10.9%, respectively.

The primary purpose for the majority of the informants' visits was general vacation. As data from the conducted interviews suggest, this vacation mainly comprised a wider itinerary through Austria and its neighbouring countries or a compressed European tour. For around 16% of the SoM location tourists, visiting the film locations was the primary purpose of their visit to Salzburg (14.7% in 2004; 17.2% in 2005). Table 4.2 provides an overview of the primary visitation motivations.

The following section contains the individual profiles of the SoM location tour participants that were interviewed by the author for the fieldwork tours. Apart from two informants (female, 52, UK; female, 27, UK), all other informants, 13 in total, were on a travel itinerary through wider Europe. The length of the general itinerary ranged from ten days to four weeks. Two informants travelling for four weeks (female, 18, UK; female, 18, UK) were Gappies who were staying in backpacker-style accommodation. Two Salzburg-stationed informants (female, 52, UK; female, 27, UK) and four informants touring backpacker-style relied on public transport, whereas the remaining stopover informants used rental cars and stayed in hotels. Eight informants stayed in Salzburg for no longer than a day. Two informants stopped in the city for two days, two other informants visited the city for four days. For nine out of 13 informants, the SoM locations were the only reason for their visit to Salzburg. Four informants stated the locations were the main reason for visiting the city. Two informants (female, 56, USA; male, 56, USA) had come to Salzburg for the SoM locations as well as for its connection with Mozart. Pre-trip information sources were travel guides, internet and word-of-mouth. All informants owned the movie DVD. Out of the 13 informants, five were Gappies and had just finished high school or college. Six informants had a university degree, while the remainder had attended high school only.

Pre-location Visit Elements

This section deals with the first phase of the film location touring cycle – the pre-visitation phase. It is split into two main blocks: the informants' travel-triggering elements and their individual tour booking decisions. Triggering elements are the effect of repeated film watching, the potential encounter of specific locations during the tour, character empathy, the influence of additional media on the travel decision and the general appeal of film location tours to the individual. The second block summarises the different booking methods and times of booking of the informants.

Repeated film watching

A major draw card of a tourism-generating film is its status as a 'classic' or 'cult' film that can sustain repeated watching (see Chapter 3). The amount of repeated movie sessions of the informants differed immensely between the individuals. The biggest range of extremes was observed with LOTR, as these tours were comprised of participants without prior knowledge of the movies, as well as fanatics who would watch and re-watch the films. One informant (female, 49, UK) admitted to watching 20 minutes every evening before bedtime. Five of the 15 LOTR informants had watched each of the movies five times or more, six had watched each movie between two and four times and four had watched each film only once. When it came to the possession of the DVDs, 12 of the LOTR informants owned all three extended editions. The remaining three informants did not own any of the three movies. With SoM, 10 out of 13 informants had seen the movie more than five times.

Salzburg Panorama Tours' visitor survey presented the following results. In 2004, 53.1% of all tour participants had watched the movie less than five times, 20.1% had watched it between five and 10 times and 26.8% had watched it more than 10 times (Salzburg Panorama Tours, 2005). This distribution is almost identical in the survey covering the months of January to July 2005. All SoM informants owned the movie DVD and it was evident from their comments that SoM is regarded as a classic family movie. A SoM movie session is often performed as a social event, either in the family circle at home in front of the television during Christmas or in a cinema during a special sing-along screening with other fans. As with the SW informants, nearly all of them had viewed the SW movies many times, particularly the original episodes (SW IV–VI). They all agreed upon the fact that the new episodes (SW I–III) lack the character and the atmosphere of the original films and for that reason, they are not nearly as frequently watched as the originals. All SW informants owned all six SW movies on DVD and video.

These figures demonstrate that the vast majority of all the informants have watched the case study movies a number of times, some even excessively. As outlined in Chapter 3, repeated film watching can be a clear indication for the perceived innovative craftsmanship or artistic value of the work (Konigsberg, 1997; Lopez, 1993). Such perception, in turn, can validate a film, making it a classic. As with cult films, classic films often enjoy a considerable following of devoted and sometimes even obsessive fans. This notion is clearly expressed by this SW informant:

SW

Author: What do films that have attracted film location tourists have in common?

Informant: I think [the film location tourists] are absolutely obsessive about a particular film to visit the location.

Author: What do you mean by obsessive about the film?

Informant: Meaning that you watched it more than three times, perhaps. You repeatedly watch it. You watch it over and over. You buy books about the film. You watch it when it comes out on DVD. You watch all the extras and all the deleted scenes and just keep watching. (Male, 42, UK)

Many of the SW informants possessed behind-the-scenes books about the films. They had also watched the deleted scenes found under the Special Features section on the DVDs and viewed all the other extra features. The extra features provide a vast pool of information about the film production, for instance the three extended DVD versions of the LOTR trilogy contain six full-length Special Feature discs, each with hours of additional material. Other means of living out a film obsession are the accumulation of film collectibles, the visitation of film-related fan conventions and the attendance of movie premieres. One SW informant travelled to both SW III premieres in Los Angeles and London within the course of a week.

Clearly, the passion for and the connection with a film can increase over time due to repeated film watching. This is most evident with SoM and SW: SoM and SW IV both started as sleepers until a cult following was later established (Pye & Miles, 1999; producer R. Zanuck, *The Sound of Music*, disc 2, 20th Century Fox). In the case of SW I, fan culture has ensured the SW movies' empirical temporality and their construction as timeless, mythic narratives. A remarkable parallel occurred with SoM in that the 'picture didn't open like a smash hit. It was a perfect example of what word-of-mouth can do to a good movie. And it opened, I would say, rather soft' (producer R. Zanuck, *The Sound of Music*, disc 2, 20th Century Fox). The secret of its success was its continuous re-attendance by moviegoers and the subsequent re-screening of the film on television. Thus, a second and third generation of SoM fans were brought up by their introduction to the movie through their parents or through frequent television screenings (Strasser, 2000). As this research exemplifies, a growing passion for films can result in an increasing empathy for the characters, admiration for the actors or the director, and it can also stir the longing to travel to the portrayed locations.

Particular locations

Some of the LOTR location tourists participated in the tour without prior knowledge of the movies. When asked about their reason for participation in the tour, the common answer was the wish to visit scenic places off-the-beaten-track that one would normally not access on a holiday. The prevailing perception was that the film-makers must have picked very attractive locations and that by participating in an organised tour, these off-the-beaten-track places would not merely be consumed as scenic locales, but would gain a new sense of place through the provided narratives around their film location nucleus. The tour participants placed the responsibility upon the guide to generate such a sense of place.

The majority of all informants, as outlined in the section above, had a very detailed knowledge about the different film production aspects. Most of these informants placed no specific priority upon the visitation of a particular location before booking a location tour. Two notable exceptions have to be mentioned: one LOTR and one SW informant were triggered in their tour booking decision by a particular location included in the tour, which is exemplified in the two quotes below.

LOTR

The most important scene or the most important place for me personally was the location of the Argonath. I have dreamt of seeing that. I didn't know if that was possible. Then I found out that it is possible with this tour and then it was clear that I wanted to book it. (Male, 26, Germany)

SW

I came here mainly to see the Dome. To see the Igloo. That was the primary reason. (Male, 35, Belgium)

While the LOTR informant found out about the accessibility of the location whilst already in New Zealand, the SW informant booked the tour from home because of the inclusion of a particular location (the Dome) on the tour itinerary.

In order to source relevant information about the locations, the informants relied on generating and transit markers. The consulted markers were mainly the Special Feature DVDs, film location guide-books, the internet and word-of-mouth. When asked about the pre-trip information gathering process, one informant stated that watching all the technical details about the film-making clearly decreased the suspense of disbelief previously created by the movie (female, 49, UK). Informants used the sourced information to evaluate the locations in terms of accessibility, cost of access and their position within the wider travel itinerary. If these aspects match with the perceived attractiveness of the location, it is likely to be selected for visitation. All these elements are also relevant when selecting an organised film location tour.

Empathy with the characters

Hyounggon and Richardson (2003) found no pre-visit connection between the involvement with the film characters and any place issues – real or imaginary – in their experiment using *Before Sunrise* (1995) (see Chapter 3). They could not find a link between character empathy, which is mainly developed over time, and repeated movie watching. As this research suggests, for some of the informants, character or even actor empathy played a part in their visitation decision, although actor empathy has less of an influence than character empathy. Nevertheless, anecdotal research conducted at the Samurai Village location from *The Last Samurai* indicates that many location visitors are driven by the desire to follow in the footsteps of actor Tom Cruise (S. Radcliffe, 2005, personal interview; personal interviews with *The Last Samurai* film location tourists). For the actual case study informants, character or even actor empathy was certainly a textual core property of their beloved film.

Many informants stated that during their booking decision process, they favoured a location tour that had a high number of locations with connections to the main or favourite characters.

Additional media influence

As previously explained, measuring the influence of the additional media exposure of a film on the decision to travel to a film location is next to impossible. Nevertheless, for some informants, the media exposure of the movie clearly influenced their decision to participate in an organised location tour. The best indication for this argument can be found in the LOTR case study. Some tour participants were not familiar with the movies, but knew about the prospect of seeing the kind of spectacular scenery shown in the film. This perception had clearly been transported by media rather than by the films themselves. A common statement was something like 'everyone knows that Peter Jackson used stunning scenery for his movies'.

Many informants could not recall when they first became aware of the connection between the imaginary world of the LOTR movies and the geographical position of their film location counterparts. The informants accredited this lack of memory to the substantial media exposure surrounding the film production and the subsequent film releases. Some LOTR informants made the connection between the movies and New Zealand only after the release of one or more of the films.

LOTR
Author: When did you find out where they had been filmed?
Informant: It was probably not until the second [movie release]. (Female, 27, Australia)

Others had consulted any information available about the filming well before the first film's release:

LOTR
When it became clear that the movies were about to be filmed and the whole media hype around it started, I began to follow the developments quite thoroughly. (Female, 38, Germany)

LOTR
I've been on the internet for a couple of years waiting for them to come out and reading One Ring.net. (Female, 56, Australia)

Most SW tour participants were very well informed, not only about the fictional aspects of the world of SW, but many also had in-depth knowledge of the film production. Interestingly, although most of the participants considered themselves fans, many had only discovered in recent years that parts of SW II–IV had been filmed in Tunisia. The SW tour participants had to consult sources other than the movies to identify their geographical positions. This was even more complicated because of the lack of media attention and lack of tourism-intended images regarding the location positions. One SW informant found relevant location information by watching the end credits of SW IV. Others sourced their information through the website of *Star Wars* fansites and, to a lesser extent, through word-of-mouth of friends and fellow fans at film conventions and similar occasions. Potential SW film location tourists had to be very active in sourcing the correct information, as there was little information widely available about the position of the Tunisian locations, with the exception of the recent *Lonely Planet* edition (Ham & Hole, 2004). The connection between SoM and Austria, on the other hand, is obvious. The opening sequence in the movie ends with the subtitle: 'Salzburg, Austria, in the last Golden Days of the Thirties' (*The Sound of Music*, DVD, 20th Century Fox). Unlike the fantasy worlds of LOTR and SW, SoM is loosely based on a true story and therefore involves real location places. The fact that fans can embark on a film location tour is widely known and either spread by word-of-mouth or readily available on the internet.

In summary, relevant information about the film locations were sourced in different ways. Some informants actively sought out information via the internet and other sources such as location guidebooks. This phase of information gathering sometimes started before the release of the movies (LOTR) or long after them (SW; SoM). Other informants became aware of the geographical position of the locations as a result of the surrounding media hype before and during the movie releases. A number of those informants were able to recall how and when this message was transported, while other informants could not cite a specific source of information that had established that connection with the film.

Prior participation in film location tours

Though being a small minority, some location enthusiasts seem to have turned film location visits into a passion and a hobby, collecting locations from all sorts of films (see Reeves, 2001). Of the 25 research informants, only five had previously been to film locations from other movies, and none had ever visited these locations on an organised tour. Among the previously visited locations were those of *Braveheart* (1995) in Scotland (female, 52, Australia, LOTR), *Puerto Escondido* (1992) in Mexico (male, 26, Germany, LOTR), *Mrs Doubtfire* (1993) in San Fransciso (female, 47, Canada, SoM), *Indiana Jones – Raiders of the Lost Arc* (1981) in Tunisia (male, 42, UK, SW), *The Sound of Music* (1965) locations (male,

35, Ireland, SW) and locations of *The English Patient* (1996) in Tunisia (male, 42, UK).

Some of the informants had already visited other locations on their itinerary before participating in the researched location tour. With LOTR, such visitations included Hobbiton (three interviewed parties), the Mount Doom location in Tongariro National Park (three interviewed parties), the locations in and around Wellington (one informant) and the location of Edoras in Central Canterbury (two interviewed parties). One LOTR informant had pre-booked four different, organised location tours before coming to New Zealand (female, 52, Australia). A couple from the UK (49 and 55) had visited Hobbiton and were about to do a LOTR location flight-seeing tour around Queenstown. One couple from the UK (female, 36 and male, 46) had encountered the Mount Doom location as a tertiary nucleus through active exploration while undertaking the popular Tongariro Crossing walking track. For them, the discovery of the location seemed to have been as beneficial as the location experience itself, which conforms to Leiper's (1990) argument.

Only one SoM informant (female, 52, UK) had been to SoM locations before. Apart from having visited some of the locations independently, she had also participated in the same tour selected for this research three times before. In two other interviews, SoM informants revealed that they had independently visited other SoM locations in Salzburg before going on the tour. Three SW participants had previously done an identical tour in 2003. For all three of them, the decision to repeat the location tour was due to the highly satisfactory experience of the first tour. None of the SW tour participants had previously been to other SW locations outside Tunisia.

Tour booking decisions

The tour-booking pattern for the three case studies differs significantly. Firstly, as there are no specialised SW location tours available in Tunisia, the opportunity to participate in an organised fan club trip tour resulted in bookings made well in advance of the commencement of the trip. With a group size of only 16, some SW tour participants booked a year or more in advance, whilst the last few places were filled only a couple of months prior to departure. For the majority of the participants, experiencing the SW locations was the primary purpose of the trip. The remaining two group members were the wives of two of the male fans. For them, the primary reason for the travel, apart from accompanying their partners, was to experience the country of Tunisia.

Most SoM tour participants included the SoM location tour in their wider travel itinerary. In five out of seven interviews, the informants stated that they had only dedicated one to two days to Salzburg while on a longer journey through Europe. This is a similar pattern to the majority of the LOTR tour participants for whom the visitation of some LOTR locations was part of their general itinerary. The date of the tour booking, in the cases of both SoM and LOTR, ranged from a few months in advance to only a day in advance. According to one of the LOTR guides, about 50% of the Southern Lakes Sightseeing customers book in advance, in some cases up to a year in advance, 30% secure their place the day before and the remaining 20% about a week in advance whilst already in New Zealand (LOTR guide I, 2005, personal interview). It is often backpacker-type tourists with a sufficient amount of time at their disposal who book at very short notice. Travellers with a relatively tight time schedule tend to secure their tour places by booking ahead and, as their organised approach suggests, most are usually older than 30 years of age (LOTR guide I, 2005, personal interview).

Short notice SoM bookings show similarities to those of the LOTR case study. Younger SoM tour participants aged between 20 and 30 form the largest market segment for Salzburg Panorama Tours, with 26% booking spontaneously. These clients are often Gappies who travel extensively through Europe whilst taking a year off before, or after, University studies (S. Herzl, 2005, phone interview). The tour operator addresses the Gappy target group by cooperating with the largest backpacker accommodation in town (S. Herzl, 2005, phone interview). Table 4.3 presents an overview of the time, place and method of the tour bookings by the LOTR and SoM informants.

Apart from the actual locations, additional elements that make up a high-quality film location tour should include supplementary elements such as meetings with people who have a connection to the film-making process, or the handling of film-related items. These aspects play a significant role in a highly competitive market, as the following remark shows:

LOTR
The props were probably quite a big factor in the [decision making process] because none of the other [tour operators] say anything about having any props. (Female, 36, UK)

Film-unrelated elements included in the selected location tours are the provision of general information about the area, the inclusion of lunch or snacks, the visitation of film-unrelated locales and the chance to participate in film-unrelated activities, such as wine tasting (LOTR), enjoying the local cuisine (SoM) or camel riding (SW). Lastly, the costs of the different tours are compared with competitive products before a customer makes a final decision. This comparison was carried out either prior to the travel using the internet, or at the destination itself with the help of on-site information such as brochures and flyers.

Table 4.3 Time, place and method of *The Lord of the Rings* and *The Sound of Music* location tour bookings

Interview party	Time of booking	Place of booking	Booking method
LOTR			
Couple (female: 36 and male: 46) UK	Few days prior	Wider destination	Through tourist information
Solo female (38) Germany	Pre-trip	From home	By email
Couple (female: 44 and male: 46) USA	Pre-trip	From home	By email
Solo female (29) Germany	Few days prior	Locally	Through accommodation
Solo female (52) Australia	Pre-trip	From home	By email
Solo male (36) USA	Pre-trip	From home	By email
Couple (female: 27 and male: 27) Australia	Pre-trip	From home	Through travel agent
Couple (female: 49 and male: 55) UK	One day prior	Locally	By telephone
Solo male (26) Germany	One day prior	Locally	Through accommodation
Mother (60) and daughter (20) USA	Pre-trip	From home	Through travel agent
SoM			
Solo female (18) USA	Pre-trip	From home	By email
Sisters (48 and 45) UK	One week prior	From home	By email
Female friends (both 18) UK	One day prior	Locally	Through accommodation
Solo female (64) USA	Two months prior	From home	By email
Mother (47) and two daughters (both 18) Canada	Three months prior	From home	By email

Table 4.3 (*Continued*)

Interview party	Time of booking	Place of booking	Booking method
Couple (female: 56 and male: 56) USA	Two months prior	From home	Through travel agent
Mother (52) and daughter (27) UK	One month prior	From home	By email

LOTR

We got one of the local i-tag tourism booklets. It lists all the companies who are doing LOTR tours here. So we ranked each one of them and chose which one we thought was the best deal. (Male, 46, UK)

One LOTR informant selected the tour purely by positive word-of-mouth feedback (female, 29, Germany, LOTR). Positive word-of-mouth feedback also resulted in booking decisions in two SoM tour bookings.

The method of booking differed significantly between the cases. All the SW tour participants, without exception, secured their places by email. The LOTR tour participants generally tended to book either by email, through a travel agent or on-site through visitor information sites or the current accommodation provider (LOTR guides I and II, 2005, personal interviews). The SoM tour participants booked in a similar fashion. Due to information restrictions imposed by the two companies, further percentages and quantifications about booking procedures cannot be provided in this book.

Part 2

The Experiences of Film Location Tourists

Chapter 5
The Spiritual Location Encounter

Spectatorial and Collective Gazing

Postmodernity is dominated by occular-centricism (Stafford, 1997). This is particularly evident in the tourism industry that selects, combines and symbolises pictures in order to institutionalise how tourist attractions should be gazed upon (Urry, 1990), photographed and framed (Albers & James, 1988). The widely accepted concept of the tourist gaze (Urry, 1990) describes 'the process through which the gaze transforms the material reality of the built environment into a cultural imag[e]' (AlSayyad, 2001: 4). Tourists visually experience and consume objects, but at the same time, the objects determine what the tourists can gaze upon. Media, such as newspapers, television productions or movies, as well as the tourism industry construct this gaze through projecting signs, 'features of landscape or townscape', onto places out of the ordinary (Urry, 1995: 132). This construction results in the creation of symbolic sites (Edensor, 2000) and sacred places (MacCannell, 1976) whose meanings as places of consumption are fluid and change over time.

The toured objects (i.e. places) are then captured and reproduced as previously imaged by representational practices. An illustrative example for such on-site gazing practice is the so-called 'sunset point' at Uluru, Australia. Representational practices initially created this vantage point, which was established as the perfect position to gaze upon, frame and photograph the famous monolith. Through the practice of gazing, tourists enter the hermeneutic circle by spreading the collected pictures. This, in turn, reinforces the general acceptance of the perfect place to gaze upon Uluru. The act of gazing at toured objects can also be regarded as a particular act of performance in the wider context of tourist performance and social practice (Edensor, 2000).

In this context, a brief explanation has to be provided for the different types of gazing relevant to this research. The 'romantic gazer' is solitary, possesses sustained immersion and his or her gaze involves a sense of awe. 'Collective gazing' is a communal activity, a series of shared encounters experienced while gazing at the familiar. For example, the gaze of a coach tour group upon the Taj Mahal is mainly collective. The 'spectatorial gaze' is similarly a communal activity, which manifests in a series of brief encounters or glances that enable individuals to 'collect' different signs. An example of such an encounter may occur when attending a staged performance of indigenous culture. As 'collective gazing' and 'spectatorial gazing' are very similar and related types of gazing, they are dealt with simultaneously in this section.

An interesting connection can be made with Edensor's (2000) theory of tourist performance. According to Edensor, performances are a meta-social commentary reproducing social norms. They are constrained by structure, such as an organised tour, and are shaped by the symbolic meanings and spatial organisation of the visited places. Edensor distinguishes between disciplined rituals, improvised performances and unbound performances. Disciplined rituals are directed, repetitive and constrained by time. Collective and spectatorial gazing, framing and photographing is a disciplined ritual. Improvised performances leave more room for spontaneity, but still rely on instructions in order to ground them in a broader framework of behaviour. As such, romantic gazing can be considered an improvised performance. Lastly, unbound performances occur when frameworks of familiar behaviour are entirely missing. Such performances usually take place in unfamiliar settings, such as an Arabian market, and can cause distress or panic or, alternatively, result in highly satisfactory experiences of adventure, discovery and excitement.

For film location tourists, the question arises where and how to gaze upon the location. As the film location tourist has collected the different projected signs via the representational practice of the film, he or she enters the hermeneutic circle in order to re-experience and reconstruct the filmic signs or objects in the real world. Collective and spectatorial gazing upon film locations can take on two different forms. The first form is only loosely connected to the filmic gaze. The term 'filmic gaze' stands for the visual consumption of a (filmic) sight (see Chapter 3). For some LOTR tour participants, it was sufficient to gaze upon a location in a symbolic way. They were not interested in adapting the exact camera position to re-create a particular shot; rather they took general photographs of the landscape surrounding the location:

> **LOTR**
> **Informant 1:** We didn't bother taking photos because everyone was taking photos of the bush. But it's a bush at the end of the day unless you know all the details of it to explain it to people. (Male, 27, Australia)
> **Informant 2:** I sort of took more photos of the landscape. (Female 27, Australia)
> **Informant 1:** Yeah, we were taking photos of the landscape and we can just show people where *Lord of the Rings* is.

Here, recording a location as a symbolic representation of the imaginary served the purpose of achieving a privileged status amongst friends and peers.

Collective and spectatorial gazing also frequently occurred at *The Sound of Music* (SoM) locations. For the majority of the SoM tour participants, the gaze upon the locations was a brief, superficial encounter. The main purpose of the encounter was to collect those signs for reasons of prestige and recognition amongst peer groups. A significant number of tour participants did not even take photographs of some of the locations, with the notable exception of the Gazebo. The Gazebo features in the romantic scenes with Liesl and Rolf and with Maria and the Captain. Liesl and Rolf sing the famous song '16 going on 17' in front of and in the Gazebo. A studio-built version was used for the interior shots. The set structure is currently tucked into a corner of the vast grounds of the Hellbrunn palace and forms the top attraction on any SoM film location tour.

The Gazebo clearly provides a prestigious stage for formal posing (Edensor, 2000). Such formal posing was expressed through the taking of family portraits or by couples kissing each other in front of the structure. The recording of these posed performances had to be picture-perfect. This was evident in one incident where the mother of a family of four meticulously cleared the ground of rubbish and debris in front of the Gazebo before posing for a photo, as can be seen in Figure 5.1.

Indeed formal posing for photographs at the Gazebo amounted to a downright competition between the SoM tour participants. Very few of them listened to the guide's explanations or took in the atmosphere of the wider setting – the picturesque grounds of the Hellbrunn palace. Everyone rushed to be the first to pose for pictures. After the formal pose was photographed, most tour participants instantly lost interest in the toured object. These observations are backed by those of Salzburg Panorama Tours. In the opinion of the tour operator, the importance for SoM tour participants is 'to be able to say that they have been there' (S. Herzl, 2005, phone interview) in order to gain privileged status. The SoM locations are therefore mainly consumed as a spectacle.

The second form of collective or spectatorial gazing upon a film location is the capturing of the filmic gaze. In order to capture the filmic gaze, the gazer has to position himself or herself where the original film camera was set up for shots. The gazer then has to face in the same direction as the original film camera lens. By capturing the filmic gaze, the film location tourist takes on the position of a spectatorial gazer who views the sight as a voyeuristic and incidental outsider (Peet, 1998). The clear (filmic) sight sets the stage where the (imaginary) action takes or took place. This form of consumption is often brief and staged as highly directed, disciplined rituals by the tour guides. An illustrative example of such disciplined gazing was observable at the different LOTR sights at Deer Park Heights, a private deer farm near Queenstown. In a very repetitive and highly directed operation, the tour guides present about 15

Figure 5.1 Setting the scene for formal posing at the Gazebo
Source: Author.

different sights in a series of brief, voyeuristic encounters with the imaginary. Once a sight is framed and photographed, the guide approaches the next sight and so forth. Because of its importance in the location consumption, a separate section in this chapter is dedicated to this form of gazing.

Gazing upon film locations during an organised tour always involves collective gazing. The close nature of both the spectatorial and the collective gaze makes it difficult for an observer to clearly distinguish one type of gaze from the other. As the location encounters are shared in the form of a communal activity, any spectatorial gazing that occurs is automatically collective. In addition, the highly directed operational nature of an organised location tour reinforces and ensures the presence of a collective gaze through structured narrative scripting. The tour guide presents the visited locations in such a way that they are recognised by the tour participants and therefore rendered as familiar. The familiar is represented by a clear (filmic) sight, which is collectively framed and captured by the interpretive community in a series of (brief) encounters. Furthermore, film location tourists on self-organised location visits can similarly be classed as collective gazers, unless they travel alone and are thereby prevented from sharing their encounters with others.

Romantic Gazing

Romantic gazing requires sufficient time and relative solitude in order to achieve sustained immersion (Urry, 1990, 1995). It seems logical that during a highly directed, organised tour with little time available at the locations, romantic gazing is difficult to sustain. The romantic gazer has to be allowed enough time to separate from the group, both physically and mentally, in order to immerse into the place. In spite of the SoM location tour being organised around a tight time schedule, the very last location, that of the Mondsee church in which Maria and Captain von Trapp's wedding scene takes place, was allocated a generous timeframe. Although the Baroque atmosphere of the building and its connection to the romantic wedding scene provided the tour participants with the opportunity to adopt the romantic gaze, many still remained spectatorial and collective gazers. The dominating performance was to quickly capture the sight of the aisle down which Maria walks in her wedding dress. After this brief encounter, the majority left the church in order to literally consume the next object signalled by the tour guide: Austria's famous apple strudel. Only a small number of tour participants took time to stroll down the aisle and sit down on one of the benches in order to take in the atmosphere.

The LOTR tour participants were generally allocated more time for romantic gazing and many were clearly emotional at particular locations. They often appeared stunned and remained silent and in awe for a few seconds when encountering a new location or sight. The guides generally reacted accordingly to the atmosphere and gave the tour participants sufficient time to process these first impressions before proceeding with the tour script. They constantly encouraged romantic gazing, particularly after each location or sight script narrative was finished, by giving the tour participants enough individual leeway. A significant number of tour participants appreciated these opportunities and separated themselves from the group in order to become immersed in the moment. The following informant split from the group a number of times and simply sat down at vantage points, silently taking in the surrounding landscape:

LOTR

Informant: I wanted to be closer to the landscape and therefore also the 'Middle Earth' of the movie.

Author: How did you try to achieve that?

Informant: By inhaling the atmosphere. And by creating my own images parallel to the movie. (Female, 29, Germany)

Compared with the SoM tour participants, most LOTR tour participants attached intrinsically deeper meanings to the locations. They acted as behavioural insiders in relation to the visited locations, involving emotional and empathetic spatial involvement (Peet, 1998). The locations were experienced as sacred places rather than as sites of spectacle. The same can be said about the SW tour participants. While they certainly engaged in spectatorial and collective gazing when first encountering new locations and sights, romantic gazing almost always followed after the initial, superficial consumption as spectacle:

SW

I'm quite happy just to go to the *Star Wars* canyon with a packed lunch and maybe just go up there and sit in the shade, have some fun and just relax and chill out. I wouldn't necessarily have to spend the whole time constantly visiting all the different places with fans and lining everything up for a photo. You can just sit down and you feel content and so happy. (Male, 42, UK)

The above comment backs up the recurring observation that the majority of the SW tour participants were actively seeking out sustained immersion by soaking up the location atmosphere. The nature of the organisational structure of the SW tour certainly fostered this type of spatial involvement. The guide never followed a script; he allocated more than sufficient time for the location encounters and made very few directional commands. When describing sustained immersion, physical solitude from the group was seen as very important for this SW tour participant:

SW

Informant: Sharing [the locations] wasn't a bonus for me. I certainly would have preferred to come on my own.

Author: Why?

Informant: I just didn't have time to reflect and take it in. You're watching all these people milling around, there's too much going on and you're very, very much aware of the group all the time. Personally, I think it would have been better on my own or, you know, to have my wife here. It's better to share it with somebody but not with a group. Not on my own, but on my own terms. (Male, 35, Ireland)

Apparently, the presence of too many people at locations, whether they are members of the interpretive community or outsiders, can distract from the mood of sustained immersion. The other interesting aspect in the comment above is that sharing such a deeply emotional and empathetic spatial involvement may not be possible even within such a tightly knit community as a fan group. As the comment evidently shows, for some film location tourists such an experience is better shared with a close friend or loved one.

Capturing the Filmic Gaze

Capturing the filmic gaze through location sights is the ultimate manifestation of the film location consumption as spectacle. The location sight provides the present object of the spectacle and, at the same time, symbolises the absent imaginary object. The absent elements of the imaginary object are the characters, set structures and digital enhancements; the present elements are the physical place features. The framing and photographing of such a sight correspond to general tourism gazing performances. The symbolic sites (re)constructed by representational practices have to be tracked down, captured and framed in person (Albers & James, 1988: 137). In this instance, the symbolic sites are constructed by a film through the incorporation of literary aspects, mise-en-scène and, in particular, compositional aspects (Baker, 2003; Campsall, 2002; Corrigan, 1994). Some sights are even reconstructed by location guidebooks, websites and on-site markers (i.e. intended images of destination-imaging), which all reinforce the film-tourism hermeneutic circle. Tour guides significantly contribute to this circle of construction, reconstruction and consumption by adhering to a script that directs the tourists towards the sights. Figure 5.2 shows a film location guide (on the left side of the photo) pointing his clients towards a specific (filmic) sight.

Figure 5.2 Guided sight directing
Source: P. Hunt.

The film still in his hand depicts the equivalent shot and supports the identification of the sight.

Tracking down the different sights and reconstructing them is highly rewarding for film location tourists. Not only can they compare the original film shot and their own reconstructed photograph for their own benefit, but by capturing the filmic gaze they gain privileged status amongst their peer groups. In saying that, privileged status is already attained purely by visiting the film locations and taking photographs of the general locations. Still, a more precise overlap between the film shot and sight photograph results in the photograph having an even higher status, thereby reflecting on the status of the film location tourist:

> **SW**
> **Author:** Is it important to photograph the exact camera angle in the movie?
> **Informant:** When you see for example Camel Head Rock, and you see it from a different location than where the camera was then it is a completely different rock. So it's not the same. (Male, 35, Belgium)

It became apparent from observation that capturing the filmic gaze brings with it such a high degree of privileged status that even seemingly uninterested sight collectors felt the need to join in. This sense of having to join in was generated either by the tour guide and his or her directional commands or through peer pressure within the interpretive community.

The emphasis on sight collection by some tour participants evoked the fear of missing out on an opportunity of photographing a prestigious sight amongst the seemingly disinterested. In order to prevent any future feelings of regret, formerly disinterested sight recorders started to capture the filmic gaze as well, although not all non-sight collectors could be converted. For some, taking photographs of the general location was sufficient to achieve privileged status. Regardless of the structure of a tour script, capturing the filmic gaze can also be a very active process for location tour participants. This was the case for the majority of the SW tour participants who identified the sights actively on their own (Figure 5.3).

Even on the relatively structured LOTR tour, some tour participants actively sought out the precise sights and even corrected the guide when they deemed it necessary. However, for one LOTR tour participant, the 'mental recording' of the sights was enough: 'I take pictures with my mind. I never look at photos afterwards, so what's the point of taking them?' (female, USA, LOTR). However, for the majority of the observed film location tourists, mental sight recording did not provide satisfactory consumption. In order to be able to present the recorded sights to peer group members, they had to be either photographed or digitally recorded. Approximately 10% of tour participants who chose to sight-record used video cameras, while the rest photographed the sights with digital cameras. The seemingly disinterested sight collectors often had very simple, disposable cameras. Nevertheless, while there was a tendency for

Figure 5.3 Unguided sight recording
Source: Author.

tour participants with a high degree of fandom to employ high-tech recording equipment, no general conclusion about the connection between the degree of fandom and the type of recording equipment can be drawn from the research.

Aside from the purpose of gaining privileged status, sight recording also serves as personal proof of the actual encounter, which may be perceived as equally or even more important:

LOTR

Author: How important is it for you to photograph the exact camera angle?

Informant: Very. It's got to look like it. If it's recognisable from where it was in the film, it's a big plus for the tour. It means that you can point it out to people when you go back. [...] I've got quite a few friends who are obsessed with *Lord of the Rings* and they expect me to go back and show them what I've got [i.e. location photos]. But more important, you point it out for yourself. (Female, 46, UK)

Most informants acknowledged the importance of recording precise sights. However, one SW informant could not give a particular reason for doing so:

SW

Author: Did you try to locate the exact camera angle?

Informant: I did. I did. Why? I don't know why. It's important, but I can't explain why. Because I guess if it wasn't complete, if it wasn't perfect, I would have regretted it. I guess I just wanted to be perfect when taking the photos. (Male, 30, USA)

This comment clearly reinforces the argument that the prestige of a collected sight increases by its resemblance to the equivalent film shot. It also signals the existence of unconscious pressure from the interpretive community.

If the recording and collection of sights is not possible, for example when access to the sight is prohibited, the film location experience can be a disappointment. Access may be prohibited due to natural spatial constraints, such as watercourses, difficult terrain or that the original position of the film camera was located on a beam. Other factors of inaccessibility are access denial by gatekeepers or simply a lack of information about the precise sight(s). The first access problem, natural spatial constraints, often poses a particularly difficult obstacle. Sometimes, it is simply too dangerous to reach a particular sight, as occurred with the Mos Eisley lookout. Due to its position on a high cliff, the sight could not be accessed. At other sights, the camera was set up on a beam, which makes it impossible to record the sight, for example at the LOTR location of Aragorn's cliff. In these cases, the sight collector can only try to record the sight from the next-best position. For example, the scene in SoM when Maria walks down the aisle in the Mondsee wedding church is impossible to sight-record, as the camera was set up on the publicly inaccessible gallery. Instead, SoM tour participants tended to photograph the main aisle from lower down, with the lens still aiming towards the altar. A similar process was observable at a LOTR location: in order to film the character of Eomer at the riders of Rohan campsite, the camera was put up on a beam. As such, the tour guide attempted to overcome this disadvantage by leading the tour participants onto an elevated rock plateau slightly left of the original camera position in order to get the next-best sight.

In cases of access denial to the general location or the precise sight, the tour participants showed disappointment. This was clearly evident at the LOTR Flight to the Ford location and the rear view of the von Trapp house. To a lesser extent, the impossibility of accessing the low angle sight facing the LOTR Pillars of the Kings location slightly decreased the satisfaction of the experience:

LOTR
Author: What do you think about the location where they filmed the Pillars of the Kings?
Informant: Oh, that was great. That was like an aerial view of it. And I suppose I thought it would have been nice to get a good bit lower down, right to water level to get the image from the film. (Female, 52, Australia)

Consequently, the tour participants did not spend much time gazing, as there was not much to gaze upon. The SoM tour participants were disappointed by the location of the von Trapp house and its inaccessibility:

SoM
Informant: I just thought it was so beautiful and magnificent, although it's kind of different in the movie. In the film, you're always looking from the backyard out at the lake, and we were standing on the other side of the lake. It was a different perspective. It sort of made it not quite as imaginable.
Author: Were you disappointed that we couldn't get closer to the location?
Informant: A little bit. I would have liked to see it closer up, to walk on the grounds because there are a lot of scenes there. That would have been really cool. (Female, 18, USA)

Formal posing in front of the lake with the house in the background had far less prestige when compared to the Gazebo. A different, disappointing experience outside the actual SoM tour was reported by an informant who could not access a precise sight within a location. This wider location is a cemetery in the city of Salzburg. In the film scene, the von Trapp family hides from the pursuing Nazi soldiers behind two tombstones in a cemetery:

SoM

I was a bit disillusioned by the cemetery, the grave. You know, you can't actually get behind it. So I was kind of disappointed about that. (Female, 27, UK)

Many LOTR tour participants refrained from taking photographs at the Flight to the Ford location, as only glimpses of the actual location were possible because pine trees formed a visual barrier along the fence. It can be beneficial at such locations to have a guide on-site. By providing narratives about the location and the filming process, the guide can make even inaccessible locations and sights meaningful, as long as glimpses of the actual place are possible:

LOTR

It is a pity that you can't access the [Flight to the Ford] location, because I think it would have been more interesting. The stories about the filming were the only thing that helped. The place itself was very unspectacular. (Male, 26, Germany)

A third sight accessibility issue is the inability to finding the exact sight due to a lack of information, which can occur at a location where contiguous markers are missing. Even the presence of contiguous markers might render the identification of sights impossible, if they lack accuracy. For example, many of the LOTR informants complained about the inaccuracy and the lack of detailed directions in the LOTR location guidebook (Brodie, 2002). Although containing relatively word-precise directions such as '[c]limb the fence on your left and walk 250 m in a north-westerly direction' (Brodie, 2002: 107), many locations and sights remain impossible to identify. Another example of on-site marker inaccuracy occurred at Deer Park Heights. The property owner has erected five signposts around the location that point out different sights. When accessing Deer Park Heights, visitors are given a map on which the signposts are marked. The map also contains brief descriptions of each sight. Although direct access to the sights is provided, three of the signposts are sight-inaccurate. It was evident from fieldwork observation that individual visitors to Deer Park Heights were very disappointed with this marker system, as it generated expectations of identificational accuracy that could not be fulfilled.

A fourth and previously unmentioned type of sight inaccessibility occurs when there is no precise and identifiable sight. In these situations, the tour participants tended to gaze upon the location in a general way. For example, the yardangs (triangular-shaped sandstone formations formed by water and wind erosion) at the SW Jedi duel site have eroded to such an extent that precise sight recording is impossible. In this yardang field, several SW I scenes were shot, the most well-known being the light sabre duel between Darth Maul and Qui-Gon Jinn.

A second example would be the SW Jawa Sandcrawler location which is just desert sand and provides no identifiable sight due to its featureless physical attributes. Both locations were photographed without attempting to record the exact sights.

Even with detailed in-depth knowledge of the film, only the provision of visual aids or on-site guidance could guarantee the identification of sights. A lack of such visual assistance on the SoM tour was negatively commented upon by this informant:

> **SoM**
>
> I should have brought my book. It would be an advantage if for every stop we make we'd have a visual – I don't know, a little TV or something – that said: this is it! That's where it happened! (Female, 47, Canada)

Other SoM tour participants complained in a similar fashion: 'They should show the scenes in the bus'. Ultimately, there are only two types of (on-site) markers that enable the film location tourist to identify precise sights: visual aids such as guidebook photographs, photo boards, film stills or a portable DVD player; and external guidance. Ideally, visual aids are combined with directional commands from a location guide. The provision of film stills during the LOTR tour was applauded by all tour participants and seen as a considerable asset to the tour. Some tour operators, as advertised on the internet, even use a portable DVD player to replay the individual scenes before the group accesses the location and experiences the different sights.

Mental Visions

A mental vision occurs when the imaginary mentally overlaps with the real: the film location tourist has a vision in which he or she can mentally see the (absent) objects such as characters or set structures:

> **LOTR**
>
> You recreate the scenes in your mind. You put yourself into the movie. (Male, 36, USA)

> **SW**
>
> I could visualise Darth Maul [i.e. the character] at that point. I actually kind of saw him flying down on his space-bike. (Male, 30, USA)

With mental visions, the cinematic suspense of disbelief manifests itself in the real-life situation at the location that serves as the backdrop for the absent objects, yet at the same time, it remains part of the imaginary. A mental vision disconnects the visionary from external visual inputs and creates mental mirror-images of the absent objects. These mirror-images are then combined with the mental replay of the relevant film scenes. Several elements support the occurrence of mental visions, the most powerful of which is the screening of the relevant scenes on DVD immediately before encountering the location so that they are freshly memorised. Another supportive element is the provision of an on-site visual aid. By comparing the on-site visual aid and the sight, mirror-images can be more easily projected onto the physical place. Narratives from a tour guide also aid the possibility of mental visions, specifically through first-person interpretation and re-enactments. In these situations, the guide serves as a connecting link between the subject and the absent object. Both of the latter issues will be dealt with in more depth in Chapter 7.

When encountering natural locations, informants more frequently reported mental visions. Natural locations often guarantee a high degree of recognition and therefore a more precise overlap between the real and the imaginary, which clearly supports mental visions; in particular, where spatial and temporal discrepancies are minimal. Specific natural elements at the location, such as atmospheric lighting conditions or extreme temperatures, contribute considerably to mental visions. For instance, the extreme conditions of the Tunisian desert reportedly added to the location experience:

SW

It certainly wouldn't have been the same if it was like Ireland, because it imprints. The heat imprints the experience. (Male, 35, Ireland)

On the contrary, remaining set structures can decrease the probability of mental visions. One reason for this is that the film location tourists concentrate on the structures as material on-site elements rather than as seeing these structures as part of the imaginary. This is particularly the case when the set structures are in a poor state. Film sets and set structures are commonly made out of cheap building materials such as plaster, chicken wire and plywood and are not built to last. It can highly distress film location tourists to see sets and set structures in disrepair and, as a consequence, they are unlikely to produce mental visions. The current personal mood of the individual is just as important as the relevant external factors. Mental visions can only take place if the visionary is in the right mood to will their occurrence.

An interesting aspect of mental visions occurred at the SW location known as Darth Maul's lookout. The same location was also used in the feature film *The English Patient* (1996), but shot from a different angle. Similarly, the SW Canyon (SW location 5) also featured in *Indiana*

Jones – Raiders of the Lost Ark (1981). These crossovers posed a problem; how was one to mentally visualise the absent objects from the different films? The solution was to progress from one film to the next and therefore separate each scene or shot both spatially and temporally:

> **SW**
> **Author:** How do you experience a location where two or three movies have been filmed?
> **Informant:** I kind of see it in camera angles. When I'm in one spot from one film, I'm seeing one film. When I'm in another spot, I'm seeing a different film. I'm kind of jumping between films as I move around. [...] One minute, I can be in *Star Wars*; next scene, I can be in *Indiana Jones*; next scene, I can be in *The English Patient*. I think like that. (Male, 42, UK)

These progressive shifts are relatively easy to achieve if the on-site filming of the different scenes was spatially separated. It becomes problematic if the exact same sight is seen in two different films, as there is no spatial separation and the scene or shot shifting becomes purely mental. Yet, as the following informant illustrates, such a mental separation is possible and can indeed result in mental visions:

> **SW**
> I wouldn't take the same picture twice. But in my head, I'm thinking about two [movies], one after the other. You have two experiences, one from each film. (Male, 42, UK)

Mental visions are also possible at locations with access restrictions. For instance, SoM tour participants reportedly had mental visions of the characters of Maria and the children at the rear view of the von Trapp house:

> **SoM**
> Actually on the tour, when we saw the back of the house, I was picturing them [i.e. Maria and the children] in the boat on the lake. I think that location meant most to me. (Female, 27, UK)

The possibility of having a mental vision at this particular location seems surprising given how far away it is from the tour's vantage point. Yet, it suggests that film location tourists can have mental visions even when they can only glimpse the actual location or sight. Mental visions were also reported at locations containing derelict film sets such as at the SW Mos Espa set:

> **SW**
> So you see Watto flying around in his shop and Anakin and Padme having this conversation. You see Sebulba sitting in the bar. You see it

when you walk in. You don't need a whole lot of imagination to recognise these places. Then, of course, I have to say, I really felt like I was on Tatooine for a split second. It is a wonderful feeling. It is a wonderful feeling. (Male, 32, Holland)

It is suggested that pre-tour determined and favourite scenes have only a small influence on mental visions. The same can be said about scene-involved characters. Regardless of preconceptions about the attractiveness of locations, favourite characters and prestigious sights, it is the actual moment of the encounter with all its imaginary elements that supports or prevents mental visions.

Mental Simulations

The transition from a mere external observer to the embodied consumer of the imaginary becomes manifest through mental simulations. A mental simulation takes place when a person disconnects from the normal perceptual inputs and behavioural outputs (Bardsley, 2002). The mental simulation determines 'what further beliefs and desires we would develop, what decisions we would make, what emotional reactions we would experience and so on' (Bardsley, 2002: 160). It is the simulation of being someone else by taking on the beliefs and desires of 'the Other'.

The advantage of mental simulations is that 'they allow us to explore safely the mental lives of others without compromising our own' (Bardsley, 2002: 160). Mental simulations take place when we immerse ourselves in fictional texts such as novels or films. In order to experience a mental simulation in connection to a film, 'I must both take myself for the character (i.e. an imaginary procedure) so that he [or she] benefits, by analogical projection, from all the schemata of intelligibility that I have within me, and not take myself for him [or her] (i.e. the return to the real) so that the fiction can be established as such (i.e. as symbolic): this is seeming-real' (Metz, 1977: 57). The seeming-realness of fictional film is identical to the aforementioned suspension of disbelief (see Chapter 3). In other words, what we experience on the silver screen, we are inclined to believe could have actually happened. Suspension of disbelief results in mental simulations: we suffer, we laugh and we celebrate with the characters. Our self-identity is suspended as we take on the identity of 'the Other'.

When engaging in mental simulations, film location tourists take on the personality of the film characters and simulate what they must feel and experience in particular scenes.

SW

You're actually trying to become one of the characters when you're standing there. And then you say: "Wouldn't it be amazing if I was actually Luke Skywalker or Han Solo?" So I tried to imagine myself inside the scenes in my head. (Male, 27, Belgium)

Mental simulations involve bodily feelings such as elation, excitement, overwhelming joy or sadness. These aspects are important elements of intra-personal existential authenticity (Wang, 1999). Existential authenticity is the authenticity of Being and is 'derived from [the] tourist's participation in the event' (Wang, 1999: 359). By experiencing places through mental simulations, the film location tourist enters existential insiderness in relation to that place (Peet, 1998). As opposed to the intended provision of mental simulations by filmic texts, film locations can pose a significant problem, as parts of the toured object, the characters, props and sets, are missing. All there is to make the simulation work is the physical location features, which signify the absent objects through their function as the symbolic.

Although mental simulations were reported throughout all three case studies, the SoM informants had less mental simulations than the other informants. The only SoM location that reportedly enabled mental simulations was the Mondsee wedding church:

SoM
I love the movie so much that I want to kind of live it in a sense. Like when I walked into the church and nobody was there and you can visualise it. For me, I was visualising the movie itself. I want to live every song, I want to hear every song, because this was a special moment. (Female, 47, Canada)

Presumably the large group sizes of the SoM tour, restricted access to the locations, the lack of accessible sights, the highly scripted tour commentary and the strict time schedule had a negative impact on the probability of mental simulations. Similarly with mental visions, the nature of the location influences mental simulations. These elements can comprise a location's natural features, its recognition value and perceptible natural elements, such as temperatures, rainfall and snowfall. Other factors involve the connection of the location to favourite or lead characters and the degree of fandom for the simulating subject. Relative solitude is an additional supportive element.

The most intense mental simulations occurred for the informants with the highest degree of fandom. Accordingly, such simulations were reported by SW informants. A very strong mental simulation took place at the Dome during the sunset visit: one SW group member deliberately separated himself from the group and walked into the sunset. He wore headphones and listened to the original soundtrack attached to this particular scene. He was deep in thoughts and observably crying. The moment of this immersion is captured in Figure 5.4.

Figure 5.4 *Star Wars* tour participant engaging in a mental simulation
Source: Author.

When later asked about this particular moment, the informant remarked:

> **SW**
> I experienced him [i.e. Luke Skywalker] in the way that he must have felt. I had the film music on with a headset. I was very much wrapped up in that moment. (Male, 30, USA)

According to one of the LOTR guides (LOTR guide I, personal interview), some LOTR tour participants showed strong emotions on some of the tours. While some people cried at Aragorn's cliff, others kissed the stone where he sits in the stew scene. These observations and comments indicate that there seems to be a connection between the intensiveness or frequency of mental simulations and the (absent) presence of a favourite or lead character.

Another interesting mental simulation was reported by one SW informant. Having a high degree of fandom for the *Indiana Jones* movies, this informant had previously visited Tunisia in order to find some of the *Raiders of the Lost Ark* (1981) locations that are scattered throughout the country. Kairouan, situated on the Mediterranean coastline, was depicted as Cairo in the 1930s in the movie because of its architecture and medieval appearance. What was surprising to the informant was that all the other visitors to Kairouan were completely unaware of its imaginary component, whereas the informant experienced Kairouan first and foremost as the fictional Cairo of *Indiana Jones*. In this case, the informant did not simulate the thoughts and feelings of a film character, but mentally simulated being immersed in a fictional place as himself.

SW

For me, in a way, it's Cairo. That's what it was in the film. When I go wandering around, with my location pictures trying to find buildings, you know, I am not really in Kairouan. I'm actually in Cairo. (Male, 42, UK)

Although mentally immersing himself into Kairouan's fictional doppelganger, the informant consciously reflected upon his 'restless movement' between the real and the imaginary:

SW

Indiana Jones is something that could have happened, but I still don't see it myself as an actual reality. (Male, 42, UK)

The acknowledgement of this constant shift confirms Torchin's (2002: 264) argument that film location tourists drag 'multiple representational files to each site' and for the informant the spatial narrative of Kairouan competes with the narrative of its setting as Cairo in *Indiana Jones*. A significant difference to mental visions is the fact that mental simulations can occur without an attachment to particular locations. Both LOTR and SW informants reported mental simulations while travelling through the wider destination:

SW

Author: Did you sometimes have the feeling, even when you were not at a specific location, that somehow you were on Tatooine?
Informant: There were times when I did. We stopped in the desert. There were sand sculptures and stuff in the middle of nowhere. It was the hottest I've ever been! I got out of the car and this wave of excitement passed over me and I thought 'this must be what it's like, you know.' And I walked away by myself and I couldn't see any of the rest of the group or hardly hear them. I stood there for a second, just to have that moment captured. It happened a couple of times, when I thought, well, this could be Tatooine in a sense, you know? (Male, 35, Ireland)

LOTR

I've been in certain parts of New Zealand that had nothing to do with the films but it felt the same way. We were horse riding on a beach and we rode over a ridge and stopped. I just imagined when I rode over the ridge, the scene when the siege is going on and the riders come over a ridge. I just wanted to charge. (Male, 46, UK)

This conforms to the notion that mental simulations, unlike mental visions, are not linked to visual consumption. This form of location consumption is purely mental and can be detached from the precise locations as long as the travelled area lies within the wider film location destination and bears some resemblance to the fictional world of the film.

Second Gazing

Whilst acknowledging Urry's (1990) notion of the tourist gaze, MacCannell (2001) proposes the existence of another gaze. MacCannell argues that Urry's notion of the gaze fails to take into account that some tourists consciously attempt to look beyond the stage and onto the backstage of experiences. A second critique is that the Urry gaze, though it intentionally set out to defeat determinism, does in fact do the opposite: it empowers the gazing subject, but renders the object of the gaze as powerless, as an 'exotic fauna' (MacCannell, 2001: 29). MacCannell proffers the existence of another gaze, which he denotes 'the second gaze'. This gaze 'is capable of recognizing the misrecognition that defines the tourist gaze' (MacCannell, 2001: 30), in other words, the tourist manages to see beyond the façade set up by the tourism industry. An example would be a stage show by an indigenous performance group, where the potential audience has the choice to either attend such a show, look for a more authentic experience or object to such an inherently inauthentic encounter altogether. Simply put, sometimes tourists refuse to gaze at all. According to MacCannell, many contemporary tourists pursue second gazing and are constantly trying to go beyond touristic representations in order to see the real.

It is important to repeat at this point that film locations are never intentionally developed as tourist attractions (Preston, 2000). Therefore, some preconditions of Urry's (1990) gaze are somewhat precluded from the outset, as the objects of the film location tourist's gaze are not initially established and defined by the tourism industry. Contrary to MacCannell's (2001) assumption, the structural side of the film location encounter does not force the subject to 'shut down its second gaze'. Apart from addressing the imaginary component, the LOTR location guides on the research tours pointed out technical aspects and stories of the filming process and they gave the tour participants enough time and room to gaze upon the film-unrelated 'ordinary'. Rather than being distracted by the shift of focus onto the technical aspect of the film, film location tourists generally appreciated this aspect of the tour. At some locations, gazing at technical aspects was preferred over the primary gaze upon the fictional or story components. This was particularly evident at locations that discouraged behavioural or existential place-insiderness. Most of these locations contained low recognition values, were situated next to distracting man-made features and were only partly accessible. In these situations, the LOTR guides adjusted their narratives accordingly and subsequently preferred technical aspects and actor naming over the narratives of the imaginary. At locations without direct accessibility, the tour guides focused on its backstage aspects (i.e. technical gaze), for example at the Flight to the Ford location and at the Pillars of the Kings location. As the sights at the Pillars of the Kings location are not accessible and the two statues in the film scenes were computer-generated, technical gazing predominated. At both locations, the guide's narratives circled around transport logistics, camera techniques and the challenges for the actors in those scenes.

Technical gazing can also occur at locations that are close to man-made features.

LOTR
I find it very interesting to see how far it is [i.e. the location] to the next houses. How they did the filming of the scenes. Bringing down the camera to a lower angle to hide the background. This is more of an interest for me at that moment. (Female, 38, Germany)

In addition, the group size influences the probability of second gazing. The SW guide explained that the increase in group size compared to the previous tours he had led resulted in more occasions of second gazing, in particular the refusal to gaze at the location altogether.

SW guide:
I realised that on the previous trips when we were smaller groups, we were more into the experience. But now, when they're going to a set, it's almost like they forget that they're at the *Star Wars* set after five minutes and they start talking about other things. I'm like: "Hey: wait, wait, wait! Wait! Think back! Take a step back! We're at a Tatooine location, you know! We're on Tatooine. We're here for *Star Wars*".

Such behaviour was observable on some of the SW locations where, due to the group size, it took a considerable time until all tour participants had taken their turn at sight recording and shot re-creation. During the long waiting periods, in order to overcome boredom, the tour participants simply started to chat to each other, discussing things other than SW. This type of non-gazing was observed at several locations. Overcrowding also reduced the chances of mental visions and simulations.

In situations of technical gazing, the tour guide has to cross a fine line between directional commanding and granting enough leeway for the alleviation of feelings of boredom or impatience. It can also be argued that locations and sights with lesser importance or meaning provoked technical gazing sooner than sacred locations or sights, as the following comment from one of the second gazers hints:

SW

Camel Rock, well I recognised it from a few films. From the *English Patient* and the *Little Prince*. Yeah. It was a mild day. It was fine. Nothing spectacular to see apart from the horizon. It just doesn't mean so much to me. (Male, 37, Ireland)

A different form of non-gazing took place at the SW Dome. In spite of being such an important location for the majority of the SW tour participants, some group members staged a Jedi duel with blow-up light sabres in front of the set structure. This performance not only ruined the atmosphere for other tour participants, but was also perceived as slightly embarrassing by the guide:

SW guide:

Last night when we were at the igloo at Nefta, they pulled out the Jedi robe and inflated the blow-up light sabres. I just distanced myself because in my opinion, that was geeky. That was like you're giving the *Star Wars* fans a bad name here.

This opinion might have been reinforced by the presence of the author, yet it was observable that such behaviour was also disapproved of by other group members. Suddenly, the highly sacred zone around the Dome was degenerated into a profane backdrop for the duellists. In a similar fashion, the 'desecration' of a sacred zone took place at Aragorn's cliff during one of the LOTR tours. Some tour participants pretended to fall off the cliff and took over-staged photographs of their performance, which was clearly frowned upon by other participants.

An entirely different notion of second gazing upon the film locations is the lack of any connection between the real place and its function as a film location. This was particularly evident with tour participants who had no pre-trip knowledge of the movies and generally a low degree of fandom. They tended to ignore the narratives of the tour guide and sometimes separated from the group entirely to take in and photograph the 'general' landscape. In one instance, a LOTR tour participant practised rock climbing on Deer Park Heights, while the guide and the rest of the group proceeded with the programme. Some LOTR tour participants preferred to take photographs of the many goats on Deer Park Heights than of Aragorn's cliff. During the second LOTR research tour, an elderly American couple without any knowledge of the movies was booked on the tour. The couple often split from the rest of the group and enjoyed the general scenery rather than listening to the guide's narratives. When stopping outside the Fighter Pilots Museum (first LOTR tour stop), where the guide displayed and explained film-related items, the couple separated from the group entirely and strolled into the museum instead.

Generally speaking, the majority of the tour participants treated the location encounter self-reflexively and consciously acknowledged the restless movements between the real place, the technical filming aspects and the imaginary component. One LOTR tour participant commented: 'It is stupid to take this photo, it's just a bit of grass. But I'll take it anyway'. The LOTR tour guides often identified problems that arose with this notion of second gazing and in order to address these, they provided narratives about the history, geography, geology, fauna and flora of the visited places. This provision of general information was approved of not only by the non-gazers, but also by all other tour participants and considered as an important asset to the tour quality:

> **LOTR**
> **Informant:** I think it was very good that we were given so much information that was not concerned with *Lord of the Rings*, but to do with wine growing or gold mining. That was good.
> **Author:** You didn't mind that this was combined with the tour?
> **Informant:** In the opposite: that was very positive. (Female, 38, Germany)

Other LOTR tour participants remarked that the provision of general, film-unrelated narratives also eased tensions in the group by satisfying tour participants with a low degree of fandom.

Spatial Location Discrepancies

Location discrepancies or distortions occur where imaginary places and real locations differ in their mutual recognition value. They concern both the location in general as well as the particular sight(s). One type of common spatial discrepancy is caused by the ever increasing use of visual effects in big budget productions, which can significantly alter the recognition value of a place. For example, while SW IV contains 360 visual effects, SW III includes 2151 (Bailey, 2005). The number of digital shots in LOTR increased from 540 in LOTR I to 799 in LOTR II and, finally, 1488 in LOTR III (Visual Effects Supervisor Jim Rygiel, LOTR III, extra disc 2, New Line Cinema). Visual effects are commonly used to create aspects of landscape or built environment; to remove disruptive elements such as intrusions of the built environment; to make small additions such as a digital bush in the foreground; or to alter some of the existing location features such as digital squashing or stretching of mountains. Another discrepancy factor is the frequent application of creative geography, a term which is used to describe the filmic amalgamation of spatially separate places into one fictional location (Beaver, 1994).

The majority of the LOTR and SW tour participants were aware that visual effects had been extensively used in the movies. Nevertheless, when encountering the locations, this awareness did not always coincide with expectations:

LOTR
Author: What was your reaction when you saw the locations and it became clear to you how much was changed digitally?
Informant: I thought that was a bit of a pity. I was probably wishing for purer landscapes, less digital enhancement because it was not really necessary. (Female, 29, Germany)

Some LOTR informants were disappointed by the absence of the two statues at the Pillars of the Kings location. One teenager reacted in a dissatisfied manner after it was explained that the two statues were digitally superimposed: 'So they superimposed the statues? I thought the statues were real'. One informant explained his difficulty imagining the statues due to the reverse perspective from which this sight was seen on the tour:

LOTR
I tried to imagine the statues of the Argonath. It was a bit more difficult, because we could not see them from the front, only from behind. I would have liked to see them from the front. (Male, 26, Germany)

The most common type of spatial discrepancy is the clever use of camera angles to disguise disruptive elements such as houses, aerials, roads and other elements of the built environment. A significant number of informants were very interested in the technical aspects of the filming process. These informants were not disappointed when encountering disruptive elements near a location or in view of a sight:

LOTR
Author: Were you distracted in any way, or did it influence you in a negative way that at many locations there were houses nearby or for example, up on Deer Park Heights that one can see Queenstown below?
Informant: No, not at all. In the opposite. I find that exciting. I find it interesting to see how close it is to the next settlement. For example down at the creek location, seeing that it is directly behind a row of houses. I find that very interesting to see.
Author: The technical side of it?
Informant: Exactly. How did they do it? Aha, bringing down the camera so that one can't see the background or so. This interests me more in this moment. (Female, 38, Germany)

Other informants tried to block these elements out, both mentally and physically:

LOTR

Author: Were you distracted in any way by all the man-made structures around the locations?
Informant: I can block that out. I mean you look down to the lake and you see Queenstown. You know it's not there in the film. But if you start thinking about stuff like that you'd just become totally distracted from everything, wouldn't you? (Male, 46, UK)

LOTR

You have to use some tricks, for example, bending your knees so the houses disappear behind the ridge. Or you position yourself in a way that the aerial is hidden behind a tree. The rest is done by imagination. (Male, 26, Germany)

The following comment acknowledges the tour participants' constant problem of how to deal with the restless moment between the real and the imaginary:

LOTR

Well, the illusion gets a little bit destroyed. But when you look to the other side, it is there again. So, it distracts and it doesn't. One side is the fantasy world which is intact. The other side is the reality which belongs to it as well. (Female, 29, Germany)

The application of various camera angles and lenses can also change the scale between the physical location and the film shot or scene. Such alterations turned the small area on Deer Park Heights into the vast film landscape of Rohan where the crew filmed various scenes from LOTR I and LOTR II within the same area. Consequently, the tour participants encountered five different sights from all three movies, which are merely ten metres apart. This example of creative geography amused the majority of the tour participants, but it did not distract from the experiential consumption of the imaginary. The application of different camera lenses and zooms manipulated the Deer Park Heights area even further in order to make it appear as a vast landscape. Many LOTR tour participants were surprised upon making this discovery: 'This all looks so much bigger on screen' (male, 26, Germany). Similar statements concerned the location of Aragorn's cliff: 'This place doesn't look as big as on screen' (female, 27, Australia). A number of astonished responses were made at the location where the refugees walk around what is, in reality, a small mountain tarn. One statement was: 'The tarn looks like Lake Wakatipu (a massive glacial lake around Queenstown) in the movie' (male, 46, UK).

Although many noted this discrepancy, the prevailing reaction was one of excitement and the participants enjoyed comparing the real and the imaginary. With the Remarkable mountains in the background, the brown grass, the picturesque rock faces and the mountain tarn, the Deer Park Heights area was perceived as a 'beautiful setting'. The tour participants also appreciated the insights into the use of landscape for the production of the film scenes: 'It's amazing how versatile they were with the filming'.

The LOTR tour participants were taken by surprise by the relatively small size of the Kawarau River at the Pillars of the Kings location. In the movie, the river looks considerably broader due to the application of low camera angles.

LOTR
Author: What do you think about the Pillars of the Kings location?
Informant: Yes. It's very beautiful but much smaller than I imagined.
Author: Smaller means...?
Informant: The river is narrower. Not as broad and not very torrential. (Male, 26, Germany)

This perception was clearly influenced by the tour's vantage point, which was high above the river and thus made the river appear to be relatively narrow and small.

A third type of spatial discrepancy takes place during the editing phase when the colours of the filmed environment are changed or digitally enhanced. In LOTR, almost 80% of the colours of the finished product were manipulated in the studio. Most of these changes are not noticeable on location, as this would require a detailed comparison between the shot or scene and the sight. In saying this, one sight where LOTR tour participants were aware of such manipulation was a sight where the grass looks much greener in the movie. In reality, it is of an ochre colour. Some tour participants remarked that the grass in the photograph of the sight could be easily adjusted at home with the help of a computer graphics program. Colour and light manipulation was similarly remarked upon at a SoM location, the Mondsee church. For some tour participants, the church appeared to be much darker than in the movie: 'I remember being surprised. Inside, it's very dark' (female, 48, UK). Natural colour manipulation influenced the shots filmed at the second LOTR location above the Kawarau River, where some tour participants commented: 'It looks murkier in the movie' (female, 27, Australia). This was due to a flash flood during the filming, which turned the naturally ice-blue water a murky grey.

The common use of flip scenes in film, which is the digital flipping of shots 180°, also causes spatial discrepancies. The manipulation of some sights into flip shots always caused brief periods of confusion amongst tour participants. The discovery of the manipulation resulted in surprised excitement, as the majority of the informants were not familiar with the concept of flip shots and scenes. Some tour participants would take a digital photo of the sight, then immediately flip it on their camera screen so as to capture the filmic gaze. The camera was then passed around to other tour participants and enthusiastically received by the group. Similar reactions were observable at locations and sights defined by creative geography. Most tour participants were surprised and excited when encountering Aragorn's cliff. The fact that the cliff face is only two metres high, and that Queenstown (and not a river valley) lies below, generated a great deal of amusement in the participants. However, this did not affect the location's imaginary appeal. Creative geography at two SW locations (the two Lars' Homestead locations) affected some SW informants who were similarly excited by their discovery:

SW
I can't wait until I see the films when I get back. Because, realising that the Lars' Homestead is two parts that are hundreds of kilometres apart, I just wonder how it will be. I'll probably just smile to myself when I see that part. (Male, 35, Ireland)

In saying that, creative geography spoiled the location experience at the von Trapp house location. For the movie, the rear side of the Leopoldskron palace was combined with front shots of an entirely different building:

SoM
It's a little bit disappointing that they didn't use one house with the front and the back. Kind of spoils the illusion a little bit. (Female, 45, UK)

A distinct, spatial discrepancy occurred at some of the SW locations containing sets or set pieces. Although having been built eight years before the location visit, the Dome and the Mos Espa set were still in a surprisingly good state. Nevertheless, they had deteriorated over the years, which caused dismay for the tour participants as it was more difficult for them to engage in mental visions and simulations when parts of the set were literally falling apart. As one of the tour participants remarked, the Mos Espa set had the feel of a ghost town (male, 30, USA, SW). An extreme spatial discrepancy involving a set took place at the Ksar Hadada set. The set was almost entirely buried by a massive sand dune, which was very disappointing for the SW tour participants. Lastly, the schizoid location of the Gazebo presents a spatial discrepancy in its own right, as the set piece has been relocated to a place completely detached from its original filming location. Nevertheless, the majority of the SoM tour participants enjoyed the Gazebo as an objectively authentic set piece:

SoM
Author: What do you think about the fact that the Gazebo is not at the original location anymore?
Informant: I don't think it's that pretty. The Gazebo itself is pretty, but the whole location is not as pretty as it gets. I'm sure it would have been on the real location. I guess it's important because of the way it's presented in the tour, you know 'this is the Gazebo'. So that makes it important. (Female, 64, USA)

SoM
Author: What did you think about the Gazebo?
Informant 1: Oh, I didn't like that, actually. (Female, 56, USA)
Author: Why not?
Informant 1: I would have liked to have the doors open and to have walked inside. I would have liked it to be it a bit more, I don't know, maybe in a different location. It sort of just sat there in the corner somewhere.
Informant 2: It was like somebody just dropped the Gazebo in the middle of nowhere. (Male, 56, USA)

One SoM tour participant was disappointed by the fact that the Gazebo is locked and not accessible: 'I wanted to dance in the Gazebo. You can't go in' (Female, 64, USA).

Another schizoid location is the Krayt Dragon Ridge. Here, the original sand dune used for the shots in SW IV has moved a number of kilometres over the last 30 years. One informant explained that the former geographical position of the cameras was not so important to him.

SW
When you come to the Grand Dune, it's a bunch of sand, so who the hell knows where they filmed. If C-3PO and R2-D2 were dropped there, or five kilometres back, or five kilometres further away, I don't know that. I don't care. (Male, 35, Belgium)

A second informant was disappointed that he was unable to identify any exact sights:

SW
I was disappointed that they didn't pinpoint it exactly. I would like to know exactly where it happened. (Male, 37, Ireland)

One SW tour participant attempted to find the original sand dune by walking out into the desert. But, for the majority of the SW tour participants, it was more important to visit the general area of the filming: 'I just enjoy the scenery and the desert here' (male, 35, Belgium).

Temporal Location Discrepancies

Temporal discrepancies occur when the filmic time of the film does not match with the real time at the location, specifically the season and time of day. In comparison to spatial discrepancies, the number of encountered temporal discrepancies at the case study locations was comparatively limited. Over the course of the fieldwork, three different temporal discrepancies were experienced. The first one concerned the lack of snow on the mountain peaks surrounding many of the LOTR Deer Park Heights locations during the time of research; as noted by one participant 'had there have been snow on them, it would have been perfect' (female, 38, Germany, LOTR). As all the scenes on Deer Park Heights were filmed in winter, a LOTR tour in summer or autumn has to deal with this particular temporal discrepancy. However, on one of the LOTR tours, fresh snow covered the mountain peaks around Deer Park Heights. The weather on this day was stunning and when standing at the location of the refugee tarn, with the snow on the peaks, the reaction was excitement and awe: 'The snow tops it off!'

Another temporal discrepancy occurred at the LOTR Gladden Fields location. The Gladden Fields scenes were filmed in winter, with the trees stripped bare of leaves. In addition, the filmic time of the scene is just after dusk. The tour visits the location during bright daylight. For some LOTR tour participants, visiting this particular location in winter would have resulted in higher satisfaction:

LOTR
It would have been nice if it was winter and it would have looked more like in the movie. (Female, 27, Australia)

In this instance, the guide's comments detracted from the visitor's satisfaction. He remarked that 'in the winter, it looks exactly like in the movie', which naturally led to tour participants feeling disappointed. One informant wished she had blue lenses on her camera so she could simulate the light conditions of the filmic time. In order to avoid a similar spatial discrepancy at the SW Jawa Rock site, a tour participant suggested re-visiting the site at dusk:

SW
I was a little disappointed that we did not go there when the sun was setting, because when R2-D2 gets shot by the Jawas, it's dark. So I would have liked to re-enact that exact time frame. (Male, 30, USA)

A third temporal discrepancy was experienced at the SW Dome. Two of the scenes at this location were shot during a real sunset. One scene portrays Owen and Beru with the infant Luke Skywalker and depicts the two adults looking into the sunset (SW III). The other scene shows the adult Luke staring into the twin suns of Tatooine (SW IV). The tour group visited the location during the day. Because of the two famous sunset scenes, the guide organised a re-visit during the real sunset later on. The tour participants encountered the same sight twice: with and without a temporal discrepancy. In order to make the recorded sight look shot-perfect, some tour participants intended to draw in a second sun later using a graphics program. It was evident that the second visit resulted in a much higher experiential satisfaction than the first.

Chapter 6
The Physical Location Encounter

Shot Re-creations

The filmic gaze and its recording is the relatively passive, visual consumption of a film location in which the gazing subject never leaves his or her position as a spectatorial gazer upon the sight. A more active role in spectatorial consumption is the notion of shot re-creation, which occurs when the subject places himself or herself in the frame in order to re-create the position of the absent character. The subject thereby leaves the audience and enters the stage by taking on the position of 'the Other'. How intrinsically this transformation is performed depends on two levels of place immersion. The first level is that of behavioural insiderness, as the sights being re-created first and foremost serve as backgrounds for the photographer. The position of the absent object provides the stage for a ritualistic re-creation of the imaginary as seen in the film shot:

> **LOTR**
> I was Legolas firing arrows at the wargs. I'm a bit like that, I like to do stuff not just look. It's nice to be a participant and not just an observer. (Female, 36, UK)

Such performative action is often supported or, moreover, expected by either the tour guide or fellow group members. The re-creation is highly directed and on the LOTR tour, the guides would often encourage the participants to re-create shots. An example for directional shot position-ing is the following command given during one of the tours whilst the tour guide tried to help one of the tour participants recreate a film shot with her digital camera:

> **LOTR guide I:**
> If you want to recreate this exactly, what you're trying to get is a little bit of ski field road on the Remarkables, the mountain coming over the top of the stone and the green hill coming in with the white spot on the side of the rock. To your left a bit! Yup, that's good. A little bit more! Yeah, that's perfect!

In other cases, tour participants did not need any encouragement in order to re-create shots. Placing themselves in the frame was actively pursued from the outset. Once a re-created shot is recorded, it is added to the sign collection as part of the visual place consumption for the film location tourist.

SW

Author: Did you recreate any scenes or pose for any specific photos or scenes?

Informant: I photographed the sunset at the Dome to recreate my own picture, like it is shown in the movies. I just took the photos to remember again when looking at them in the future. 'That's right, it was like that and it looked like that'. (Male, 32, Holland)

Shot re-creation which might include posing as Legolas while standing on a rock from which the character spots the wargs (wolf-like creatures), is just another proof of 'having been there'. The collection of a prestigious sight is pursued in order to gain privileged status for oneself amongst peers.

The second, deeper level of immersion – place insiderness – often occurs simultaneously with behavioural insiderness, but beyond active cognitive control. In these situations, the subject actively or uncontrol-lably immerses himself or herself in mental visions and mental simula-tions: he or she sees through the eyes of the character, for example through the eyes of Legolas. Here, the subject has indeed left the gazing audience, has entered the stage and mentally simulates the cognitive inputs and behavioural outputs of the imaginary object. In other words, the subject becomes the (imaginary) object and mentally disconnects from the real environment. In addition, the subject extends upon the visual images constructed in the film as, suddenly, he or she is able to consume the imaginary beyond the filmic gaze.

The following comment by a *Star Wars* (SW) informant serves to further illustrate this deeper level of place immersion while taking on the position of a character:

SW

I've been there. I've been there. It's that kind of feeling. You watch the film and as soon as it comes up with a scene where you've been, you probably just look at it a bit more closely and you know in your mind, you've seen what's on the other side of the building or on the other side of the Dome. You know what's there. You see a three hundred and sixty degree view of that location, whereas everybody else runs the scene on screen. (Male, 42, UK)

Not all sights are suitable or favoured for re-creating shots. Access to the particular sight must be possible and safely achieved. It has to be a sight with a small number of characters, preferably lead characters who are depicted in the foreground of the action. The sight loses appeal for shot re-creations if it is a wide angle shot or contains too many distracting elements around the lead character(s). The depicted lead character(s) must be at the centre point of the shot and clearly outlined in the foreground of the action and it is essential that the film location tourist can re-create the pose of the character. Finally, the recognition value of the location has to be accurate, as too many spatial and temporal discrepancies can deter from a matching shot re-creation.

One of the preferred sights for shot re-creations on the LOTR research tours was that of Frodo, Sam and Gollum hiding under the thorn bush, with Frodo being the most re-created character. Éowyn and Merry conversing at the campsite proved to be another popular scene re-creation. Several participants asked the tour guide to take a photo of them positioned as the hobbit Merry is in the film, and two couples wanted to have the exact shot re-created with the two of them pretending to be Merry and Éowyn. The shot with Legolas firing arrows at the approaching wargs was re-created to a lesser extent. More popular were the shot re-creations of Legolas spotting the wargs, Legolas, Gimli and King Theoden glancing down the edge of Aragorn's cliff, and finally the stew scene with Éowyn and Aragorn. With regard to the last sight, most tour participants posed as Aragorn and sat on the same stone.

Shot re-creations of the thorn bush scene, the conversation between Merry and Éowyn, the cliff scene and the stew scene were especially popular with couples. These re-creations were always gender-specific with the man posing as Aragorn or Merry and the woman posing as Éowyn. The connection between favourite characters as named by the informants and the informant's shot re-creations was apparent. For instance, informants whose favourite character was Legolas re-created the shots of Legolas spotting the wargs and Legolas firing arrows. Fans of Aragorn re-created Aragorn in the stew scene by sitting on the same rock. This connection was also backed up by both LOTR guides (personal interviews). Only one tour participant wanted to re-create the Gollum character by crawling under the thorn bush and he sustained several scratches in doing so. Consequently, everyone else opted for either Frodo or Sam.

While the inaccessibility of the exact character positions at *The Sound of Music* (SoM) locations prohibited the re-creation of shots, the SW locations offered plenty of opportunities. The most popular shot re-creations were Luke Skywalker walking up the stairs at the Lars Homestead interior, Luke Skywalker gazing into the sunset at the Dome, Darth Maul on his lookout (Figure 6.1) and the Jedi duel between Darth Maul and Qui-Gon Jinn.

The only SoM location suitable for shot re-creations were the Mirabell Gardens. Of those, the Do-Re-Mi steps were the only sight selected for such performance, which involved the re-creation of the characters' dance up and down the stairs.

Figure 6.1 Shot re-creation of Darth Maul at his lookout
Source: Author.

Successful shot re-creations were generally applauded by the tour participants and often, the re-creations recorded on digital cameras were passed around and commented on. In the case of the flip scene with Legolas spotting the wargs, tour participants with digital cameras flipped the photograph digitally in order to match it with the shot. The flipped photograph was also handed around and was the cause for much hilarity, applause and enthusiasm about the recognition value of the shot re-creation.

Filmic Re-enactments

In a further transitional step towards existential place insiderness and existential authenticity, the subject transitions from formal bodily fixed posing to filmic re-enactment. Filmic re-enactment is a process of both engaging in a mental simulation, and thus a transition of self-identity, as well as the involvement of the bodily behavioural outputs of the simulated object. In the tradition of Edensor's (2000) performance theory, filmic re-enactment can be regarded as unbounded performance. Filmic re-enactment is not necessarily the re-enactment of particular scenes. On the contrary, this process is often completely disconnected from precise scenes. The existence of such imaginative consumption has been previously acknowledged by Winter (2002), using the example of the World Heritage Site of Angkor in Cambodia and its portrayal in the movie *Tomb Raider* (2001). Winter (2002: 334) cites one female informant who climbed around the ruins in a precarious way in order to feel 'like Lara Croft exploring the jungled ruins of Angkor'. The woman not only consumed and experienced the imaginary place through mental simulations, but also through the full embodiment of filmic re-enactment.

During the fieldwork, filmic re-enactments were performed only in rare situations. One particularly expressive re-enactment was observable at the Lars Homestead interior location. Some of the SW tour participants dressed up in Jedi robes before entering the location. They proceeded into the room where Luke Skywalker, his Step-Aunt and his Step-Uncle drink blue milk and have a conversation about Luke's future. Not only did the dressed-up tour participants formally pose around the table, but they also re-created the character conversation and drank blue milk. Although there are no Jedi Knights involved in that particular film scene, the re-enacters mentally and bodily simulated the feel of being in Tatooine and in Luke's home:

SW

It's a feeling that somehow, it puts you into the film. It's like a re-enactment in your head. You're a part of that film. (Male, 42, UK)

The sorts of re-enactments mentioned above were very rare, as they require a number of supporting elements. As internal and external surveillance often restricts the boundlessness of performances, particularly when travelling collectively (see Edensor, 2000), the momentary surveillance has to be such that it admits and supports such 'unbound performances' (Edensor, 2000). External distractions such as noise or onlookers should be as minimal as possible. Filmic re-enactments are more likely to occur when the re-enacter is determined to perform at a specific place before embarking on the tour. A high spatial and temporal recognition value of the general location is also beneficial.

Apart from the previously illustrated instance, the only other SW re-enactment took place at the Dome during the sunset visit. All the previously listed, supportive elements came together in this instance. Some SW tour participants re-enacted Luke Skywalker as he comes out of the Dome, walks over to the rim of the homestead pit and gazes into the twin suns of Tatooine. One SW tour participant also re-enacted Obi Wan Kenobi from the SW III scene where he gazes into the sunset (Figure 6.2).

SW

I did recreate one scene. I experienced Luke Skywalker at the igloo with the sunset. I was living that moment. And I did experience Obi Wan Kenobi because at the end of *The Revenge of the Sith*, he delivers the babies. And he just has this look on his face like "this is the end!"

Figure 6.2 Filmic re-enactment of Obi Wan Kenobi
Source: Author.

He has his hand on his face and he looks in a certain direction.
I actually used the Jedi robe for that one. (Male, 30, USA)

Another example of filmic re-enactment occurred on a SoM tour. One of the tour guides revealed in an interview that he had once had an elderly woman on the tour who told the guide that her long-held dream had been to visit the Gazebo and re-enact the character of Liesl as she dances in the pavilion and leaps from bench to bench. At the Gazebo, she was able to fulfil her dream: inside the pavilion she did indeed dance and sing, but her re-enactment was cut short when she slipped from a bench and broke her leg (since then, the interior is no longer accessible to the public). Another filmic re-enactment at a SoM location was experienced by one of the female informants (18, UK) who admitted that she had walked down the aisle in the Mondsee church, imagining herself as the soon-to-be wedded Maria.

For outsiders, the feelings and beliefs of the re-enacters in these moments are not possible to ascertain. The re-enacters are in their own, secluded world of imagination, entirely disconnected from normal perceptual inputs. In these situations, the re-enacter becomes the absent character who is gazed upon by the other tour participants who themselves record the re-enactment. Sometimes, such recording was consciously noticed by the re-enacter(s). In other cases, where the re-enacters were completely immersed in the imaginary, the recording remained unnoticed.

Interaction with Site Markers

Immobile on-site markers

Despite substantial promotional efforts, many LOTR locations lacked the necessary on-site markers. Out of roughly fifty publicly accessible locations (apart from Hobbiton), there are just two sites with immobile on-site markers: the location of Rivendell at Kaitoke Regional Park, East of Wellington and on Deer Park Heights. At the Rivendell location, a couple of directional signs point towards the exact site of the filming. There, a larger information board provides some facts about the location. On Deer Park Heights, the property owner has erected five signposts pointing towards the exact sites. Two of these are intended to pinpoint the sights, but are not placed accurately (Figure 6.3).

In addition, the tourists accessing Deer Park Heights can pick up an information sheet containing a map with the five signposts drawn in, yet visitor satisfaction was not as high as might be expected. The inaccuracy of the sight markers resulted in disappointment, as it was not possible to identify the sights. In addition, the meagre sight descriptions provided by the information sheet also prevented any possibility of proper sight identification. It was observable that many independent visitors on Deer Park Heights appeared confused and helpless when encountering the

Figure 6.3 Directional signpost on Deer Park Heights, Queenstown, New Zealand
Source: Author.

different sights. Sometimes, they would come over to the touring group and ask for help with the sight identification.

Most LOTR tour participants acknowledged the benefit of a guide on-site when compared to the prospect of sight identification with other markers: 'I can't imagine coming up here and trying to figure it all out myself' (Male, 55, UK). One informant expressed the advantage of a guide very clearly:

LOTR

Author: Have you noticed the signposts?

Informant: At Deer Park Heights? Yes, I did. But it was much better with a personalised guided tour with a personal narration. (Male, 26, Germany)

The LOTR guides would regularly make the tour participants aware of the challenge of finding all the exact sights. At some sights, the only means of identification were specific patterns of lichens, the structure of nearby rocks and rock faces or the shape of the mountains in the distance. The guides constantly pointed out these natural on-site markers and compared them to their position in the film stills provided. In a rare instance, one informant overrated the usefulness of the signposts on Deer Park Heights and underrated the advantage of an on-site tour guide:

LOTR

Author: Did you see the signposts?

Informant: Yeah. I saw them and thought: Ah! If we'd driven up on our own, we could have done this ourselves! (Female, 36, UK)

Another informant regarded the signposts as distracting elements when recording a sight. The father of two made his children stand in front of the two signposts at Aragorn's cliff when photographing their formal pose, in order to hide the signposts from view. Clearly, the signposts on Deer Park Heights not only fail to precisely pinpoint the sights, but they also distract from experiencing the imaginary component fully by their intruding presence.

A different type of immobile on-site marker is the photo billboard. This marker contains various photographs that were taken during location filming. Photo billboards are used at Hobbiton in Matamata and the Samurai village in Taranaki (*The Last Samurai*) (Figure 6.4). In both instances, the tour is partly based on the information provided on these boards.

Some problems are inherent in this technique of nucleus marking. First, the displayed photographs were taken by the landowners who had no specialist knowledge of film location tourism. Consequently, they did not take their photographs from the position of the film camera in order to record the sights. Second, each of the photo boards contains various

Figure 6.4 Photo board at the *The Last Samurai* location of the Samurai village in Taranaki
Source: Author.

photographs with various contents. This results in information and sight overflow as the various sights around the photo board are difficult to compare with those on the board. Only by very careful, step by step sight-guiding can this problem be addressed. Finally, some tourists got bored with staring at the numerous photo boards, which are somewhat detached from the nucleus. As previously illustrated in Chapter 5, film location tourists want to stand in a location with a clear sight in front of them.

During the course of the fieldwork, three specific, immobile on-site markers gained meaning and recognition for the tour participants. At the SoM Gazebo, a nearby information plaque signifies the objective authenticity of the set structure and was therefore often consulted and subsequently photographed by SoM tour participants. Objective authenticity refers to the authenticity of originals. Correspondingly, authentic experiences in tourism are equated to an epistemological experience (i.e. cognition) of the authenticity of originals (Wang, 1999).

MacCannell (1973) first introduced the concept of authenticity into the sociological side of tourism research. His notion of inauthenticity or staged authenticity forms a juxtaposition to the concept of authenticity. Since then, issues of authenticity have played a major role in tourism research (Cohen, 1988; Harkin, 1995; Jamal & Hill, 2002; Selwyn, 1996; Silver, 1993; Wang, 1999). Further developing MacCannell's concept of staged authenticity, tourism researchers borrowed from objectivism as well as from constructivism to introduce the two notions of objective and constructive authenticity. Objective authenticity refers to the authenticity of originals, which is the toured object. Constructive authenticity refers to 'the authenticity projected onto toured objects by tourists or tourism producers in terms of their imagery, expectations, beliefs, powers, etc' (Wang, 1999: 352). A toured object can therefore possess various versions of authenticity.

Other significant on-site markers also contained clear name connotations. At Hobbiton, the first stop on the location tour is a hilltop overlooking the location. A signboard reads 'Welcome to the Hobbiton movie set'. In the distance behind the signboard, the location is clearly visible and recognisable. The tour participants perceived the signboard as an important signifier. Formal posing in front of it was a more common reaction than recording the actual location behind it (Figure 6.5).

A similar phenomenon took place at Aragorn's cliff on Deer Park Heights. Next to the directional marker on the cliff, a second marker connotes 'Aragorn's cliff'. While all LOTR tour participants ignored the

Figure 6.5 Formal posing in front of a name connotation marker: 'Welcome to the Hobbiton movie set'
Source: Author.

directional marker, some of them formally posed with the connotation marker of Aragorn's cliff or simply photographed it. The two latter examples suggest that on-site markers with name connotations contribute to the objective authenticity of a film location or sight.

Transportable markers

Transportable film location markers include location guidebooks and other printed film location-related information. On the research tours, some transportable markers were brought along by the tour participants, while others were provided by the tour guides. Transportable markers included the LOTR location guidebook (Brodie, 2002) and self-made information folders containing set photographs and film shots about SW. The LOTR tour guides provided colour-printed film stills on-site and copies of the original call sheets with maps and general information about the filming. The SW guide provided a folder with maps, photographs and other general information about the locations, which he had prepared himself. None of the SoM guides provided transportable markers.

Without a guide on-site, transportable markers are very important for the location experience. Ideally, transportable markers direct film location tourists to the locations, pinpoint the exact sights and provide narratives about the technical aspects and the imaginary component of the film. They should contain directions, location maps, sight photographs, location and sight descriptions and technical filming information. The sight identification of the LOTR location guidebook (Brodie, 2002) was criticised by some LOTR tour participants:

LOTR
Informant: I've been slating it. I thought the guidebook was really not that helpful.
Author: So you didn't use it during your trip?
Informant: No.
Author: Why did you buy it then?
Informant: We bought it when we first got to the South Island with the view to us maybe driving around those places, but the book didn't make it easy for us to do that. Because of the way it's laid out, the structure of it, the directions and all of that are so unhelpful, that it was like 'right, a guided tour then', because I'm not prepared to drive round and round in circles trying to find the right places. (Female, 36, UK)

The film stills provided by the LOTR guides substantially increased the objective authenticity of the locations as participants were able to compare matching identifiable location features, such as lichen patterns, rock structures or background features, with the provided film stills. This was expressed by these informants:

LOTR
Informant 1: I was inspired actually, having the movie stills. (Female, 46, UK)
Author: That was quite important for you?
Informant 1: Definitely.
Informant 2: I think that was excellent. But it was evidence as well. It was evidence. (Male, 55, UK)
Author: Evidence of what?
Informant 2: It happened there. I mean, how many people on tours are often told a lot of lies.
Informant 1: Yeah. They really matched everything up where it was.

The film stills used as pictorial cues on location also increased the existential authenticity of the location, as they identified positions for shot re-creations and filmic re-enactments. Tour participants would often photograph the film stills either with or without the sight in the background. This ensured the possibility of photo and thus sight identification at a later stage. The LOTR guides used a second type of transportable marker on the tours, namely copies of some of the original call sheets that they employed at some locations, not only for providing obscure and personal narratives, but also to prove the proper identification of a location. The call sheets significantly raised the objective authenticity of the locations for the tour participants, as they served as visual proof of their originality.

Handling of Film-related Items

Some film location tour operators provide the opportunity to handle film-related items on their tours. This can be a decisive incentive during the tour selection process (see Chapter 4). The selected LOTR tour company presents copies of some of the original call sheets, copies of the original scripts of LOTR I and LOTR II, a number of replica weapons plus a helmet and one original prop used in the film. The latter item is the elven cloak of the hobbit Sam. Although the weapons and the helmet are replicas made under license in Taiwan, they have the exact look and form of the original film props and are made of the same material. The selected SoM tour operator hands out Edelweiss seeds to all participants at the conclusion of the tour. The Edelweiss flower is a national symbol of Austria and is paid homage to in the movie's song 'Edelweiss'.

The LOTR weapon replicas are introduced by the guides, who provide much detail about the fictional history of the weapons, the meanings of their inscriptions, their appearance in the different scenes and background stories from the filming. After the weapons are laid out, the tour participants have the opportunity to photograph the collection and the chance to handle and pose with them. The strongest reactions, expressed through body language, facial expressions and behavioural actions, were observed when handling the LOTR scripts and the elven cloak. Clearly, the objects considered more 'authentic' possessed more meaning for the tour participants than the replica weapons. Most tour participants handled and treated scripts and cloak with the utmost awe and respect.

The recording of this handling was very important. For instance, costumed formal posing in front of a location was the prevailing action used to capture the connection between the posing subject and the elven cloak. The significance of the cloak's objective authenticity was expressed by two informants:

LOTR
I think the cloak was more important because it's authentic. Everything else was an imitation. I know they are great imitations, but to me it was Disneyland. And the cloak was actually worn by actors, so that had power. It was unique. But the swords had no part in it whatsoever. They weren't used in the movie. I need the real thing. (Male, 55, UK)

LOTR
Unfortunately, it was all replicas apart from the cloak. I found the cloak really great. It had really been used in the movies. Fantastic! You become even more a little bit of a part of it. It sounds silly but it is totally fascinating! (Male, 26, Germany)

As the informants remarked, wearing the cloak made its bearers feel even closer to the imaginary. In order to eliminate distracting elements, the poses were staged to hide most of the contemporary clothing underneath the cloak, which was also encouraged by the guides. When formally posing with the cloak, the background was important: most tour participants posed for a shot re-creation whilst either carrying a weapon replica, wearing the cloak or doing both. Where this was not possible, full satisfaction could not always be achieved, as one LOTR tour participant indicated to the guide: 'You [the guide] should not show the weapons and props here (in the Fighter Pilots Museum) but in the landscape' (Male, 26, Germany). Most LOTR tour participants selected Frodo's weapon, known as 'Sting', when posing with the cloak. Sting seemed to possess more meaning than any of the other presented replicas:

LOTR
Author: The first weapon you took in your hands at Deer Park Heights was 'Sting'. This was very evident. Was there a specific reason for that?

Informant: It's probably the most recognisable weapon because it features very often in the film, it is called by its name and there is a constant focus on it. For example the knives of Legolas, you see them quite often, but they are not really highlighted. (Female, 38, Germany)

The importance of Sting is built up by its recognition value in the movie, namely, its relatively long screening time. This special meaning was transferred to the actual location experience when people held the weapon in front of them whilst wrapped in the cloak (Figure 6.6).

For tour participants, this experience went far beyond mere formal posing:

LOTR
Author: What would you say was the most fascinating moment for you today?
Informant: The most fascinating moment was probably when I put on the cloak. The cloak and 'Sting' in my hand, Frodo's sword. The cloak and Frodo's small sword, yes.
Author: Why?
Informant: Because I had the feeling that I am even closer to it through the cloak and the sword. Maybe simply because I could feel like the character. (Female, 29, Germany)

Figure 6.6 Costumed posing with Sting and elven cloak at a *Lord of the Rings* film location
Source: Author.

This example demonstrates that formal posing can go far beyond the notion of disciplined rituals or Urry's tourist gaze. Many LOTR tour participants attached intrinsic feelings to this particular moment in time and space, which resulted in strong mental simulations.

There is no evident connection between the favourite characters the LOTR tour participants named, and the weapons presented on-site that held the most meaning for them. When handling a film-related item, its meaning and importance was attached to the emotions surrounding the item as it appears in the movie, as well as its screening time, whereas the connection with the character owning the item played only a minor role.

Miniature Positioning

A special form of visual place consumption occurred during the SW location tour. Some of the tour participants transported SW miniatures with them in order to place them in front of some of the locations and sights. Such miniature positioning was performed at Obi Wan Kenobi's Hermitage and the Dome. At the Dome, the two droid miniatures of R2-D2 and C-3PO were placed in a direct line before the dome structure (Figure 6.7). In order to have both elements in 'real' scale on the photo, the camera was lowered down to the ground, with the miniatures situated at a distance from the Dome.

Such use of forced perspective enabled one participant to recreate the precise sight at Obi Wan Kenobi's Hermitage with the land speeder model in the photograph:

SW
Informant: I went to Ben Kenobi's house. I had a model of a land speeder. I had my friend hold it up in the approximate position in the film. I lined up the camera so I got the land speeder and the house in the right position and I photographed that. Some of the people took photos of the R2-D2 and C-3PO figures. Some of these worked really well, especially out in the sand dunes.
Author: What impulse is behind that?
Informant: It's a funny picture that you show to your friends. (Male, 42, UK)

It is suggested that the positioning of miniatures in front of locations and sights may serve as a substitute for the absent, imaginary object(s) of the character(s). By miniature positioning, the imaginary is reconstructed as accurately as possible. This, in turn, gives both the photo as well as the photographer additional status amongst his or her peer groups. In the shots shown in Figure 6.7, in which toy miniatures are positioned to look

Figure 6.7 Miniature positioning in front of the Dome (*Star Wars* location)
Sources: Author and M. Lefebvre.

like the characters form the film, the recorded photographs were shown to members of the tour group and loudly applauded.

Souvenir Collection

The collection of souvenirs is part of the physical consumption of a place (Meethan, 2001). Typically, souvenirs are divided into pictorial images (photographs, video footage, postcards), pieces-of-the-rock (pieces of the natural environment such as rocks, pine cones, sand), symbolic shorthand (manufactured souvenirs), markers (souvenirs with word inscriptions) and local products (arts and craft; food produce) (Gordon, 1986). The acquisition of souvenirs is an essential part of a satisfactory film location experience. The prestige of the acquired souvenir largely depends on its objective authenticity value: the higher the value, the higher its prestige. Pieces from original set structures possess the highest objective authenticity, followed by on-site pieces-of-the rock and marker souvenirs. The example of the provision of Edelweiss seeds during the SoM tours exemplifies that pieces-of-the-rock film location tour souvenirs tend to possess less meaning if detached from specific locations:

SoM
Author: What will you do with the Edelweiss seeds?
Informant 1: I'm going try and grow it. They only grow on the top of a mountain so I don't think they'll grow in our garden. But I'll try. (Female, 48, UK)
Author: Is it different from just going somewhere and buying a normal souvenir?
Informant 2: No. No. (Female, 45 UK)
Author: It has no connection to the movie for you?
Informant 2: Just a little connection.
Informant 1: Again, it was sort of a bit of a laugh really, wasn't it? You know, the guide coming round giving you the Edelweiss seeds. It wasn't meaningful.

This is different with detached marker and symbolic shorthand souvenirs. For instance, some LOTR tour participants bought symbolic shorthand LOTR souvenirs such as replica weapons and LOTR stamps in a shop in Queenstown at the end of the tour. Other LOTR tour participants purchased the location guidebook (Brodie, 2002) at the New Zealand Fighter Pilots Museum (first LOTR tour stop) and had it signed by the author Ian Brodie. One informant explained that he intended to buy the book upon return to his home country:

LOTR
Informant: I think I will buy it in Germany.
Author: Why will you buy it then? You won't be able to use it.
Informant: Well, at least, I can use my imagination when it says: 'This and this is near Wellington'. I know what the landscape roughly looks like. When I see a specific photo, I might be able to say: 'Okay, I have seen something very similar from the bus'. (Male, 26, Germany)

The acquisition of the LOTR location guidebook was time- and place-independent for most tour participants. Due to the nature of the connection between the marker representing the general experience of New Zealand as an imaginary place and the personal encounter, the location guidebook was a very meaningful reminder of that experience. The same reason animated SoM tour participants to purchase marker and symbolic shorthand souvenirs in the town of St. Gilgen during a tour stop.

The following quote suggests that the acquisition of a detached marker or symbolic shorthand souvenir through a third party is regarded as an unbiased proof of achievement:

LOTR

Informant 1: A little presentational thing would have been nice. You know, we did a heli-hike and as part of that, when you come down, you get given a booklet that's got a certificate in it to say: I've done a helihike on Franz Josef glacier. And those are the important things, when you travel a long way and you spend a lot of money. It's nice to have that sort of tangible object. (Female, 36, UK)

Informant 2: Tangible. Yeah. That kind of reconfirms it. That you haven't actually obtained it yourself, it's given to you. It's like 'yeah, I've done that'. (Male, 46, UK)

Rather than through self-acquisition, the presentation of the film-related souvenir marks a neutral symbol of acknowledgement and achievement, which, in turn, can increase its status. The majority of the acquired souvenirs, however, were collected on location. Apart from pictorial images, whose acquisition has been thoroughly dealt with in the previous sections of this chapter, the main bulk of collected souvenirs were pieces-of-the-rock souvenirs, ranging from stones pilfered from Aragorn's cliff to the collection of pine cones at the Flight to the Ford location, rock chippings from the Jawa Rock to bags of sand from various SW locations. The pine cones, for instance, were intended to be used for their seeds, which might grow LOTR pine trees. Many SW tour participants collected sand in purposely brought plastic bags (Figure 6.8). Part of the sand was intended for a personal collection, while the rest was put aside for sale to other SW fans.

Pieces-of-the-rock souvenirs that are obtained on-site form a very strong symbolic link between the real and the imaginary:

SW

Author: What's behind the desire to have a piece of the location?

Informant: It's as close as you can get. This is sand where the Jedi walked. This is where the jawas ran. This is sand where Anakin Skywalker flew over on his speeder bike. Of course, it's just an idea and the sand is a metaphor. It's a metaphor for 'I've been where *Star Wars* was filmed. I've been to Tatooine. This is sand from Tatooine.

Figure 6.8 Packing sand at a *Star Wars* film location
Source: Author.

This is not sand from Tunisia, this is not sand from a beach in Florida. No, this is sand from the planet Tatooine'. (SW guide)

Contrary to the LOTR and SoM tour participants, the SW tour participants had the rare opportunity to collect pieces-of-the-set souvenirs from the remaining film sets and set structures. Some of these were bought from locals, namely the Krayt Dragon bone fragments, as shown on Figure 6.9.

Only a small minority of the SW tour participants collected a set piece from the Ksar Hadada set, although there were plenty of fragments lying around. The reasons for this may be that the set has almost completely disappeared under the dune and, therefore, it can no longer be appreciated as an intact and recognisable film set. In addition, the set structure is a reproduction of the real building used for most of the scenes, which can be found in the settlement of Ksar Hadada near the South-Tunisian coast and was visited earlier on in the tour. Finally, the scenes involving the set have no strong significance in the storyline of the films, as the screening time of the set is very limited.

At some locations, set pieces were acquired by raw force. The tour participants simply ripped parts off the set structures, in particular at the Mos Espa set. The guide insisted in the interview that on his previous trips, no set pieces had been ripped off the set structures. This time, due

Figure 6.9 *Star Wars* souvenir obtained from locals
Source: Author.

to the bad state of the Mos Espa set, participants' inhibition levels were much lower:

SW guide:
On the first trip, everything was still in primo condition. The only thing we took was sand. Then, on the second trip in 2003, the sets had deteriorated and some things had actually fallen down, or broken off or whatever. They were thrown on a pile. We didn't take anything from the walls or stuff like that. We just took things out of that pile. Now, this is the final trip, and we can see that many of the sets are deteriorating very fast now. They're not being kept tidy. It's almost like it's only half there, you know. There are buildings that have been destroyed, roofs that have collapsed, walls that are gone, doors that are gone. People are now like "I should take it with me because tomorrow it's gonna end up in a pile. It's gonna be destroyed, it's gonna be gone forever. So I'll take it with me".

All the SW tour participants based their justification for taking pieces by force on the bad state of the Mos Espa set. As soon as one tour member started to rip off a piece of the set, all inhibitions were overcome and most group members joined in the action of set piece acquisition. Few wanted to miss out on this opportunity to collect film relics.

SW

What happened today at the Mos Espa scene? I have to say that I took a piece from the set with quite a bit of force. But you know it's the last time we'll be here, everybody wants a piece and if you see everybody else doing it... At the beginning I said "oh, please don't do that! Leave it!" But when everybody starts tearing things off the wall and tearing the place apart, then you think: "Why not?" (Male, 27, Belgium)

Remarkably, none of the SW tour participants ripped pieces off the Dome structure. It was observable that the sacredness of the set placed a strong taboo on the physical collection of set pieces. When asked about the future of the collected pieces-of-the-set souvenirs, the informants stated that they would be framed and displayed (Figure 6.10).

SW

It just seems to be a part of the trip here that you bring something home. I mean, I will. I'll frame it. I'll frame the pieces I took from Mos Espa. I already have an idea for that. (Male, 35, Ireland)

SW

Author: What will you do with the bits and pieces you tore off the set?
Informant: I'm rebuilding my house and actually one big room is only for *Star Wars*. Only for me. Nobody else is allowed to come in there. Yeah, my *Star Wars* friends, but... (Male, 27, Belgium)

Two main drivers are behind the acquisition of pieces-of-the-rock as well as pieces-of-the-set souvenirs: they symbolise the connection

Figure 6.10 *Star Wars* film location trophies

between the real and the imaginary component, and they signify the pilgrimage of the film location tourists to the worshipped film location and make the experience tangible.

SW

Author: Did you rip off any parts of the set?

Informant: Yes, I did.

Author: Why is it important for you to have a set souvenir?

Informant: For me, it makes it touchable. I don't need a whole metre of door or big pieces. No, just little pieces makes it real for me. I'm going to watch the first of the six movies again. Just to experience and think 'that's where I've been! Look at this part on this evaporator: I've got it! I've got it! It's in my collection'. (Male, 32, Holland)

SW

Well, isn't that ironic? It's not different from my grandmother bringing back something from Lourdes. Maybe in the days before cameras, before books, we also needed to show that a place has had an impact upon our lives. You've gone to do a pilgrimage and we took a piece of relic hoping that the relic, whatever the piece is, will magically transform us even more. (Male, 37, Ireland)

The collected souvenirs raise the status of the film location tourist amongst the wider fan base not only through its material possession, but also through its meaning as a signifier for the location pilgrimage.

Chapter 7

The Social Location Encounter

Group Interactions

The appeal of watching a film, amongst other factors, is to share the experience within an interpretive community (Feuer, 1992). As anecdotal research in film tourism suggests (Aden *et al.*, 1995), this shared experience is also sought at the film location when participating in a location tour. This research indicates that being part of a group of like-minded people is an essential part of the whole experience. The benefits of visiting a film location within an interpretive community are manifold. First of all, members of such a community can share general information about the films as well as particular information about the locations:

> **SoM**
> Other fans may have some information that's not in the books you've been reading about the movie. Sometimes people on the tour might actually tell you something you didn't know. (Female, 52, UK)

Information is shared either as visual data – photographs, location guidebooks, maps or simply internet printouts – or as narratives. Narratives are exchanged in the form of public, obscure or personal information (Lugosi, 2002). Public information regarding film locations can be obtained via Special Features DVDs, the print media or other public sources of general information. In order to acquire obscure information, specialists or people with personal knowledge or experiences about a particular film have to be consulted. These include fan clubs, fan groups or people involved in the filming process.

When comparing all three case studies, the most intensive exchange of information took place within the *Star Wars* (SW) community. There was certainly less time at hand for *The Lord of the Rings* (LOTR) and *The Sound of Music* (SoM) participants to share information. On the other hand, both LOTR and SoM tour participants relied heavily on the guides for obscure information. The SW tour participants had a far greater in-depth knowledge about the filming and the locations than the other tour participants. Some of the SW participants had obtained more obscure information about SW than the guide himself had. In addition, the guide and three of the tour participants were able to share information due to their participation in previous trips. The least exchange of information took place within the SoM community, as the SoM tour participants had little in-depth knowledge about the filming

181

and the locations. This might be the case because there simply is not as much publicly accessible obscure information about SoM as there is about LOTR and SW.

Exchanging information benefits both sides of the exchange process: the information provider can boast about his or her in-depth knowledge and the information receiver relishes the discovery of new information. As this research suggests, hunting down new information about a film and its locations is an important factor in the experiential consumption of film locations within an interpretive community.

Another benefit derived from being part of an interpretive film location community is the mutual drive between the members to actively participate in formal posing, improvised and even unbound performances. As an interpretive community always consists of heterogeneous members, some members are more active than others. Through observation, it was noted that the more active members had influence over more hesitant members regarding posing and performing. For instance, even tour participants seemingly uninterested in recording sights started to join in with the active recorders. A similar phenomenon occurred with the re-creation of shots, the handling of film-related items and interactions with the guide and other group members. The active members reduced the notion of embarrassment when re-creating shots or capturing the filmic gaze by opposing such feelings from the outset. The fact that some LOTR tour participants were embarrassed in those situations was expressed by some informants who considered themselves as fans, but not as 'crazy' or 'mad' fans. Certainly, the presence of a researcher on the tours might have had an impact.

Informants with a higher degree of fandom all agreed that the experience of a film location tour is highly dependent on the consistency of the interpretive community:

LOTR

What makes the tour is the people who are on the tour, and there is no way you can change that. It was lucky that we had a nice group of people. (Male, 55, UK)

The problem arising with passive members is that it can decrease the quality of the location experience for the more active members. This is especially the case if the passive members predominate:

LOTR

What would have been good, which was not the case today, would have been to be around other fans. This is something which I enjoy very much. Being around other fans and exchanging stories. (Female, 38, Germany)

In these situations, it is the responsibility of the guide to mediate between the different group members and to balance their needs and wants accordingly:

LOTR guide I:
If they haven't seen the films and if it's just them on the tour, it's not a problem. But if they are on a tour with people who are really interested, it's very hard for them to feel included because you need to give all the information to the real fans. All you can do is just make sure you give them a lot of other general knowledge to keep them happy as well.

Another significant bonus of experiencing film locations within an interpretive community is the very sense of community felt by participants when encountering the locations. The experience of the restless moment between the real and the imaginary is the common denominator between the tour participants or community members, which aids them in establishing a bond with each other and reinforces the experience through the sharing of emotions:

SW
It's really lovely to have your friends around you, or people around you to share the experience of standing where the movie was made. I admit that we do bring the movie magic with us. (Male, 37, Ireland)

In the case of SW, the location tour established strong friendships between some of the tour participants. The link between group bonding and single locations was very strong at some locations and weaker at others. Out of all the locations visited, the two locations that evoked the strongest sense of community were the Western summit of Deer Park Heights (LOTR) with its spectacular views onto Queenstown, Lake Wakatipu and the surrounding mountains, which incorporated the filmic sight of the Bay of Belfalas, and the SW Dome at sunset. With the Deer Park Heights sight, several elements came together to make it special as a communal experience. Here, the real and the imaginary match perfectly, making the sight very recognisable. As such, the real place is visually spectacular and provides stunning scenery to gaze upon and to conjure an 'imaginary reality':

LOTR
It's just become reality now. Everything here is living history, is part of a real "Middle Earth". Because if you're a fantasy fanatic like I am anyway, you actually believe. (Female, 52, Australia)

An interesting sense of community evolved at the SW Dome during the group's second visit at sunset. During the first visit in the middle of the day, the tour participants were first and foremost interested in taking photographs of the location, capturing the filmic gaze, re-creating shots and posing in front of the film sets. The location had a hectic atmosphere to it as each tour participant tried to take his or her photographs without anyone in the viewfinder. During the second visit in the evening, the atmosphere changed entirely:

SW

We'd been there in the afternoon so everybody took that picture, so that was over with and we were there as a group and we enjoyed it. We were there in the same moment for the same goal. (Female, 31, Holland)

It was apparent that it was a moment of communal bonding and a mutual sense of belonging to the community, as well as to the place itself. Despite this sense of community, everyone experienced this moment in mental solitude through mental visions and simulations. This was also expressed physically; some tour participants simply sat down on the sand and watched the sun disappear, while others stood up on the crater rim, imitating Luke Skywalker in SW IV. There was only one brief period of renewed frenzy: when the sun was about to set, everyone wanted to take a photo with the Dome in the foreground.

Experiencing film locations within an interpretive community can also have some negative consequences, one being that sights can become too crowded for the purpose of romantic gazing and the seeking of solitude:

SW

There is something about solitude that really makes me enjoy the moment. No distractions. (Male, 30, USA)

In addition, the positions for sight recording as well as shot re-creation are heavily competed for. It takes some time before everyone is satisfied with the recording. Such waiting periods can result in boredom, impatience or annoyance:

SW

You just have to be patient if you don't like pictures with other people in them. You can yell "get out of the picture!" I yelled that sometimes. (Male, 27, Belgium)

One SW informant explained that the sharing of the location experience slightly decreased its value (male, 35, Ireland, SW). He would have preferred to come on his own terms in order to experience the locations in solitude, which clearly expresses a wish for romantic gazing. For him, the other tour participants distracted too much from that experience.

Guide–Participant Interactions

The primary roles of the professional tour guide are mediation, interpretation and fulfilling a leadership function (Lugosi, 2002). The film location tour guide shares information about the locations, interprets them spatially and creates a sense of community through encouragement and intimacy. The format of the tour determines the accessibility and intimacy of guide–tour participant interactions (Lugosi, 2002). A high accessibility is achieved if the guide is open to individual and group interaction and shares personal information. The more intimate this interaction is, the richer it becomes in affective qualities and existential authenticity. To Edensor (2000: 339), the structure of a guided tour determines 'the extent to which directors or choreographers [control] the range of manoeuvres available'. Tour guides suggest places for photographic and gazing performances and provide scripted commentary. Whilst these elements sound slightly determining, a guide also provides live interpretation and is a very effective and flexible on-site marker. Guides convey information but also add elements of amusement and personal touches to the tour.

A distinction can be made between third-person and first-person interpretation. The third-person interpreter usually wears contemporary clothes, uses normal language and does not act anything out. The first-person interpreter is often costumed and lives the role to a greater or lesser degree of reality (Howard, 2003). The quality of the tour guide as a live interpreter is based on three complexes, namely training, translation and reproduction (Lugosi, 2002). Through formal training, the guide is educated for the tour. Formal training can include the participation in tours with experienced guides, followed by training tours supervised by the company management and the learning of a tour script. The second part of the educational process is to learn through experience and to consult different sources of information for the tour commentary. The original tour is then reproduced in an individualised way 'where guides, influenced by personal characteristics, specific perceptions of the guide role, and the different people on the tour will reshape their tours' (Lugosi, 2002: 337).

As opposed to all other markers, the mobile marker 'tour guide' actually mediates between the toured object and the tourist by directing, commanding, narrating and re-enacting. The guide's role is not simply to prove objective authenticity and to provide constructive authenticity, but also to convey existential authenticity. Besides the passion, enthusiasm and drive of the individual tour guide, existential authenticity is essentially achieved by first-person interpretation. First-person interpretation in film location tourism puts the guide in an immediate, mediated position between the subject and the toured object. As the toured object includes both the real-place features as well as the absent, imaginary objects of the sets and the film characters, first-person interpretation shifts the imaginary components into the mental vision of the subject. The following, running commentary was recorded during a LOTR tour. It illustrates how the tour guide switched back and forth between first- and third-person interpreter when explaining the location of Aragorn's cliff. The underlined sentences indicate where the tour guide has slipped into his role as a first-person interpreter, re-enacting the relevant scenes.

LOTR guide I:
So what happened? Aragorn has jumped on Sharku's warg, giving him the Glasgow kiss. They fight, he throws Sharku off. You see Aragorn while he's still fighting, riding the warg across in front of those Matagauri bushes over there where we were standing. Then, a little bit later, you see him dragged around the same Matagauri bushes. He's then dragged down this slope here, up to the cliff edge and goes over and then there's silence in the film. The music stops and half the audience is sitting and thinking "I can't remember any of this in the book!" Major change to the novel. Peter Jackson invented the whole warg battle. It's not in the novel. The only time the wargs are really mentioned is south of Rivendell on their way to Moria. They are heard in the background. So, it's silent. The camera then focuses on this warg on the ground here. Gimli comes up with his axe and graaa! – Kills the Warg. The camera then focuses on the riders of Rohan; the soldiers of Rohan milling around in the grass down there. You see a warg chased up the gully, a warg is chased up that little slope up onto the ledge and there are soldiers milling up in that area there. Here is the still from that scene. This is taken a little bit higher up. The camera cuts back and King Theoden is here, looking around. The camera then goes over here. There is a dead horse here and Legolas is standing here, suddenly spots the camera on him, starts walking. He walks up and he goes: "Aragorn?" Looks around. The camera then focuses over here on Gimli.
And Gimli is standing here. He goes: "Aragorn?" Looking around. The camera then goes back to Theoden who is still, more desperately now, looking around but quietly. You then see Legolas walk up here. Follow me up! Legolas hears laughter and on this tussock grass here, lying down, is Sharku the orc. Gimli comes up and says: "Tell me what's happened and I'll ease your passing!" And in a very dodgy accent he goes: "He's dead. He took a little tumble off the cliff!" Legolas comes up and grabs him and shakes him and says: "You lie!" Legolas shakes Sharku and he goes: "CHHhhhh" and he dies. He opens his hands, and in his hands is the Evenstar...

Figure 7.1 A *Lord of the Rings* guide engaged in first-hand interpretation
Source: Author.

When the tour guide slipped into first-person interpretation, all the narrated quotations were acted out by the guide, as can be seen in Figure 7.1, which shows him re-enacting the dying orc Sharku.

The guide not only altered his voice to imitate the characters, he also cited their lines and re-enacted their facial and body movements. He took on the different roles of the characters and transformed himself into them. Such re-enactment enabled the tour participants to have clear mental visions of place and character(s):

> **LOTR**
> **Author:** When you were standing at the locations and the guide explained them to you, did you see the characters in your mind?
> **Informant:** Yes, yes. I could see the characters.
> **Author:** What do you mean by 'you saw them'?
> **Informant:** I saw the film scenes in front of me. I could recall every scene and every moment.
> **Author:** Is the guide very important as a connection?
> **Informant:** Yes. He basically transforms into the different characters. (Female, 29, Germany)

The comment above illustrates that film location tourists are able to mentally project the features of the interpreted characters onto the tour guide so as to imagine the absent object.

All tour guides on the research tours named the characters rather than the actors in order to carry the cinematic suspense of disbelief over to the location. This naming procedure was also implemented in situations of third-person interpretation. The LOTR guides as well as SW guide agreed that character-naming considerably enhances the experience of the imaginary:

LOTR guide I:
Most of the people who are on the tour almost believe that the characters are real people. That's the magic of the book. You're doing the tour of a film set, so people suspend their disbelief to the extent that they almost believe it's a true story. So therefore, you follow that. It just feels right to me to talk about the characters rather than the actors.

SW guide:
You have to use the character names because you're in that make-believe world so you have to use the make-believe character names. It enhances the experience.

The informants were very appreciative of this naming procedure, as this remark demonstrates:

SoM
If you named the actors it would take away from the scenes themselves. If you say Julie Andrews the whole time, it would give the tour more of a rational feeling. But if you refer to the characters, it's nearer to the original movie. I think it was good the way they did that. I liked that better than saying Julie Andrews and, you know, whoever the other actors were. Then you don't even think it's a real story. Then you think: "Oh, Julie Andrews touched that fountain. I don't want to touch that". But if it's Maria.... (Female, 18, USA)

All the guides slipped into actor-naming when taking on the technical gaze. The actors were connected with stories around the filming of particular scenes, funny remarks about their filming experiences and other information. All in all, character-naming, first-hand interpretation and re-enactment of scenes can shift the restless moment towards the experience of the imaginary. The film location tourists are able to have mental visions and are more likely to immerse themselves in the place.

The leadership function makes the guide responsible for directing the group, and also for establishing positive relations amongst the group members. The smaller the tourist to guide ratio, the easier it is for the guide to get a feeling for the degree of fandom of the individuals and to achieve an intimate sense of community. The same can be said about the structure of the tour. A tight script prevents the guide from establishing a sense of personal accessibility and intimacy. For example, due to the tight time schedule and the large group sizes of the SoM tour, the guides always remained complete outsiders to the tour participants. It was not possible to create intimate and positive relations between the guide and the tour participants, nor between the group members. The opposite effect was observed during the SW tour. As the guide was working on a non-profit basis and acting as a true *primus inter pares,* a high intimacy between the guide and the tour participants, as well as amongst the group members was established. This intimacy helped to overcome feelings of embarrassment or otherness in situations of improvised or unbound performing. Ideally, the guide's leadership function should be loosely based upon a script with directional commands, but also leave sufficient leeway for romantic gazing, experiencing solitude, mental simulations, filmic re-enactments and interpersonal, communal ex-change. An intimate, emotive manner of guiding can be achieved by a small guide to tourist ratio, a high level of enthusiasm and passion from the guide, the provision of personal narratives and through first-person interpretation of important locations and sights.

A significant challenge for the guide is created when the consistency of the group is heterogeneous in its varying degrees of fandom. Tour participants without a particular interest in the imaginary have to be entertained with film-unrelated narratives. This does not pose a problem when moving between geographically separated locations, particularly when travelling in a vehicle. During the location encounter, however, the guide has to provide the tour participants with narratives of the imaginary as well as technical aspects about the filming. The danger of losing the attention of disinterested tour participants in these situations is far greater than during the transport phase, as the uninterested tour participants are likely to drift off, engage in second gazing and therefore spoil the experience for the others. The film location guide has several means of averting this threat to the location experience. He or she can cut short the time spent at the individual locations, ignore the group members engaged in second gazing, or try to get them interested through interactive and emotional guiding. The LOTR case shows that interactive, interesting guiding can turn initial disinterest into increased approval. LOTR tour participants who admittedly booked the tour without previous knowledge of the movies often became increasingly interested and engaged during the course of the tour.

Direct LOTR tour interactions between the guides and the tour participants often involved technical questions posed by the tour participants, such as 'did they take the fences down for filming?' or 'what did they do about the houses?' One recurring question posed to the LOTR guides referred to their own participation in the filming process as an extra or to personal interactions with cast and crew. The status of the guides increased significantly if one of these questions was answered positively, demonstrating that the connection between toured object and subject becomes more immediate due to the involved role of the mediator. Direct guide–tour participant interactions during the SoM tours were limited to a few remarks about the organisational issues of the tour. Lastly, the interactions between the SW guide and the tour participants generally took place on a level of mutual friendship.

Interactions with Outsiders

Utilising Edensor's (2000: 327) performance theory, one could say that performances of film location tourists tend to be 'exclusive affairs, designed only to reinforce communal solidarity among the participants'. Non-members (this term does not include the location guide who is regarded as a communal member with different rights) are perceived and treated as outsiders. These outsiders can be separated into three groups: other film location tourists who are not part of the tour group, general sightseeing tourists and locals. Solidarity within the group is achieved by physical separation from outsiders by moving closer to the group, through the use of name connotations unfamiliar to outsiders or the general disregard of others.

At the research locations, two incidents with other film location tourists were encountered. The first incident frequently occurred at Deer Park Heights. Independent travellers can enter Deer Park Heights on their own account as it contains a clustering of sights, is easy to find and to access and therefore a number of independent LOTR film location tourists turn up there every day. Many of these carry the location guidebook (Brodie, 2002) in order to identify the precise sights, yet as explained in Chapters 5 and 6, such identification is made difficult for them. This was evident to the LOTR tour participants not only by pure observation, but it was also pointed out by the LOTR tour guides. The result of this awareness was a feeling of superiority over the individual film location tourists, as the tour participants felt privileged to have access to the precise sights. An interaction between both parties took place when independent film location tourists followed the tour group in order to eavesdrop. In these situations, both guides and tour participants secluded themselves from these outsiders in order to maintain the status of privileged knowledge. As a result, even the attempt to eavesdrop did not lead the independent tourists to successful sight identification. This, in turn, resulted in 'schadenfreude' amongst the tour group members and it also strengthened the bond of the group by separating the group members from the underprivileged 'others'.

The second incident took place at the Mos Espa location. About 25 minutes after the group had entered the Mos Espa film set, a number of jeeps from a local tour operator based in the nearby oasis of Touzeur stopped at the set and released a number of tourists. Although they were booked on a full-day, general sightseeing tour of the wider area, one of the itinerary stops was the film set of Mos Espa. The SW tour group reacted very indignantly to the newcomers. The jeep drivers parked the vehicles right in front of one of the set streets leading out into the desert (Figure 7.2). It spoilt this segment of the set for the SW tour participants who were eager to record it on camera, as it represented a clear sight:

SW

Author: Do you think that at times there were too many people around? Did it distract you from the experience?

Informant: At the Mos Espa set, when all the tourists came and they were all walking around and then they parked the jeeps right in front of the evaporators I thought 'why do you have to park your cars at this spot?' (Male, 27, Belgium)

The whole film set was suddenly teeming with people and it became difficult to take photographs without anyone in the picture. The SW group members did not concede the newcomers the right to be at the location, as they perceived that they did not possess a high degree of fandom. Their spectatorial gazing performances were viewed as a desecration of the place.

Figure 7.2 Outsiders at the Mos Espa film set
Source: Author.

Direct on-site contact with general tourists were much fewer. Naturally, as most research locations are relatively secluded and off the beaten track, such encounters were very limited. During these encounters, both parties usually followed their own paths. As the general sightseeing tourists were either not aware of the additional meaning of the visited place or not interested in it, the feeling of privilege was not very strong amongst the tour group. It can be said that general sightseeing tourists pose no threat to the status of film location tour participants.

A different point of contact was the presentation of film-related items in public. Passers-by would often stop and watch the LOTR tour participants wielding and displaying the weapons and the cloak. Sometimes, this interaction resulted in a slight uneasiness amongst the group members, as they felt exposed and slightly embarrassed about their performances. It is the responsibility of a location guide to avoid such situations entirely. At the SoM locations, the group members mixed with and blended-in with the general sightseeing tourists, particularly at the Mondsee church. Here, the tour guide released the group before entering the church. As the tour participants tended to experience the location individually, the danger of exposing group performances was non-existent. On the other hand, being part of a group provides anonymity for the individual film location tourist:

SoM
Author: Do you think that there is a difference between a do-it-yourself tour and experiencing it with a group of other fans?
Informant: All the people who are there, they like the same thing as you. So you don't feel stupid. (Female, 47, Canada)

At the Gazebo, the general sightseeing tourists visiting the castle grounds were not interested in the set structure and simply ignored it. As formal posing is a generally accepted expression of touristic performance, the disciplined rituals performed at the Gazebo did not draw much attention from the outsiders.

At some locations, locals posed a threat to the quality of the location experience. This was particularly the case at SW locations, where locals tried to sell desert roses at the Dome. The placement of the little stall next to the dome structure spoilt its authentic look and the vendors tried to sell their products in a very persistent way, which was perceived as a nuisance by the tour participants who literally had to fend them off.

SW
They distract you from the experience. They were pulling on your arm: "Sir, Sir, buy this!" It can happen once, it can happen twice, and

Figure 7.3 Locals selling Krayt Dragon bone fragments to the *Star Wars* tour participants
Source: Author.

maybe three times. But when you say five times: "I don't want it!" and they still keep pulling on your arm... (Male, 35, Belgium)

After a while, the locals gave up and watched the group from a distance. It was apparent that they did not know how to interpret the actions of the tour group. An even stronger interaction between locals and the SW tour group occurred at the Mos Espa set. The handful of locals stationed at the set offered to rip off remaining set pieces for money. They acted in a very aggressive and persistent way in their efforts, which almost caused a fight between them and some of the group members. In the end, one local tried to chase the group off the set.

A contrary interaction was observed at the Krayt Dragon Ridge. The locals at this location offered fragments of the Krayt Dragon bones which were the remains of a set piece resembling the skeleton of a giant dragon in a SW IV scene that they had dug up from underneath the sand. The interaction between both parties resulted in lively negotiations over the price of the fragments (Figure 7.3). In this case, the tour participants enjoyed the interaction, which was perceived as entertainment:

SW
That was fun. Because the locals there were trying to sell us things. There was one little kid that wore a *Star Wars* t-shirt and it was very

cool to see somebody out in the middle of the desert wearing a *Star Wars* t-shirt. (Male, 30, USA)

The interaction resulted in the purchase of some of the bone pieces, leaving both parties highly satisfied.

A different tour group–local interaction took place at the von Trapp house location. A local vendor had set up a wooden front panel depicting Mozart and his wife Constanze, with two holes cut out for the heads, behind which people could stand and have their photographs taken in character. The SoM tour participants were invited to put their heads into the holes and have their photographs taken, yet on all seven research tours the SoM tour participants simply ignored the vendor.

Part 3
Conclusion

Chapter 8
Characteristics of the Film Location Encounter

Preconditions for Film Location Tourism

In tourism literature, much has been speculated about the film's textual preconditions for film tourism and film location tourism (Cousins & Andereck, 1993; Riley & Van Doren, 1992; Riley, 1994; Riley *et al.*, 1998; Tooke & Baker, 1996). There is no doubt that the filmic text itself is the inciting factor for the majority of people who consider travelling to portrayed film locations. As anecdotal evidence derived from the literature suggests, it is the interconnected, symbolic system of the non-verbal and the verbal that signifies meaning in a filmic text (Barker & Schaik, 2000). The concept of film (location) tourism-inducing film icons, as put forward by Riley *et al.* (1998), does not reach far enough to understand a film's power to attract film location tourists: magnetic resonance research has proven that visual elements address general brain areas, whereas intrinsic film messages provoke individual reactions (Hasson *et al.*, 2004). This is supported by the list of tourism-inducing feature films provided in Chapter 3, of which the majority of these include textual core properties of the genres of drama or romance. A key element within both genres is the development of empathy with the lead characters who struggle through familiar life situations. The more believable the fictional setting for these situations, the more strongly it addresses our emotions. Literary precursors or underlying real-life stories and historic figures further enhance the believability of such settings. This intrinsic film element is then combined with visual icons, which have to portray attractive and spatially identifiable and accessible locations.

Cousins and Andereck (1993), as well as Riley *et al.* (1998), also assume that the box office success of a feature film relates to the number of attracted film (location) tourists. This supposition can be clearly rejected, for as Table 3.3 reveals, a significant number of the listed tourism-inducing feature films are not included in the top 350 box office records list. Some of those feature films reaped relatively modest revenues at the box office. For example, the film *Highlander* (1986) grossed just under US$6 million in the USA. Yet Eilean Donan Castle in Scotland, portrayed as the lead characters' home, has since experienced a constant influx of film location tourists (Stenson, 2008, via email). This assumption is also backed by the significantly increased tourist visitation to the Greek island of Cephalonia, location for the feature film *Captain Corelli's Mandolin* (2001), which turned into a film-induced attraction in spite of the film's modest box office success (Hudson & Ritchie, 2006b).

The number of repeated film sessions gives another indication about the likelihood of a film's tourism-attracting power. For instance, 20.1% of the participants of Salzburg Panorama Tours' SoM tour in 2004 had previously watched the movie more than four times and 26.8% had seen it more than 10 times. Repeated film watching was also reported by *The Lord of the Rings* (LOTR) informants, with the average number of times each informant had seen the movies being five to six times. Apart from the women accompanying their partners, all SW tour participants had watched the movies numerous times. Some informants admitted to having seen them so often that they had lost count. Re-watching a film on numerous occasions can evidently increase character and place empathy.

The geographical identification and access-promotion of film locations is based on several factors. Under normal circumstances, films and their accompanying media exposure are unofficial place promotion tools, as it is not their intention to promote tourism to the portrayed places (Preston, 2000). In some cases, destination marketers and tourism enterprises jump on the bandwagon and combine these unintended images with their own, intended images. Ideally, such tourism promotion efforts commence with the first window of the film exhibition cycle and consequently follow through the complete cycle (Grihault, 2003). New, short peaks of public enthusiasm within the issue-attention cycle generated through media gossip and the film's postproduction exhibition cycle create excellent opportunities for the tourism industry to establish sustainable film location tourism. Tourism New Zealand's campaign 'Welcome to New Zealand – Home of *Middle Earth*' is an impressively successful example of such business demeanour. Yet, as the case study on *Star Wars* (SW) demonstrates, film location tourists can also be attracted to locations at geographical positions that are not widely publicised. In this case, the internet-based, obscure information about a non-profit location tour reached individuals with a high degree of fandom. This and other examples from this book suggest that potentially interested film location tourists with a high degree of fandom actively inform themselves about the geographical location and access issues of film locations. Such information is obtained via fan-based websites, film end-credits, official film production compendia, location guidebooks or through word-of-mouth.

The actual travel decision depends on several considerations. First of all, the type of film location attraction nucleus determines the purpose of the travel (see Chapter 3). For instance, the SW locations were primary nuclei for the tour participants as they were the decisive element for booking the tour. For the majority of the LOTR and the SoM tour participants, the film locations formed secondary attraction nuclei as they were not influential in the participants' wider destination choice. Yet, for most tour participants, the visitation of the film locations and the participation in location tours was decided upon prior to the trip. Some LOTR locations were also encountered as tertiary nuclei under two different premises. Under the first, four of the LOTR tour participants had no knowledge about the movies, yet upon arriving in Wanaka, they decided to partake in the film location tour in order to experience places off the beaten track. Under the second premise, some LOTR informants revealed that they had discovered individual locations purely by coincidence during their travels through New Zealand. They also stated that stumbling upon these locations generated as much excitement as actually experiencing them. Macionis (2004) tackled this aspect from a different angle and introduced the threefold distinction of the specific, the general and the serendipitous film location tourist. The specific film location tourist is someone who specifically travels to a destination to visit a film location, whereas the general film location tourist incorporates a location visit within a wider itinerary but does not select the trip based on film location visits. The serendipitous film location tourist happens to encounter a film location by coincidence, for instance by passing a signpost that marks a specific place as a film location.

Once the decision for a location visit is reached, the question of whether to participate in an organised location tour or whether to experience the locations independently is a central determinant. For all tour participants, the decision to book on an organised tour was made due to several factors: ease of access to the locations, including the organisation of transport and accommodation in the case of SW, the chance to experience the locations with an interpretive community, and guided interpretation. The SoM- and LOTR-interested location tourists were able to choose from different tour operators. In the case of SoM, Salzburg Panorama Tour's main draw card is its association with the film crew of SoM, which is extensively promoted. The major assets of the Southern Lakes Sightseeing tour are the clustering of a large number of visited locations on Deer Park Heights and the chance to handle film-related items. Costs also played a significant part in the booking decision and tour participants were apt to carefully weigh up the perceived value-for-money of each tour.

In some situations, a particular film location can influence the tour booking decision as well. Besides the substantial clustering of SW locations in Tunisia, the remaining film sets and set structures were an additional asset to the locations. This is backed up by Singh's (2003) finding that a motivating factor to visit the Hobbiton film set was its remaining set structures.

When taking all the above arguments into account, it is fair to say that there is no single decisive trigger for film location tourism. In most cases, it is a combination of factors that initiates a travel decision. These triggers may encompass: (1) an exposed attractive, identifiable and accessible location where one or more scenes have been shot on-site. (2) The exposed place is tied into an emotional story with intrinsic elements of drama or romance. (3) The storyline is either based on a true story or on a popular novel. (4) The film has become a classic or cult film and is watched time and again. Additional triggers can be: (5) believable and multi-layered characters, dependent on high-quality acting and directing. (6) An imaginative and detailed world, in which the storyline and characters are embedded. Ultimately, the accompanying media, film awards and touristic structures in place influence potential film location tourists to travel to screened locations. In saying that, there are cases where film location tourists turn up solely through active exploration or word-of-mouth propaganda.

Characteristics of Film Location Tourists

While it is not the intention of this book to establish a typology of film location tourists, a summary of the characteristics of the informants does indicate some interesting tendencies.

The informants were generally culturally aware and well-informed about the destination they were visiting and sought to participate in existentially authentic activities and experiences. These ranged from nature excursions and adventure activities (i.e. New Zealand, LOTR), to close encounters with the local culture (i.e. Tunisia, SW), to the appreciation of architectural treasures and local cuisine (i.e. Austria, SoM). The informants were, without exception, part of the free independent traveller (FIT) market segment. FIT characteristics amongst the informants included the general preference of individual travel arrangements, the relative flexibility in the actual itinerary and a good knowledge of the host culture through pre-trip research. Pre-trip information was obtained mainly through word-of-mouth and by consulting popular travel guides such as *The Lonely Planet*. The internet played an important role in the general pre-trip information process and for tour booking decisions. In addition, internet and email accounted for a significant share in the actual tour booking methods.

The informants' itinerary pattern can be interpreted as an exploration of the main attractions and activities in several regions, with relatively little time spent in one place. If the film location formed a secondary attraction nucleus in the wider holiday, the location visits were incorporated in the general itinerary. In this scenario, location clustering in a convenient position in relation to the itinerary significantly influences the selection of a location tour. If location visits are the main part of the travel, other attractions and activities are included in the itinerary as well.

The informants covered all age groups, ranging from teenagers to seniors over 60. However, the middle brackets between 20 and 50 years were prevalent. They either had sufficient disposable income for the general holiday or, in the case of the backpacker-style travellers, invested their funds in activities such as film location tours rather than in more expensive accommodation, food and transport. The vast majority of informants came from Western countries, with the USA, the UK, Australia, Germany and Canada being the largest segments. This might be attributed to the fact that all three case study movies were mainly produced for these markets and address issues appealing to the Western world. However, both the LOTR as well as the SoM tour operator had recently experienced a slight increase in customers from Asia, in particular from South Korea, Japan and China (personal interviews with both companies). Most informants had completed or were undertaking an undergraduate university degree. All these general statements also conform to the findings of other researchers on LOTR (Carl, 2005; Croy, 2004; Singh, 2003).

Despite these general characteristics, as this book has shown, each tourism-inducing film attracts an individually distinct type of fan. Of the informants, 90% had never done a location tour before and were not interested in doing so in the future. Yet, several informants had previously visited other locations from the same film or were considering experiencing more locations during their remaining holiday. Four informants had done exactly the same location tour previously. The three case study movies are attractive to differing age brackets, which is revealed in the ages of the partaking tour members. As the LOTR case shows, the three prevalent age brackets reflect the different revival stages of the book. The predominant age bracket of the SW tour participants, ranging from 31 to 40 years, correlates with the target audience for the first three episodes (SW IV, V and VI), which were released in the late 1970s and early 1980s. What was surprising was discovering that the largest SoM age bracket is that between 21 and 30 years. This can be partly attributed to the fact that the SoM location tour is heavily advertised in the different backpacker hostels in Salzburg, with discounts being readily available. It also shows that the family film *The Sound of Music* has not lost its appeal with the younger generation. The gender distribution of the different cases illustrates a film-dependent distribution. SW appeals mostly to males, while LOTR attracts slightly more female location tourists. SoM, arguably, addresses a female audience (Strasser, 2000), which is also expressed in the number of female SoM location tour participants. Regarding the mode of travel, the majority of

LOTR and SW tour participants were individual travellers, although many of these had partners at home. The majority of SoM tour participants were couples, followed by solo travellers. While for some, sharing this experience with a partner or good friend was essential, others preferred to visit film locations by themselves in order to eliminate any detracting factors, as might be experienced if a disinterested partner or friend had accompanied them. The degree of fandom, measured by the number of repeated film sessions, the possession of the film on video or DVD and the in-depth knowledge of and around the film, was the highest with the SW tour participants, followed by LOTR and lastly SoM. This suggests that a high degree of fandom generates primary location attraction nuclei, which, in turn, result in longer, more intensive location encounters.

The Existential Attractiveness of Film Locations

The majority of the informants were aware of the fact that many locations had been altered in the film scenes. Film watching is an established part of social leisure activities and, due to the ever-growing distribution of Special Feature DVDs, many people are familiar with technical aspects of film making:

LOTR
Author: Were you aware of the fact that they had changed quite a lot by computer?
Informant: Yeah, yeah, well, we've watched the extended DVDs. So as part of that you watch the making of stuff so we know all about the blue screen and the blue suits and all of that kind of stuff. (Female, 36, UK)

In accordance with Carl's (2005) findings, pre-trip research generated realistic expectations about the location encounter for most tour participants. All LOTR informants were aware of the fact that there were no remaining film sets left to see on the tour. Despite this, some tour participants remarked on the potential attraction of set visits. On the other hand, the beauty of the natural locations visited on the LOTR tour ranked it above one participant's previous visit to Hobbiton due to its poor state of repair:

LOTR
The obvious thing [for the Hobbiton management] to do is to take more care of the film set because what they're offering now is, in fact, an anticlimax. (Male, 55, UK)

All LOTR informants who had visited Hobbiton previously, preferred the natural locations of Deer Park Heights over the partly reconstructed

Hobbiton set. When asked about the most attractive features of Hobbiton the lake and the party tree were cited as the most memorable features of the location. The finding that natural locations can be preferred over film sets is backed by the SW case study. The Mos Espa set was promoted to the SW tour participants as follows: 'The sensation of being here cannot be described in words, I'm afraid. You just have to be there to know what I mean. When walking these streets – truly in the middle of the desert [...] – you get this very weird feeling of walking on another planet'. Yet, for some, the set did not meet the generated expectations:

SW

I think when you walk around Mos Espa and see that everything is just made of chicken wire and wood, you really know it's just a set. You wander around and everything sounds hollow. (Male, 42, UK)

An interesting observation was that repeated encounters of the same locations altered the attractiveness of the locations. The SW guide's own favourite location shifted from the Lars Homestead interior to the SW Canyon over the course of his three tours:

SW guide:

After having done the trip three times, the place that gives me the most satisfaction now is the *Star Wars* Canyon – Djebel Krefane – which is just a natural canyon. There is nothing there, no set buildings or set pieces. It's just a beautiful piece of nature, but it is also very recognisable.

For repeat visitors, the beauty of natural place features seem to become more important to the location's attractiveness than the existence of original set pieces. The following comments indicate that repeated visits not only change the perceived attractiveness of the locations, but can affect the overall experience in a negative way:

SoM

I don't think I'll do it again, I mean, I've done it with each member of the family. Salzburg is beautiful but I think there are only so many times you can see it. (Female, 52, UK)

SW

It probably would be best if I didn't come back. Last time I came my expectations were met, but I think that this time I became more jaded by it and some of the magic is now kind of gone. (Male, 37, Ireland)

For one SW informant, repeated visitation with a tour group changed the encounter from a more personal experience to that of participating in the emotions and feelings of the other group members:

SW
It's a big thrill to see it the first time. Now, the second time, a lot of the thrill was seeing other people's faces because I knew what they were feeling. It's how I felt for the first time a couple of years earlier, so for me that was a new experience. (Male, 42, UK)

The same respondent felt that on his second visit some of the magic of the locations had worn off:

I noticed myself that I was taking less pictures or wanting to actually stand on the same locations and re-create actual scenes and poses.

Research with the informants clearly determined that natural locations with stunning scenery, high recognition values and sets in a good state of repair with a connection to important scenes in the storyline, can provide high satisfaction levels. They provide beneficial opportunities for mental, visual and physical consumption. Too many repeat visits can decrease the value of such consumption and, therefore, result in dissatisfaction.

Natural location features

According to Kelly and Nankervis (2001), attractive landscapes and places contain the following features: water bodies, a sufficient degree of variety and an interpretive pattern and personality. This set of criteria is partly drawn from the fine arts, in particular the subjective attractiveness of paintings. In order to be perceived as attractive, film locations should also incorporate some of these elements. The tarn sight (LOTR) has an alpine pond, the Bay of Belfalas sight (LOTR) a glacial lake and the Mirabell Gardens (SoM) a fountain. All three sights possess a high degree of variety, namely various morphological features and surface colours at the tarn and the Bay of Belfalas sight, and myriads of sculpted plants and blooming flowers in the Mirabell Gardens. The greatest asset of the Bay of Belfalas sight is its incorporation of a 180-degree vantage point over a stunning landscape:

LOTR
Informant 1: It's just a stunning view, isn't it? In fact, it looks much better in reality than it does in the film. (Male, 46, UK)
Informant 2: Because it's just the place itself. The film shows you really stunning sites but we know they've been manipulated, so you actually come to places and see that that place is stunning,

like it is in the film, but in fact, it's even more stunning. (Female, 36, UK)

The SW Canyon comes alive through its fascinating geomorphology, but also in the constant transition between light and shadow, which takes place in the gorge. For one informant, the canyon was the embodiment of '*Star Wars* in 3D', the 'real stuff' as opposed to a set (Male, 27, Belgium, SW). Other descriptions used to characterise this location were 'monumental', 'ancient' and 'dramatic' (Male, 37, Ireland, SW). The comments during the visit suggested that the extreme heat in the canyon further reinforced the experience.

Remaining sets and set structures

The Lars Homestead interior location (SW) and the Dome (SW) comprise remaining set structures and decorations. Set structures and decorations can be a very important asset to a location, as they are normally part of the absent features of the imaginary. Being genuine film structures, they possess a high degree of objective authenticity. However, if set structures are not maintained, the result can be a disappointing location encounter. This was the case with the Mos Espa set, which for some SW tour participants did not convey any deeper connection to the imaginary:

SW

It's a lot of cardboard in the middle of the desert. It didn't have any emotion or an impact on me at all. (Male, 37, Ireland)

As highlighted in Chapter 5 in relation to the Gazebo, set structures can also cause disappointment if their appearance on location differs from their perceived authenticity as generated by the movie. By contrast, when the set is in good condition, as with the Lars Homestead interior location, the remaining set pieces add significantly to its attractiveness as a whole, anchoring this part of the set into the restless moment between the real and the imaginary components.

Recognition value

The recognition value of the tarn sight, Aragorn's cliff, the Bay of Belfalas sight, the Lars Homestead interior, the different SW Canyon sights, the Dome and the Mirabell Gardens sights are very high. As one LOTR informant remarked, the tarn sight is attractive due to its high recognition value:

LOTR

It was pretty much just photographed. It has not been manipulated much. (Female, 38, Germany)

The Mirabell Gardens made a similar impact as a result of its high recognition value:

SoM
Author: What would you say your favourite location on the tour was and why?
Informant 1: It's the Mirabell Gardens for me. The first time I saw it and I was just like 'wow!' Just being able to walk in amongst all of this is fantastic. (Female, 27, UK)
Informant 2: When I came here, I knew where everything was. We walked in and I thought 'well that happened there and that's up there'. (Female, 52, UK)

A high recognition value of locations and sights is important for the quality of the location experience, as it fosters the likelihood of mental visions and mental simulations. In addition, the re-creation of shots is more prestigious than at sights with a low recognition value. Locations with a very low recognition value, where the built environment of the location has been changed significantly, such as the Mos Eisley cantina (SW) or the Stormtrooper checkpoint (SW), have relatively low attraction values.

With regard to the above-listed locations and sights, the spatial and temporal discrepancies that occurred were minimal. Apart from minor details, such as the lack of snow on the mountain peaks or a low water level at the tarn sight, all these locations and sights were instantly recognisable and comparable to the equivalent film scenes or shots.

Connections to the lead characters

This research indicates that for some film location tourists, a connection exists between the appeal of a location and character empathy. The LOTR informants who admitted to having favourite characters would often re-create the shots in which their favourite characters had featured. Through observation, it was noted that teenage girls tended to favour Legolas, while women aged over 20 were most fond of Aragorn. This was also backed up in the interviews with the two LOTR guides. Consequently, younger girls on the tours often re-created shots at two specific Deer Park Heights sights: Legolas firing arrows at the approaching wargs and Legolas spotting the wargs. Female tour participants aged 18 and above tended to favour the re-creation of the stew scene involving Aragorn. Sitting on the stone where the character Aragorn sits in a film scene became a ritual for them, as the following comment illustrates:

LOTR
Like today, in the scene with Aragorn and Éowyn, I touched the rock, because Aragorn has sat there. I suppose it's that sense of

thinking some of the magic of the sites could rub off, really. (Female, 49, UK)

Another example of an existing link between the attractiveness of a location and a favourite character is illustrated by the following:

SW

Author: Did you relate differently to locations where your favourite characters featured, than to other locations?

SW guide: Absolutely because for example, the house of Obi Wan Kenobi, he is my favourite character, but his house is one of the least spectacular sets on the tour. It's just a small fisherman's house and there is nothing to see there. Nevertheless, this is for me one of the highlights of the trip because it's so recognisable and it's my character's place. It gives it an extra dimension.

In this case, even though the location of Obi Wan Kenobi's Hermitage was never mentioned as an attractive location by any other SW informants, for the SW guide, it presents a very important location due to its link to his favourite character. It seems plausible that locations or sights imbued with the imaginary presence of some of the lead characters can be perceived as attractive due to this connection.

Importance for the storyline

The importance of the place settings for the storyline is expressed through their relational position to the story (Le Héron, 2004). Place processes and forces can form the background for the story, impact upon the relationships between the characters or even influence the action. Of the cited sights, the place settings that influence relationships, or even the action are: Aragorn's cliff, the Lars Homestead interior, the SW Canyon, the Dome and the Mirabell Gardens. The Dome location features repeatedly in SW II, III and IV. Some of the Dome scenes are key scenes, such as the last scenes in SW III and the sunset scene with Luke Skywalker deciding over his future fate (SW IV). In particular, the latter two scenes imbue the Dome location with very intrinsic values, as this comment shows:

SW

Luke's home. It's a simple little igloo and it's on a salt plain which is as wide and far as the eye can see. When the sun sets, it's incredibly beautiful – a very humble, religious experience. It's the home of the saviour of the universe in *Star Wars*, so it has spiritual connections, as if Jesus Christ was born there. I remember the first time I saw it I thought differently – I mainly saw the technical cougar and all the droids which was quite exotic at the time. But George [Lucas] was clever enough to let us breathe for a moment and let Luke see into the future when he shows the sunset with two suns. You think of all the possibilities that could happen if Luke left the farm. It's a human moment. (Male, 37, Ireland)

Two key scenes which show Obi Wan Kenobi (SW III) and Luke Skywalker (SW IV) gazing into the sunset give the location its powerful meaning. The Mirabell Gardens, on the other hand, have no significant part in driving forward the storyline. Nevertheless, they are accredited with considerable importance within the plot due to their connection with one of the most memorable songs – the Do-Re-Mi song:

SoM
It's a very important location in the film. It's probably the scene that most people really remember from the film more than anything. (Female, 45, UK)

The fact that the SoM tours do not always visit this location should be addressed. As opposed to the other locations included in the tour, the Mirabell Gardens actually present the opportunity to record sights and re-create shots, in particular the Do-Re-Mi steps.

Incorporated sacred sights

As outlaid in Chapter 3, a sacred site is a place where the physical environment is connected with deep meanings and therefore gains a quasi-religious status. In addition to MacCannell's (1976) concept of the sacred site, the sacred sight is a temporal and spatial consumption of an ocular view, such as the midnight sun seen from the North-facing North Cape in Norway (Jacobsen, 1997). According to Jacobsen (1997), the experience of this sacred sight is perceived as objectively authentic, has an aura of the transcendental and marks a transition between the past, the present and the future. The different factors that render a filmic sight sacred are objective authenticity, attractive physical features, recurring scene appearance and involvement of key characters and key scenes.

All the sights incorporated in the attractively perceived film locations researched for this book are objectively authentic, as they perfectly match with the arrangement of the film scenes themselves. The refugee tarn sight and the Bay of Belfalas sight incorporate breathtaking scenery, water bodies and a high degree of variety. The Lars Homestead interior sights are sacred due to their recurring appearance in SW II and IV, the involvement of key characters and the remarkably good state of the set decorations of the location. The SW Canyon sight is sacred because of its objective authenticity and the tangible, visual existence of the (imaginary) Jawa Rock. The Do-Re-Mi steps have a sacred status due to their part in the beloved song and the involvement of the key characters at this sight. Yet, it is the two Dome sights that possess the highest degrees of sacredness due to their significance in the scenes, for both mark transition times in the lives of the key characters. This is symbolised by the sunset, which is a very powerful transition marker, the existence of the film set and the aura of the location, which all combine to complete the powerful force of the place. It is apparent that all sacred sights are shown for a sufficient amount of time in the equivalent film scenes. This provides sufficient time to render it a key scene as well as to make the sight recognisable later on.

The Location Encounter

Film location tourists engage in the actual location encounter with different, underlying expectations and motivations. Some tourists are more interested in technical aspects than in the imaginary component of the locations. Some accompany their children, partners or friends without having any personal interest in the film(s). The majority of film location tourists however, have one thing in common, regardless of the underlying film genre: the longing to connect with the imaginary world through visiting the real places, which, in turn, serve as the symbolic link between the real and the imaginary. They want the location visit to address that longing, which renders it similar in nature to a pilgrimage. Such a notion has also been suggested by Grihault (2003) and Beeton (2005).

A film location visitation is always twofold, comprising of an outer as well as an inner journey. The outer journey is the physical travel to and from the location. The inner journey comprises the mental travel to the imaginary world of the film. This conforms to Crouch's (1999) assumption that touristic space must not necessarily be concrete, but can also be metaphorical and even imaginative. The more intrinsic the underlying longing for a location visit and thus, its experiential consumption is, the stronger and more intense are the inner journey elements, such as mental visions, mental simulations and filmic re-enactments.

However, film locations are often simultaneously consumed as spectacle and as sacred places. Specific expressions of the spectatorial consumption of film locations are shot re-creations in their spectatorial form and sight recordings. The degree of fandom can influence the meticulousness with which the exact camera positions, and thus sights, are re-created. The sacredness of a location depends on its intrinsic ties to the film. The degree of tour participant fandom, the nature of the location tour and the different location settings, rendered the consumption of the SoM locations mainly as spectacle. The majority of the SoM tour participants never left the stage of spectatorial gazing and hardly ever engaged in mental simulations. For the most part, they remained incidental outsiders to the visited places. The majority of the LOTR and SW location tourists went beyond mere spectatorial gazing. Their attachment to the fictional world of the film(s) was far deeper, emotional and intrinsic when compared to the majority of the SoM location tourists. Many of the LOTR and SW tour participants positioned themselves as behavioural insiders in relation to the visited places, which clearly indicates their emotional and empathetic involvement with the locations. This might be attributed to the fact that the LOTR trilogy, as well as the SW saga, was released over a period of time, resulting in an overall screening time of 12 hours or more each. In addition, LOTR is based on one of the most popular books of the last 60 years (Gilsdorf, 2003).

On-site factors significantly influence the experiential consumption of the individual locations. In particular, the nature of an organised location tour has a great impact on the encounter with both the real and the imaginary. Ideally, the tour script provides a good amount of obscure and personal information and allocates sufficient time for romantic gazing, thus allowing participants to savour intrinsic aspects of their inner journey to the imaginary. A professional location tour should also contain passionate first-hand interpretation and re-enactment, point out (sacred) sights via visual aids and provide general, film-unrelated information about the area.

The second influential factor is the individual attractiveness of a location. As summarised earlier, the perceived attractiveness of a location is defined by its natural features, the existence of film set remains and their condition its recognition value, connections to the lead characters, importance to the storyline and incorporated sacred sights. External factors also impact on location attractiveness, these include on-site markers, the presence of outsiders, accessibility and weather conditions. Figure 8.1 displays the elements that define the existential attractiveness of film locations.

The interpretive community is the third major factor influencing the experience of the location encounter. The consistency of the community's various degrees of fandom is a key point in a satisfactory experience. If the degrees of fandom within the community vary too widely, the results can lead to second gazing or to complete disinterest by members with lesser degrees of fandom. If the consistency of fandom is relatively equal, the experience is likely to be more communal and thus positive, as the different members can reinforce each other and dismiss what might otherwise be perceived as embarrassing performances. The communal nature of the group also strengthens their solidarity against outsiders. On the other hand, interpretive communities, as well as guides, put peer pressure on individual group members. Such internal and external surveillance limits the scope of performances by emphasising conventions of appropriate tourist behaviour (Edensor, 2002). For instance,

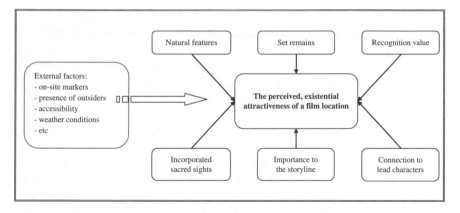

Figure 8.1 Elements defining the existential attractiveness of film locations

passive sight recorders feel pressured by active participants to photograph objects that hold no meaning for them. As peer pressure mounted, some SW tour participants began to rip off set parts despite their initial conviction not to do so. Some LOTR tour participants only dressed up in the elven cloak after a great deal of encouragement by other tour participants. In some situations, even equable fandom consistencies within communities can lead to extensive second gazing. This is particularly the case where large group sizes disrupt the experience at sights everyone wants to photograph, which can result in long waiting periods for the inactive members. The presence of a guide can somewhat alleviate the negative consequences through the provision of stories to the presently inactive members.

The fourth element defining the location experience is the existence of external disruptions. These are occurrences that are unrelated to the location features and involve, in particular, the presence of locals or other tourists on-site. Resulting disruptions can occur in several ways. Locals can try to sell products and thus distort from the experience, or other on-site film location tourists can attempt to sneak up on the group in order to grab valuable bits of information. In addition, general sightseeing tourists can dismiss the tour participant's performances as inappropriate behaviour and thus prevent the participants from becoming fully involved with the place. It is the responsibility of the tour guide, if available, to minimise such disruptions as much as possible.

Regardless of the degree of experiential satisfaction, film location tourists want to bring some of the magic back home. This is achieved not only via mental images and photographs, but also by obtaining souvenirs. These can be off- or on-site. On-site souvenirs are deemed almost holy relics, brought home from a successful pilgrimage and subsequently framed and displayed in an altar-like fashion. In particular, physically rooted pieces-off-the-rock and pieces-off-the-set souvenirs (see Chapter 6) are extremely valued in that regard, probably because they signify the highest objective authenticity possible. The benefits from acquiring such souvenirs are not only self-pride and satisfaction, but also the generation of a feeling of distinction from other film fans who have not been able to undertake the journey themselves. The person in possession of such a relic gains a privileged status amongst peers, which, in turn, raises the satisfaction of the location encounter. Such a process indicates remarkable parallels with religious pilgrimages such as the Hadsch to Mekka, or the Camino to Santiago de Compostela. The film location tour can be a spiritual journey leading to sacred places in our postmodern world. Once the boon is found – achieved either by encountering a pre-journey determined favourite location(s) or by having a highly satisfying location experience – the pilgrim has reached his or her goal. All that remains is the (outer and inner) journey back home.

The journey comes to a full closure when re-watching the film after the location encounter. The visited, real locations are re-visited when seeing the equivalent film scenes again. This renewed stance on the filmic places is accompanied by three notions. First, the film spectator now has the knowledge of how the real place setting is assembled. Second, the filmic gaze is extended, as the gazing subject is familiar with the setting beyond the camera lens. This extension concerns both the look of the imaginary in the film as well as the look of the real place beyond the camera. Third, re-watching the film is a renewed proof of achievement of the physical journey to the real place. The spectator recognises the relevant scenes and acknowledges his or her presence at the real location, as well as the imaginary filmic place. The photographed locations and sights as well as the obtained souvenirs reinforce the sense of connection.

The danger that travelling to the real places might spoil the illusory fictional world of the film was expressed by some informants, whereas the majority expressed their utmost satisfaction at having undertaken this twofold journey. To use the words of a SoM location tourist: 'I'll be so proud that I saw the steps that [Maria and the children] stand on, and the fountain. Oh yes!' (Female, 56, USA).

Experiential Benefits of Visiting Film Locations

Three experiential benefits can be derived from a film location encounter. The first benefit has to do with the actual location visit. Film location tourists with an existing degree of fandom are able to make a closer spiritual connection to the imaginary than is possible in the cinema or in front of the television at home. Consequently, the encountered LOTR locations for instance, are considered part of Middle Earth. The intensity of this connection varies with each individual. Some are content with spectatorial gazing, as was the case with the majority of the SoM tour participants. Others need to experience mental simulations in order to satisfy this longing. The consumption of the locations as sacred rather than as spectacle was important for the majority of the SW tour participants as well as for many LOTR tour participants.

Tour participants who were not interested in the movies, but had booked a location tour in order to encounter places off the beaten track – or else because they were accompanying a partner, a family member or friend on the tour – still derived benefits. As one seemingly uninterested informant (a mother accompanying her daughter) reported after the tour: 'That was very nice. A window into another world' (female, 60, USA, LOTR). Simultaneously, the tour guides enabled the participants to glimpse behind the backstage of the imaginary through the narration of technical aspects around the location filming, and by providing insider gossip about the actors.

The film location is consumed mentally, visually, physically and via narratives. This consumption is recorded and carried back home. The film location consumption cycle comes full circle by re-watching the film, which generates the second experiential benefit: 'The fun will be to find these locations when we watch the movies again'. Even tour participants who had never seen the movies before, explained that the location encounters stimulated them to watch the movies after the tour. By re-watching the movies, the experiential consumption of the film location is directly compared to the seeming-real filmic places. The benefit derived from this process is the achievement of having been 'there':

SW
I think I'll be able to just feel more complete and say "hey, I was there!" (Male, 30, USA)

LOTR
Informant: I've been there! I stood there!
Author: Which means?
Informant: How fantastic is that? I've been where Aragorn has been, tripping out into the world of fantasy. (Female, 36, UK)

SoM
It makes the movie more special. It makes it closer to you because you can say "I've actually been to that spot before". (Female, 18, USA)

The question that arises at this point is what 'there' actually means. Most informants stated that for them, 'there' was the location where the corresponding scene was filmed. It is a place portrayed via a moving image that really exists, a place to which one can actually travel:

LOTR
Author: Let's take the example of the refugee trek around the tarn. When you see it next time in the movie, what do you think your reaction will be?
Informant: I was there!
Author: Meaning what?
Informant: Meaning that I was travelling with those people – you know, playing the same part, literally breathing the same air and walking on the same ground. Maybe not at the same time, but it's like a pilgrimage, something that has a lot of meaning. (Female, 52, Australia)

LOTR
Informant: You kind of went there in reality. Although it's only a film, of course. We know that Aragorn is not sitting there now, but maybe seven thousand years ago he was. Quite a few people go to see any sort of ancient monument. They look at old stones like Stonehenge, or whatever. (Female, 46, UK, LOTR)

SW guide:
It's Tatooine. When I see the movie again, it's not like "oh, and that was shot in Touzeur and that was there". No, it's actually: "I stood there on Tatooine. I stood there". And I mean on Tatooine – in that fictional world. I realise in the back of my mind it was Tunisia and it was shot there but in your mind, you want to feel, you want to experience "I was there on Tatooine".

Tour participants of a lesser fandom regarded the film locations in a more rational manner. For them, the film locations simply represented places where a film crew produced a film:

LOTR
When we show photos we can say "Look! This is where *The Lord of the Rings* was. We were there, we were standing at this spot where that shot was taken". (Male, 27, Australia)

SoM
I think it was sort of surreal. All the actors were standing on that place there on the set. (Female, 18, USA)

For some, re-watching the movie(s) can inspire a new focus on the technical aspects of filming:

SoM

I'm going to look at it from a different angle. I'm going to look at it more technically. "Oh yeah, they did that because it was raining. The Gazebo was never there, it was there". (Female, 47, Canada)

For the following SoM informant and repeat-tour participant, re-watching the film scenes caused her to focus on the background scenery rather than the action in the foreground:

SoM

Rather than watching it as a whole I look more at the scenery rather than the actual action. (Female, 52, UK)

A repeat-SW tour participant explained that re-watching the movie after the tour had a negative impact on the seemingly-real nature of the places depicted in the scenes:

SW

In my own experience, when I've been to the location and then went back to the movie, the movie is a little bit different and I can't tell you why. It's perhaps that the illusion of the movie is gone because you know, just beyond that camera lens, there is actually a town where there should be a barren waste, but the town is just hidden from view. (Male, 37, Ireland)

Amidst all this excitement about the encounter of the physical locations, some informants consciously reflected about the implications on their future perception of the equivalent film scenes:

SoM

Author: Were you disappointed in any way?

Informant 1: You can't stand behind the grave. You know, when they hide behind the tombstone? (Female, 52, UK)

Informant 2: There is nothing, there is no room at all and I was like 'oh!' (Female, 27, UK)

Informant 1: It takes a bit of the magic away.

For others, the narratives provided by the guide also somewhat destroyed the filmic illusion:

SoM

You watch the movie and then you come on a tour and they tell you that Christopher Plummer wasn't actually singing, the voice was dubbed and the scenery wasn't there, it was actually in Hollywood. It kind of breaks the illusion. (Female, 47, Canada)

The third experiential benefit is the achievement of privileged status amongst peer groups. For some tour participants, this was the major benefit of the location encounter, apart from the actual visitation experience:

LOTR
When we are back we will watch the movies again, then we can say we've been there. (Male, 55, UK)

SW
Author: After having done this trip do you somehow feel privileged as a *Star Wars* fan?
Informant: Absolutely. I'll definitely be rubbing it into any *Star Wars* fan I meet. (Male, 35, Ireland)

SW
Author: Do you think that having been on the tour was something special?
Informant: For me it is, because there are thousands of *Star Wars* fans and there are only a few hundred who came here, so it's quite an experience. (Male, 27, Belgium)

By having been to the place 'where it all happened' – encompassing both the on-location shooting of the film as well as the imaginary story – film location tourists are privileged over other fans of that particular film.

A Sense of a Film-imagined Place

Three key elements form the sense of a place. These are the physical attributes of a place, the underlying structures of power – both on the local as well as on the global scale – which, in turn, form a consensus about the character of a place through social integration, and the personal construction of meaning with the subsequent on-site experiences of the individual. The latter establishes the organic image of such a place.

If a fictional medium is written, produced or filmed at a destination in certain localities, it alters all three off-site elements of a sense of place. It changes the power structures as they react to the place exposure with their own tools, such as provision of infrastructure and the promotional usage of the new, autonomous images imposed on this place. It also alters the self-perceptions of the place, as it is depicted as a fictional, re-imagined place set in a restless moment between the imagined and the authentic with which people assert certain meanings. All these issues impact upon the tourists' actual on-site behaviour and experience. Figure 8.2 summarises the configuration of the sense of a place that is subjected to the intrusion of a fictional medium.

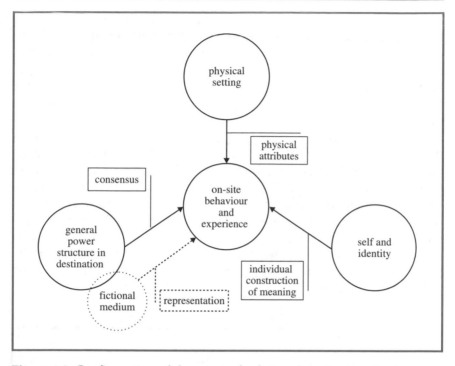

Figure 8.2 Configuration of the sense of a fictional media-imagined place

A further refinement of this configuration must be made when looking at the sense of a film-imagined place. The intruding element of the general fictional medium is replaced with the element of fictional film. The element of film has impacts on the sense of place on several levels. First of all, the physical setting might be altered through the erection of set structures. Also, an on-location film production is influenced by the prevalent power structures. Both the destination-internal and destination-external consensus about the film itself generates media exposure, recognition of the medium and its establishment within the accepted canon. One of the key impacts is that the film represents the exposed place in a restless moment, where the visitor shifts between the real and the imaginary notion of the film location (Couldry, 1998; Torchin, 2002). Through film watching, we construct our own, individual sense of a cinematic place. Films influence us through the development of place and character empathy (Dyer, 1992; Knight, 1994; Papadimitriou, 2000). They present us with the prospect of escapism into a fictional world through the suspension of disbelief (Dyer, 1992; McHale, 1987; Papadimitriou, 2000). Lastly, films enable us to share emotional and intrinsic experiences in an interpretive community (Feuer, 1992).

A second off-site element coming into play is the tourism industry itself, which acts as an influential factor within and outside the general power structure of the affected destination by altering all the components of the sense of a place. Although this institution is only an agent facilitating the creation of a filmic sense of place, it supports the establishment of a filmic sense of place through its representational practices. Image managers draw on the autonomous, unofficial place images deployed by a film and combine them with their own purpose-designed overt or covert images (Gartner, 1993) in order to generate visitation. In addition, contiguous marker placing and the provision of touristic infrastructure can alter the physical setting. Finally, the actual encounter can be influenced by offering on-site experiences provided by immobile markers, tour guides or other means. The subsequent refinement of a sense of place, as illustrated in Figure 8.3, can be manifest through physical alterations such as marker placing, through the provision of staged on-site experiences and through place re-imaging and place packaging.

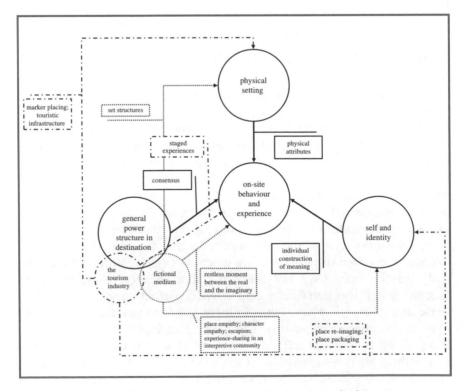

Figure 8.3 Configuration of the sense of a film-imagined place

Three of Peet's (1998) notions of place positioning need to be mentioned at this point. 'Vicarious insiderness' (Peet, 1998) occurs while watching a film, as the portrayed places are experienced second-hand. The third and fifth notions of Peet's (1998) place positioning – 'behavioural insiderness' and 'existential insiderness' – come into being during the actual visit to a film location. When combined with the uses-and-gratification theory in media studies, several notions of a film location experience can be assumed: escapism (Grihault, 2003), gaining privileged status, place empathy (Hyounggon & Richardson, 2003), empathy with the characters (Hyounggon & Richardson, 2003), the sharing of place experience within an interpretive community (Aden *et al.*, 1995) and curiosity about aspects of the location shooting (Singh, 2003).

Ultimately, the off-site intrusions from the fictional medium and the tourism industry can have a significant impact on the perception of the affected place. They can create a new sense of place and can provoke people to travel to the portrayed and re-imagined locations. Such travel becomes manifest in an outer, physical journey to the real locations, as well as in an inner journey of experience into the world of the imaginary, which, in turn, determines the on-site behaviour and experiences.

Chapter 9
Implications and Future Directions

Over the last two decades, film tourism has slowly left its shadowy existence as a small disregarded niche within the tourism industry. As this book shows, film tourism can play an important part in influencing the image of a destination. This insight has been taken into account by the British Tourism Organisation, VisitBritain, for several years now. VisitBritain has granted film tourism considerable space in its overall marketing portfolio, knowing that for around 40% of potential international visitors to the UK, their destination image is influenced by films (VisitBritain, 2008, via email).

As noted in the introduction, the aim of this book was to pick up the loose ends in film tourism research and expand the basis of knowledge on that topic. When conducting research for this book, it quickly became evident that a considerable amount of studies so far had been conducted through quantitative approaches (Riley, 1994; Tooke & Baker, 1996; Riley *et al.*, 1998; Busby & Klug, 2001; Croy & Walker, 2001; Singh, 2003). Others had focused on the areas of host community impacts (Mordue, 1999; Beeton, 2000, 2001a, 2001b; Mordue, 2001; Costley, 2002; O'Connor, 2002; Wright, 2004), destination image formation (Schofield, 1996; Bordelon & Dimanche, 2003; Hyounggon & Richardson, 2003; Croy, 2004; Connell, 2005a, 2005b; Frost, 2006), demarketing strategies (Beeton, 2002) and the intersectional relations between film and tourism stakeholders (Preston, 2000). Very few studies had examined the perspective of the film location tourists themselves, with the notable exceptions of Carl (2005) and Connell (2008). By concentrating on the experiences of film location tourists from a cultural geographer's perspective, this book also complements Sue Beeton's (2005) book on film-induced tourism, which is written from a social sciences stance and provides the reader with a comprehensive overview on the topic.

This book makes a contribution to the literature on film tourism in three ways. It is the first major research project focusing on the film location tourism encounter by applying a multiple, comparative case study inquiry, consisting of a multitude of different qualitative fieldwork instruments. Participant observation, semi-structured interviews, image-based researcher-found and image-based researcher-created data were combined within the research design in order to record first-hand experiences.

The second, major contribution is of an exploratory nature, as thus far research on film tourism has not yet examined the behaviour and experiences of film location tourists from three different film genres. In addition, this research spans three different continents, thereby taking into account the globalised nature of the tourism and the film industries.

A third contribution is of a more theoretical nature. This is the first attempt to analyse film locations as spatial and temporal constructs. Chapter 3 presents the results of the application of theories of space and place to film locations as imagined places, and thus spatial and temporal constructs. New leads explore the concepts of attraction nuclei (Leiper, 1990), sight sacralisation (MacCannell, 1976) and the issue-attention cycle (Downs, 1972). In addition, the various trigger elements likely to be responsible for initiating film (location) tourism are dealt with in a more detailed way than in any of the previous film tourism studies. These comprise the intrinsic qualities of the filmic text itself, the role of box office success, the impact of its media exposure, repeated film watching, touristic promotion and the importance of literary precursors. Another novelty is the establishment of a spatial configuration of film locations, the end result leading to the depiction of how the sense of a film-imagined place is constituted.

Contributions to tourism research in particular, are generated through new insights into the entity of the film location tourist. This is achieved by assessing socio-demographic aspects such as age, type of travel accompaniment, country of origin, gender, education and current occupation. So far, many studies providing such data have concentrated on a single movie, for instance those of Singh (2003), Croy (2004), Carl (2005), or Connell (2005a, 2005b, 2008). Yet, the findings derived from this research go even further by looking into the research subject's general travel behaviour, visited points of interest along the general itinerary, film location tour booking pattern and degree of fandom. An even more significant contribution in that regard is that the book identifies social and spatial interactions at film locations under the umbrella of the accepted theories in tourism research, such as gazing (Urry, 1990), second gazing (MacCannell, 2001) and performance theory (Edensor, 2002). The fieldwork analysis also borrows from film theories such as the concept of mental simulations (Bardsley, 2002).

The general goal of scientific research has always been to contribute to our knowledge of the world, but it has also injected ideas into the communities and therefore spanned the arc from a theorem to a real-life implementation. This book is no different in that regard, as its main purpose is, first and foremost, to incorporate various theorems from different perspectives into film tourism research. However, its results also benefit the industry for several reasons. Many industry-relevant aspects are examined here, particularly in Chapters 2 and 4, which deal with the issues of film-related destination marketing, film-related product development and the general profiling of film location tourists. The fieldwork results aim to help the industry to understand the depth of emotions film location tourists go through on site, and how these emotions should be addressed when developing film-related tourism products. This book also backs up the fact that film tourism can have many positive effects, as can be summarised by the following:

- strengthened relationships between film and tourism industry;
- contribution to a film-friendly attitude from residents;
- opportunity to support the film industry to promote the production (tie-ins);
- contribution to a wider destination brand;
- revived influx to established tourist attractions;
- film location tourism attracts independent and interactive travellers;
- potential sustainability (cult films, renewed windows of exhibition).

All these potential effects are important arguments for destination marketers and film commissioners alike, in order to politically lobby for investment in this area. It also clearly depicts its broad effects to the community, as well as its intersectoral position between two important industries. That is to say that any investment in film tourism-related campaigns, strategies or products has to be addressed in a professional manner due to its highly emotional content. The following sections attempt to provide the industry with a number of tools in order to achieve exactly that: a professionalised film tourism industry.

Implications for Tour Operators

The first implication for tour operators concerns aspects of marketing. The potential film location tourist regularly uses the internet for general pre-trip research, as well as for the selection of a specific film location tour operator. Many film location tour bookings are consequently secured by email. As the interviews have revealed, the provision of a detailed, well-designed and appealing website by a film tourism stakeholder attracts considerable attention. Such a website should contain the following features: the number of locations visited, good photographs of some of the sights encountered during the tour ideally matched with the equivalent film shots, and pieces of obscure or personal information about the filming that is not readily available. Also important is an emphasis on the inclusion of film-unrelated activities. If applicable, the opportunity to handle film-related items should be emphasised, as well as any existing link between the company and its guides to the filming process.

The second aspect of customer marketing should be direct on-site promotion through the display of brochures or flyers at local accommodation providers, tourism information centres and tourist attractions. The content of the brochure or flyer should reflect the features listed on those of the company website. A continuous corporate identity contributes to recognition effects and helps to differentiate the business from its competitors. Lastly, marketing efforts worth considering include advertisements on fan websites the product inclusion in the *Lonely Planet* and *Rough Guide* travel guides, as well as in existing location guidebooks, and the placement of advertisements in the general tourism promotion tools of the responsible destination marketer organisation.

In the case of *The Lord of the Rings* (LOTR), location tourists with a high degree of fandom tend to visit locations throughout the country and participate in several location tours. The most popular locations served by tour operators are Mt. Potts (Edoras location) in Central Canterbury, the locations in and around Wellington and the Hobbiton film set near Matamata in the central North Island. It is advisable for the operating tour companies that serve these locations to combine their marketing efforts. This can be done by offering special, combined tour packages, the mutual display of brochures and by organising joint stalls at tourism trade fairs.

With regard to the structure and content of the tour, several main factors are essential to provide a satisfactory experience. Arguably, the existential attractiveness of the visited locations is an essential part of the business. A location tour also needs to contain either a cluster of locations or one very important key location of sufficient, spatial scale. In addition, the latter ideally comprises remaining film sets and a number of different identifiable sights. Needless to say, it is important that access to the different locations and sights should be possible, indeed it can be a bonus if such access is privileged access – a fact that should be emphasised to the customers. Small group sizes enhance the location experience considerably, as there are fewer disturbances from within the group. They also foster a stronger bond and reduce the waiting time during periods when locations and sights are photographed and film-related items are handled. In a very practical way, small group sizes also reduce waiting times during hop-on and hop-off phases and during meal breaks.

The running commentary should include both general and little known, obscure and personal information, such as personal stories and gossip about the actors' antics during location filming as well as technical production details. The guides should be knowledgeable, passionate and if possible, should have a link to the film production; they might, for example, have played an extra in the film. The provided location details should go beyond the information accessible via fan websites and Special Feature DVDs. As important as the running commentary is vivid first-hand interpretation at attractive locations, where the guide re-enacts scenes by quoting lines from the film and by re-creating the characters' body movements, facial expressions and tone of voice. By dressing up in a film-related costume, the guide can further enhance first-hand interpretation.

Visual aids add to the objective authenticity of the locations. These can be location maps, film stills or even the re-playing of the relevant DVD scenes immediately before the location encounter. Small, portable DVD players can easily be integrated into the tour van or bus. The same can be said for the film soundtrack. A CD player should be fitted to the vehicle of transport so that the film music can be played in situations where film location tourists might feel an emotional involvement with the visited place(s). The track played during the location encounter should match with the one played during the film scene.

The prospect of handling film-related items can be a decisive factor in the tour selection phase. The provision of original items such as call sheet copies or props used in the film considerably raises the perceived value of such handling. Consideration should also be given to the distribution of souvenirs with a connection to a specific location. Such an unbiased souvenir raises the status of the tour participants amongst peers, acknowledges their achievement of having been to the location and serves as a visual proof of the actual encounter.

Lastly, film location-unrelated practicalities are the use of modern, comfortable, air-conditioned vehicles, the provision of general information about the history, geography, fauna and flora of the wider area and other activities included in the tour. In summary, all the above-mentioned elements closely correspond to the assumption that general tourism attraction nuclei should include good storytelling, dynamic assets, participatory experience, tourist-relevant experience and a focus on quality and authenticity (McKercher & du Cros, 2002).

Implications for Destination Marketing Organisations

In a survey conducted with 140 destination marketing organisations around the world, Hudson and Ritchie (2006a) found that 96% of the respondents admitted that they should be more active in drawing on tourism-inducing film productions. A total of 60% stated that they had experienced visitation increases due to the implementation of film tourism promotion. The three main benefits of film tourism were considered to be the amplification of the destination image, increased economic benefits and an increased number of tourist visits (Hudson & Ritchie, 2006a). The researchers recommend destination marketing organisations to collaborate with film commissions more closely, in particular during the pre-production stage.

From the outset, destination marketing organisations have no influence over the images portrayed in a film (Preston, 2000). In addition, predictions about the potential of a film to attract film location tourism prior to its release are vague at best. It requires a specialist in niche marketing and, in particular, in media-imagined marketing, in order to take all necessary factors into account when initiating a film-based destination marketing campaign.

The impacts of such promotion affect several areas, namely visitor expectations, impacts on local communities, business alterations for film location tour operators, tourism planning issues and environmental effects. It is not the purpose of this section to treat these different impacts in detail. Rather, it serves as a warning of what could go wrong when using a film production for destination marketing. First of all, the portrayed images have to correspond with the generated expectations. For instance, Tourism New Zealand's marketing campaign, which used film clips from LOTR to promote New Zealand as Middle Earth (www.newzealand.com/travel/about-nz/culture/lotr-2003/introduction. cfm, accessed 25 January 2009), can generate disappointment, as the used images differ from the real places. The images displayed in this campaign lack information, as in reality there are very few sets left intact because most locations have been returned to their natural state. Similarly, location access issues remain unmentioned.

In 2006, the homepage of Tourism New Zealand promoted the connection of two areas with recently screened feature films: the Whanganui River with its connection to the feature film *River Queen* (2005), and Central Canterbury with its connection to *The Lion, the Witch and the Wardrobe* (2005). In the case of the first connection, the website highlighted that the 'film depiction of this untouched wilderness didn't require special effects or retouching – what you see is exactly how it is'. Here, the generated expectations are kept realistic in terms of the location settings. The problem with this place promotion is that no web link or information could be found about the geographical position of the precise locations themselves. With *The Lion, the Witch and the Wardrobe* connection, the film locations were geographically located, but the information provided was not sufficient to actually find them.

In contrast to Tourism New Zealand, the Tunisian Tourism Organisation does not promote the existence of the *Star Wars* (SW) locations and its remaining set structures. Quite clearly, it has missed out on a big opportunity to attract film location tourists. This is even more astounding given the fact that the film production company was initially asked by the government to leave the sets intact with the ulterior motive of generating additional tourism. In the meantime, the sets have deteriorated so badly that their promotion without prior restoration measures would result in disappointment. However, the promotion of remaining film sets can attract significant numbers of tourists, as the example of Hobbiton in New Zealand illustrates (Tenbrock, 2005).

While such visitation increases pose a lesser problem to privately owned location attractions, the situation is different for locations set in fragile areas, such as national parks or nature reserves. For instance, if the LOTR set of Edoras had been left behind for tourism, this remote valley might have been a new attraction nucleus for many of the large tour companies and the visitation increases would have had significant impacts on the environment.

Place promotion of a television production or feature film can also have impacts on the local host community, such as an increase in property prices (Yeabsley & Duncan, 2002; Hudson & Ritchie, 2006a), parking congestion (Mordue, 1999; Tooke & Baker, 1996), an increase in car thefts (Mordue, 1999), the replacement of traditional shops with film paraphernalia stores (Sciolino, 2003) and a general shift in the quality of the prevailing tourist (Beeton, 2005). It is up to the responsible tourism marketer to take these potential impacts into consideration before starting a film-based destination imaging campaign.

In the past, destination marketing organisations have often waited too long in order to maximise the spin-off effects provided by film tourism (Beeton, 2005; Hudson & Ritchie, 2006a). It is suggested that destination marketers get behind the filming process at the earliest possible stage. Closer working relationships with the responsible film commissions in the area would ensure early notification of location scouting and film production location enquiries, thereby simplifying the process of evaluating the tourism-inducing potential of a film production. As many real-life examples have proven, an important precondition for professional film tourism is copyright clearance, which has to be negotiated between the involved tourism stakeholders and the responsible film production company from early on. Because of copyright laws and intellectual property issues, a laywer specialised in media law should be engaged before spending any funds on film tourism promotion material.

The next step after the initial research phase is the establishment of a film tourism strategy, comprising marketing and/or product development tools, as well as a visitor management plan. Figure 9.1 outlines the development of such a strategy.

Tourism Australia has provided a recent example of how to establish a professional film tourism campaign from early on. Drawing on the feature film *Australia* (2008), the destination marketing organisation commissioned the film's director, Baz Luhrmann, to produce a series of film commercials loosely related to the feature film. In conjunction with a worldwide campaign implemented by marketing agency DDB, the film commercials tried to capture the sense of the movie with its main themes of romance, adventure and transformation. The tag line consequently read 'Arrived with a thousand things on our minds. Departed without a care in the world' (www.utalkmarketing.com/pages/Article.aspx?Article ID = 12742&Title = Tourism_Australia_pushing_rejuvenating_experience, accessed 20 January 2009). Other marketing tools included billboards, themed postcards, a fold-out film experiences map and a 24-page booklet

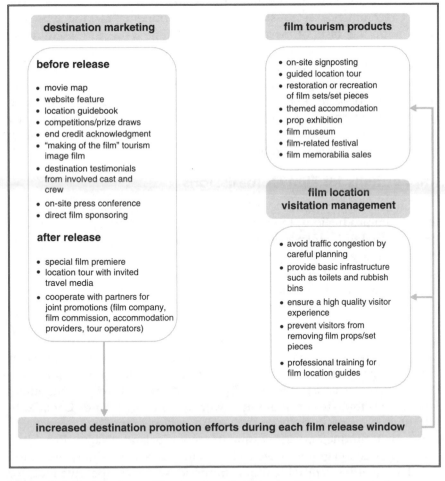

Figure 9.1 Developing a film tourism strategy and management plan

containing motivational destination content. It was hoped that the cost of the campaign that amounted to US$34.5 million, would counterbalance the predicted slump in 2009 (news.ph.msn.com/lifestyle/article.aspx?cp-documentid = 1879753, accessed 25 January 2009).

It is also recommended that research should be undertaken on the impact of film tourism. Hudson and Ritchie's 2006 survey showed that out of 140 international destination marketing organisations, only 18% measured the impacts of film tourism on their destination (Hudson & Ritchie, 2006a). So far, there is little evidence of the degree to which film-related marketing activities contribute to the overall market. Even in the UK, where film tourism is at its most professionalised and part of the organisation's marketing portfolio, a recent report has found that there is a real need for market research in this area (Olsberg/SPI, 2007). The report recommends establishing a 'Screen Tourism Tracking Observatory' with the task of permanently collecting data and conducting research on film tourism. The authors of the report suggest the implementation of a comprehensive economic study to evaluate the value of film for destination marketing. This recommendation backs up the assumption that too little is known about the monetary contribution of film-related tourism to destinations, which is part of the reason why film tourism is still treated as the poor cousin by many destination marketers and tourism stakeholders.

Implications for Film Commissions

Film commissions promote their region to film-makers in order to attract film productions, the most important reason being to benefit from primary economic effects generated by location shooting. In addition, the positive image effects for the region is a complimentary bonus. The central factors in attracting film productions are cost, ease of production, skills and facilities available on location, tax incentives and the variety of locations at close hand. The reason that New Zealand is such a successful recipient of recent runaway production money from the USA can be attributed to all of these factors. It has a considerable variety of different landscapes with reasonable access, all within close proximity to major cities, a high-quality, creative workforce, professional production facilities on both islands, film-friendly authorities and very competitive labour costs that are considerably lower than in Australia or Canada. In addition, the central Government established a competitive tax scheme for screen productions (Investment New Zealand, 2007). Providing screen production grants as well as tax schemes is increasingly becoming standard in order to provide film commissions with competitive tools for the purpose of attracting film productions.

Interestingly, the knowledge of film commissions about long-term secondary effects of film tourism remained relatively superficial until the late 1990s (Preston, 2000). A 2004 survey amongst Tyrolean destination managers revealed that none of the managers intended to include film tourism in their marketing strategies (Geir, 2005). The main reasons for this neglect were a lack of time, a lack of budget and knowledge deficits in film tourism opportunities. Some informants could not see any benefits in film tourism marketing at all. The results also showed that the surveyed managers had no regular contact with the Tyrolean film commission, Cine Tirol, and not a single destination manager had any knowledge of current film projects in the region (Geir, 2005).

Film commissions have clearly addressed this lack of knowledge considerably within the last eight to ten years, as demonstrated by the inclusion of film tourism in the 2008 International Conference of the Association of Film Commissioners International (AFCI). It is apparent that increasing numbers of film commissions around the globe recognise the potential value of long-term tourism effects generated by film productions. By establishing close working relationships, the tourism industry and the film industry can both profit from film productions. A useful side aspect of such a network could be the support of the private tourism sector in the relevant area in terms of flexible transport and accommodation options for film crews. Ultimately, the ideal situation for a film commission would be to attract film productions that have some reference to the hosting destination, thereby also benefitting tourism stakeholders.

Further Research Opportunities

With two feature films based on J.R.R. Tolkien's book *The Hobbit* currently in production, New Zealand could experience a new wave of media and fan attention within the next four to five years. Set to screen in 2011 and 2012, the two movies could have the potential to extend the *The Lord of the Rings* film location life cycle. The thousands of fans still thinking about travelling to New Zealand in order to visit the locations of the LOTR movies may well be triggered to do so as a result of the renewed hype. *The Hobbit* would make an ideal case study for the conduction of a longitudinal study, whether from a qualitative or quantitative stance. As anecdotal evidence on LOTR suggests, the degree of fandom of the film location tourists can decrease over time. The LOTR tour participants with the highest degree of fandom booked shortly after the release of the first two movies and again after the world premiere of LOTR III in Wellington (LOTR guide II, 2005, personal interview). Longitudinal research could therefore examine the change of location behaviour and experiences over time in relation to decreasing degrees of fandom, with the example of the two new *Middle Earth* movies. It could also reveal possible changes regarding socio-demographic details. This, in turn, would contribute to a higher probability of accurate predictions about the lasting on-location tourism effects of film productions.

The tourism inducing on-site postproduction effects of film productions have not been given enough consideration from academia or from within the industry. As Croy argues (2004: 15), 'the process of film-generating post production effects is generally not appreciated and thus understated when assessing the effects of films on a destination'. Beeton (2004) also acknowledged this lack of research. The main reason for this neglect is the problem of costs and time involved (Investment New Zealand, 2004). The accurate measurement of the influx of film tourists and film location tourists to a destination involves a vast amount of temporal and monetary dedication. Only major tourism organisations would have the means to conduct a destination-wide survey. A joint cooperation could help to overcome some of these obstacles.

Another approach to researching the touristic postproduction effects of film could be an on-site investigation before, during and after the location shooting. Such a project could supplement already existing investigations, as carried out by Beeton (2000, 2001a, 2001b, 2002), Costley (2002), Walker (2002) and Wright (2004), which solely concentrated on the filmic impacts after the film production was completed. Admittedly, such a course of action would involve a good deal of networking with involved stakeholders in order to identify film locations before the commencement of filming. In pursuing such a project, the on-site social and economic impacts of a film production could be closely monitored. One major focal point of such an investigation could be the community perceptions about an on-location film production before, during and after the production process. It would be interesting to investigate if and how these perceptions change throughout the different phases. Finally, the researcher could return to the field several years later in order to investigate sustainable postproduction effects.

More research should focus on disguised film locations. Although some preliminary research on a *Last Samurai* (2003) location in Taranaki, New Zealand, was undertaken, it was not the purpose of this book to look into this aspect of film location tourism. It could be an interesting academic research project to examine the success of disguised film location tourism in its two forms. For instance, a researcher could look into the impacts of a feature film such as *Cold Mountain* (2003) by collating data at the film location, as well as at the real location depicted in the movie (and book). Research in this direction could provide more insights into the marketing of disguised places in their two forms and uncover subsequent postproduction effects for tourism.

A further, interesting research project would be to make comparisons between the tourist encounter at both on- and off-locations, focusing on the same film. Although a few investigations have dealt with the off-location film tourism encounter (Moutinho, 1988; Braun & Milman, 1994; Roest *et al.*, 1997; Harvey & Zibell, 2000; McClung, 2000; Beeton, 2005), no comparative studies have been conducted between the two different tourist encounters. Such an undertaking would provide information about the differences and similarities of the motivations and experiences of the tourist encounter as well as other data, such as general travel behaviour, preferred activities or socio-demographic data.

One particular field that has been overlooked so far in terms of film-related tourism opportunities is that of computer games. Computer games are nowadays of such a high visual quality that game developers have started to release film-related games based on movies such as *James Bond – Quantum of Solace* (2008) or *The Lord of the Rings* (2001–2003). In addition, some games have been turned into feature films, including *Resident Evil* (2002) and *Max Payne* (2008). The fact that there are significant overlaps between these two media forms was acknowledged at the annual convention of the Association of Film Commissioners International in 2008, when a special session was held on the topic of how the video game revolution affects the media industry and how film commissioners can get involved. At this point, the question arises as to whether computer or video games can also trigger tourism in the future. This question certainly opens a whole new field for tourism researchers and practitioners.

Final Remarks

Film locations are not only consumed as places of spectacle – with all its inherent premises of mass tourism consumption – but simultaneously as sacred places, the extent of devotion depending on the degree of fandom of the consumer and the existential attractiveness of the location. This ambivalence of consumption runs through the entire location encounter: film locations are encountered as real as well as imaginary places for they are actively consumed within a shared community as well as in individual isolation, and the derived benefits address both intrinsic as well as extrinsic needs. Some of these aspects have previously been anecdotally recorded by Aden *et al.* (1995) in their research on the feature film *Field of Dreams* (1989). However, this book claims to be the first of its type that has identified the different threads of consumption in-between these ambivalent zones. The consumption of film locations as spectacle is mainly expressed through bodily performances, such as formal posing, shot re-creation, the capturing of the filmic gaze and collective consumption within an interpretive community. On the other hand, when interacting with film locations as sacred places, people engage with the places in a more intrinsic way, leading to mental visions, mental simulations – and as a bodily expression – shot re-creations and filmic re-enactments. Film location tourists with a relatively small degree of fandom can often be identified due to their higher degree of second gazing. Another outcome is that film locations as fantasy lands, as is the case with LOTR and SW locations, particularly encourage romantic gazing with all its inherent forms of consumption.

It is evident that for the majority of consumers, film locations are places integral to lived space (Lefebvre, 1991), despite their inherent zones of ambivalence. Film location tourists are especially aware of the ambivalent zone between the real and the imaginary, as they actively change from one zone to the other and vice versa. For example, they mentally blend out elements that disturb the consumption of the imaginary, such as elements of the built environment. The majority of the informants were well informed about potential location discrepancies before going on the tour due to extensive pre-trip research. Regarding location discrepancies, two major elements can have a negative influence on the location experience. The first is the prohibition of direct access to the location. In this instance, the location can neither be experienced as spectacle, nor as sacred. The second element is the non-existence of film sets: some LOTR informants expressed the attraction potential of remaining sets. However, if remaining sets are not maintained, this can lead to a negative experience. As such, some LOTR informants who had previously visited the Hobbiton set preferred the natural LOTR locations. It can be concluded that natural locations can foster the mental consumption of a film location more than remaining film sets, if all other elements of the existential attractiveness of a location are existent. The only exception to this rule was the SW Dome. This film set held such an important significance as a sacred place for the SW tour participants that its state of repair stepped into the background. As it was viewed and recorded from a distance, it served merely as a prop to guide the imagination.

The encounter of a film location is an emotional and intrinsic experience for most film location tourists. Any tourism stakeholder that uses film locations either for marketing purposes or for a business venture has to ensure that the emotional needs of film location tourists are addressed on-site. As outlined in this chapter, essential measures for a satisfying experience include guaranteed accessibility of marketed film locations, the presence of on-site markers to identify the exact sights, the maintenance of remaining film sets, first-hand interpretation, visual aids, the handling of film-related items, the opportunity to acquire physical on-site souvenirs and the inclusion of existentially attractive locations in a guided location tour. If the majority of these elements are addressed, the satisfaction levels can be extremely high, which, in turn, significantly contributes to a satisfactory, general travel experience. The example of LOTR in New Zealand indicates that due to a selection of highly professional tour location operators, visiting LOTR locations has become part of a wider New Zealand holiday for around 2–5% of all international visitors. A similar phenomenon occurs with visitors to Salzburg and their participation in a *The Sound of Music* (SoM) location tour. Several examples suggest that a small number of films can lead to a sustainable and long-lasting film location tourism issue-attention cycle.

In conclusion, I would like to refer back to the concepts of place as a social construct, as outlaid in Chapter 2. The analysis of film locations in this research through a cultural-geographic lens reveals that such locations are indeed formed through a combination of the environment (i.e. physical attributes), the overlaying culture (i.e. power structures) and individuals (Harvey, 1985). Once on-site, the general place consumption – including the consumption of film locations – involves a range of mental and physical performances. Although film location tourists do bring anticipated images to the visited locations, those places do not fall under the concept of touristic non-places (Augé, 1995).

The actual location encounter is a highly individual, localised, intrinsic and emotional experience for film location tourists, as they are very meaningful places. This can go as far as a film location consuming a person's identity completely (Urry, 1995), so that the gazing subject is consumed in the fiction of a film location and becomes part of the gazed-upon object, taking on the identity of Luke Skywalker, if only for a moment.

References

Abercrombie, N. (1996) *Television and Society*. Cambridge: Polity Press.

Adams, P.C. (1992) Television as gathering place. *Annals of the Association of American Geographers* 82 (1), 117–135.

Aden, R.C., Rahoi, R.L. and Beck, C.S. (1995) Dreams are born on places like this: The process of interpretive community formation at the *Field of Dreams* site. *Communication Quarterly* 43 (4), 368–403.

Aitken, S.C. and Zonn, L.E. (1994) Re-presenting the place pastiche. In S.C. Aitken and L.E. Zonn (eds) *Place, Power, Situation, and Spectacle: A Geography of Film* (pp. 3–26). London: Rowman & Littlefield.

Albers, P.C. and James, W.R. (1988) Travel photography: A methodological approach. *Annals of Tourism Research* 15 (1), 134–158.

Alsayyad, N. (2001) Global norms and urban forms in the age of tourism: Manufacturing heritage, consuming tradition. In N. Alsayyad (ed.) *Consuming Tradition, Manufacturing Heritage. Global Norms and Urban Forms in the Age of Tourism* (pp. 1–33). New York: Routledge.

American Film Institute (1998) America's Greatest Movies. On WWW at http://www.afi.com/Docs/tvevents/pdf/movies100.pdf.

Augé, M. (1995) Non-places. Introduction to an Anthropology of Supermodernity (J. Howe, trans.). London and New York: Verso.

Bailey, E. (2005) Nostalgia nothing; this is business. *Otago Daily Times* 14–15 May, p. MAG 10.

Baker, F. (2003) Film study guide for *To Kill a Mockingbird*. Seeing the film through the lens of media literacy. On WWW at http://medialit.med.sc.edu/TKAM/Framework.pdf.

Baloglu, S. and McCleary, K. (1999) A model of destination image formation. *Annals of Tourism Research* 26 (4), 868–897.

Bardsley, K. (2002) Is it all in our imagination? Questioning the use of the concept of the imagination in cognitive film theory. In K. Stoehr (ed.) *Film and Knowledge. Essays on the Integration of Images and Ideas* (pp. 157–173). Jefferson, NC and London: McFarland & Company.

Barker, P. and van Schaik, P. (2000) Icons in the mind. In M. Yazdani and P. Barker (eds) *Iconic Communication* (pp. 143–160). Bristol: Intellect Books.

Barnett, S. (2005) 'Skylights'. *The Listener*, 10–16 September, p. 68.

Baudrillard, J. (1983) *Simulations* (P. Foss, P. Patton and P. Beitchmann, trans.). New York: Semiotext(e), Columbia University.

Baudrillard, J. (1994) *Simulacra and Simulation* (S.F. Glaser, trans.). Ann Arbor, MI: The University of Michigan Press.

Baudrillard, J. (1998) *The Consumer Society: Myths and Structures*. London: Sage.

Beaver, F. (1994) *Dictionary of Film Terms*. New York: Twayne.

Beckett, J. (2000) *Tatouine on Location Tours*. A guidebook to Star Wars locations in Tunisia. Unpublished word document, received from the author by email.

Bee, S. (1999) Movies that inspired tourism. On WWW at http://www.simplyfamily.com/display.cfm?articleID = film2.cfm. Accessed 24.4.04.

Beerli, A. and Martín, J. (2004) Factors influencing destination image. *Annals of Tourism Research* 31 (3), 657–681.

Beeton, S. (2000) It's wrap! But what happens after the film crew leaves? An examination of community responses to film-induced tourism. In N.P. Nickerson, R.N. Moisey and K.L. Andereck (eds) *Conference Proceedings, TTRA National Conference – Lights! Camera! Action!* (pp. 27–136). Burbank, CA: TTRA National Conference.

Beeton, S. (2001a) Smiling for the camera: The influence of film audiences on a budget tourism destination. *Tourism, Culture & Communication* 3 (1), 15–25.

Beeton, S. (2001b) Lights, camera, re-action: How does film-induced tourism affect a country town? In M.F. Rogers and Y.M.F. Collins (eds) *The Future of Australia's Country Towns* (pp. 172–183). Victoria: Centre for Sustainable Regional Communities, La Trobe University.

Beeton, S. (2002) reCAPITALizing the Image: Demarketing Undesired Film-Induced Images. TTRA Conference Proceedings, CAPITALizing on Tourism Research, CD ROM.

Beeton, S. (2004) Rural tourism in Australia – has the gaze altered? Tracking rural images through film and tourism promotion. *International Journal of Tourism Research* 6, 125–135.

Beeton, S. (2005) *Film-induced Tourism*. Clevedon: Channel View Publications.

Best, S. (1989) The commodification of reality and the reality of commodification: Jean Baudrillard and post-modernism. In J. Wilson (ed.) *Current Perspectives in Social Theory* (Vol. 9; pp. 23–52). Greenwich, CT and London: Jai Press Inc.

Bettig, R. and Hall, J. (2003) *Big Media, Big Money: Cultural Texts and Political Economics*. London: Rowman & Littlefield.

Bloss, S. (2007) Auf den Spuren des Da Vinci Codes in Paris. Analyse des Filmtourismus, dargestellt am Beispiel des Kinofilms Sakrileg (2006) und dessen Schauplätzen in Paris/Frankreich. Dip Geog thesis, University of Trier.

Blumer, H. (1969) *Symbolic Interactionism. Perspective and Method*. Englewood Cliffs, NJ: Prentice-Hall.

Bly, L. (2004a) Third Man walking; Vienna tour is for fans of noir. *USA Today*, 27 February, p. D.04.

Blythe, J. (2000) *Marketing Communications*. Harlow: Pearson Education.

Bognár, D.K. (1995) *International Dictionary of Broadcasting and Film*. Boston, MA and Oxford: Focal Press.

Bolan, P., Crossan, M. and O'Connor, N. (2007) Film & television induced tourism in Ireland: A comparative impact study of Ryan's Daughter and Ballykissangel. In *Proceedings of the 5th DeHaan Tourism Management Conference* (pp. 226–252). Nottingham: Christel DeHaan Tourism and Travel Research Institute.

Boniface, P. and Fowler, P.J. (1993) *Heritage and Tourism in 'the Global Village'*. New York: Routledge.

Bordelon, B. and Dimanche, F. (2003) The Relationship between Motion Pictures and Tourists' Expectations of a Travel Destination. Travel and Tourism Research Association, 34th Annual Conference Proceedings, 15–18 June, St. Louis.

Bordwell, D. (1988) *Narration in the Fiction Film*. London: Routledge.

Bordwell, D. (1989) *Making Meaning: Inference and Rhetoric in the Interpretation of Cinema*. Cambridge, MA: Harvard University Press.

Bordwell, D. and Thompson, K. (1997) *Film Art: An Introduction*. New York: McGraw-Hill.

Boulding, K. (1969) *The Image. Knowledge in Life and Society*. Ann Arbor, MI: University of Michigan Press.

Bouma, G. (1996) *The Research Process* (3rd edn). Oxford: Oxford University Press.

Bradley, F. (2003) *Strategic Marketing in the Customer Driven Organization.* Chichester: Wiley & Sons.

Braun, B.M. and Milman, A. (1994) Demand relations in the central Florida theme park industry. *Annals of Tourism Research* 21 (1), 150–155.

Britton, S. (1991) Tourism, capital, and place: Towards a critical geography of tourism. *Environment and Planning D: Society and Space* 9, 451–478.

Brodie, I. (2002) *The Lord of the Rings Location Guidebook.* Auckland: HarperCollins.

Brooker, W. (2002) *Using the Force. Creativity, Community and Star Wars Fans.* New York: Continuum.

Bryant, J. and Zillmann, D. (eds) (2002) *Media Effects. Advances in Theory and Research.* Mahwah, NJ: Lawrence Erlbaum Associates.

Buhalis, D. (2000) Marketing the competitive destination of the future. *Tourism Management* 21 (1), 97–116.

Burgess, J. and Gold, J.R. (eds) (1985) *Geography, the Media & Popular Culture.* London: Croom Helm Ltd.

Business & Economy (2005) On location. Tourists flock to places featured in hit movies. On WWW at http://web-japan.org/trends/business/bus050120.html. Accessed 1.4.05.

Busby, G. and Klug, J. (2001) Movie-induced tourism: The challenge of measurement and other issues. *Journal of Vacation Marketing* 7 (4), 316–331.

Butler, R.W. (1990) The influence of media in shaping international tourist patterns. *Tourism Recreation Research* 15 (2), 46–53.

Cameron, S. (2003) Cinema. In R. Towse (ed.) *A Handbook of Cultural Economics* (pp. 114–118). Cheltenham: Edward Elgar.

Campsall, S. (2002) Analysing a Moving Image Text. On WWW at http://www.englishbiz.co.uk/downloads/filmanalysis.pdf. Accessed 21.10.05.

Canter, D. (1977) *The Psychology of Place.* London: The Architectural Press.

Carl, D. (2005) Cultural representation of New Zealand's landscapes in the films of The *Lord of the Rings* and its implications for tourism. MS Geo thesis, Victoria University of Wellington.

Carl, D., Kindon, S. and Smith, K. (2007) Tourists' experiences of film locations: New Zealand as Middle Earth. *Tourism Geographies* 9 (1), 49–63.

Casey, E. (1996) How to get from space to place in a fairly short stretch of time. In S. Feld and K. Basso (eds) *Senses of Place* (pp. 13–52). Santa Fe, NM: School of American Research Press.

Clark, H. (2001) Maximising spin-offs from The Lord of the Rings. Questions and Answers. On WWW at http://www.executive.govt.nz/minister/clark/lor/qa. Accessed 18.3.04.

Clinton, P. (2001) Review: Dazzling, flawless Rings a classic. On WWW at http://archives.cnn.com/2001/SHOWBIZ/Movies/12/18/hol.review.rings. Accessed 10.10.05.

Cohen, E. (1988) Authenticity and commoditization in tourism. *Annals of Tourism Research* 15 (1), 371–386.

Collier, J. and Collier, M. (2004) Principles of visual research. In C. Seale (ed.) *Social Research Methods* (pp. 277–281). London and New York: Routledge.

Connell, J. (2005a) What's the story in Balamory?: The impacts of a children's TV programme on small tourism enterprises on the Isle of Mull, Scotland. *Journal of Sustainable Tourism* 13 (3), 228–255.

Connell, J. (2005b) Toddlers, tourism and Tobermory: Destination marketing issues and television-induced tourism. *Tourism Management* 26 (5), 763–776.

Connell, J. (2008) Balamory revisited: An evaluation of the screen tourism destination-tourist nexus. *Tourism Management* 30, 1–14.

Corrigan, T. (1994) *A Short Guide to Writing about Film*. New York: HarperCollins College.

Coshall, J. (2000) Measurement of tourists' images: The repertory grid approach. *Journal of Travel Research* 39 (1), 85–89.

Costley, N. (2002) The impact of film. Expectations of the *Lord of the Rings*. PGDipTour thesis, University of Otago.

Couldry, N. (1998) The view from inside the simulacrum: Visitors' tales from the set of Coronation Street. *Leisure Studies* 17 (2), 94–107.

Cousins, A. and Andereck, K.L. (1993). Movie generated tourism in North Carolina: Two case studies. Poster presentation at the Travel and Tourism Research Association Conference, Whistler, BC, June 1993. *Proceedings of the 1993 Travel and Tourism Research Association Conference*. Wheat Ridge, CO: Travel and Tourism Research Association.

Crang, P. and Jackson, P. (2001) Geographies of consumption. In D. Morley and K. Robins (eds) *British Cultural Studies* (pp. 327–342). Oxford: Oxford University Press.

Cresswell, T. (2004) *Place. A Short Introduction*. Oxford: Blackwell.

Cresswell, T. and Dixon, D. (eds) (2002) *Engaging Film. Geographies of Mobility and Identity*. Lanham, MD: Rowman & Littlefield.

Crompton, J.L. (1977) A systems model of the tourist's destination selection decision process with particular reference to the role of image and perceived constraints. PhD thesis, Graduate College of the A&M University.

Crompton, J.L. (1979) Motivations for pleasure vacation. *Annals of Tourism Research* 6 (4), 408–424.

Crouch, D. (1999) Introduction: Encounters in leisure/tourism. In D. Crouch (ed.) *Leisure/Tourism Geographies: Practices and Geographical Knowledge* (pp. 1–16). London: Routledge.

Croy, G. (2001) The ideal spot: The appraisive component of destination image. In P. Holland, F. Stephenson and A. Wearing (eds) *2001: Geography: A Spatial Odyssey. Proceedings of the Third Joint Conference of the New Zealand Geographical Society and the Institute of Australian Geographers* (pp. 412–418). Dunedin: Department of Geography, University of Otago.

Croy, G. (2004) The Lord of the Rings, New Zealand, and tourism: Image building with film. On WWW at http://www.buseco.monash.edu.au/depts/mgt/research/working_papers/workingpapers04pdf.php. Accessed 24.5.04.

Croy, G. and Walker, R. (2001) Tourism and film: Issues for strategic regional development. In M. Mitchell and I. Kirkpatrick (eds) Conference Proceedings, New Dimensions in Managing Rural Tourism and Leisure. CD ROM, Scottish Agricultural College, Auchincruive.

Cooke, M. (2000) Play stations. On WWW at http://www.findarticles.com/cf_0/m3094/4_35/62169851/print.jhtml. Accessed 8.8.08.

Curran, J., Morley, D. and Walkerdine, V. (1996) *Cultural Studies and Communications*. New York: Arnold.

DeFleur, M. and Ball-Rokeach, S. (1989) *Theories of Mass Communication*. New York and London: Longman Inc.

Demetriadi, J. (1996) The tele tourists. *Hospitality* October/November 14–15.

Denscombe, M. (1998) *The Good Research Guide: For Small-scale Social Research Projects*. Buckingham and Philadelphia, PA: Open University Press.

Dettmer, J-M. (2005) Southfork Ranch bei Dallas zieht Touristen an. On WWW at http://www.rundschau-online.de/kr/KrCachedContentServer?ksArtikel.id=110438953504&listID=1035900687823&openMenu=103883...&calledPageId=null. Accessed 4.10.05.

Dimanche, F. (2002) The contribution of special events to destination brand equity. In K. Wöber (ed.) *City Tourism 2002* (pp. 73–80). Wien and New York: Springer Verlag.

Dishneau, D. (1999) Blair Witch Town Embraces Commerce. On WWW at http://www.halloween-news.com/haunted/Halloween_places_001.html. Accessed 20.10.05.

Dodd, J. and Sandell, R. (1998) *Building Bridges: Guidance for Museums and Galleries on Developing New Audiences*. London: Museum and Galleries Commission.

Dodwell, P.C. (1956) Studies of the visual system. In B.M. Foss (ed.) *New Horizons in Psychology* (pp. 15–44). Harmondsworth: Penguin.

Dominick, J.R. (1999) *The Dynamics of Mass Communication*. Boston, MA: McGraw-Hill.

Downs, A. (1972) Up and down with ecology – the issue attention cycle. *The Public Interest* 28, 38–50.

Dredge, D. (1999) Destination place planning and design. *Annals of Tourism Research* 26 (4), 772–791.

Dyer, R. (1992) Entertainment and Utopia. In R. Dyer (ed.) *Only Entertainment* (pp. 2–13). London: Routledge.

Eames, E. (2005) Tourism & Change Come to Southern Tunisia. On WWW at http://www.travelintelligence.com/wsd/articles/art_168.html. Accessed 5.5.05.

Echtner, C.M. and Ritchie, B. (1991) The meaning and measurement of destination image. *The Journal of Tourism Studies* 2 (2), 2–12.

Eco, U. (1986) *Travels in Hyperreality*. New York: Harcourt Brace & Co.

Edensor, T. (2000) Staging tourism. Tourists as performers. *Annals of Tourism Research* 27 (2), 322–344.

Edensor, T. (2002) *National Identity, Popular Culture and Everyday Life*. Oxford, New York: Berg.

Eisenhardt, K. (1989) Building theories from case study research. *Academy of Management Review* 14 (4), 532–550.

Ellis, J. (1992) *Visible Fictions*. New York: Routledge.

Empire State Building (2009) ESB in the movies. On WWW at http://www.esbnyc.com/tourism/tourism_facts_inthemovies.cfm?CFID = 13395299 8&CFTOKEN = 60310504. Accessed 6.10.09.

Epstein, E. (2005) Hollywood-By-The-(Secret)-MPA Numbers. Worldwide Studio Receipts. On WWW at http://www.edwardjayepstein.com/mpa2004.htm. Accessed 1.12.05.

Fakeye, P.C. and Crompton, J.L. (1991) Image differences between prospective, first-time, and repeat visitors to the lower Rio Grande Valley. *Journal of Travel Research* 30 (2), 10–16.

Faulkner, B. (1997) A model for the evaluation of national tourism destination marketing programs. *Journal of Travel Research* 35 (3), 23–32.

Feighey, W. (2003) Negative image? Developing the visual in tourism research. *Current Issues in Tourism* 6 (1), 76–85.

Feuer, J. (1992) Genre study and television. In R. Allen (ed.) *Channels of Discourse, Reassembled: Television and Contemporary Criticism* (pp. 138–159). London: Routledge.

Filzmair (2004) Film-induzierter Tourismus durch Location Placement. Dip Tour Mgt thesis, IMC Fachhochschule Krems.

Fisher, R. (ed.) (2001) Austria. Where to stay, eat, and explore. Smart travel tips from A to Z. *Fodor's New Edition*. New York and Toronto: Fodor's Travel Publications.

Fodness, D. (1994) Measuring tourist motivation. *Annals of Tourism Research* 21 (3), 555–581.

Frost, W. (2006) Braveheart-ed Ned Kelly: Historic films, heritage tourism and destination image. *Tourism Management* 27 (2), 247–254.

FutureBrand (2008) *Country Brand Index 2008: Insights, Findings & Country Rankings*. New York: FutureBrand.

Gallarza, M., Saura, I. and García, H. (2002) Destination image. Towards a conceptual framework. *Annals of Tourism Research* 29 (1), 56–78.

Garrod, B., Fyall, A. and Leask, A. (2002) Scottish visitor attractions: Managing visitor impacts. *Tourism Management* 23 (3), 265–279.

Gartner, W. (1993) Image formation process. *Journal of Travel and Tourism Marketing* 2 (2/3), 191–215.

Geir, R. (2005) Film und Tourismus – Handlungsempfehlungen in Bezug auf Wertschöpfung von Film- und Fernsehproduktionen in Tirol. MA (FH) thesis, FHS Kufstein Tirol.

Giddens, A. (1991) *Modernity and Self-Identity. Self and Society in the Late Modern Age*. Cambridge: Polity Press.

Gilsdorf, E. (2003) Lord of the Gold Ring. On WWW at http://www.boston.com/news/globe/magazine/articles/2003/11/16/lord_of_the_gold_ring/. Accessed 26.10.05.

Gledhill, C. (1985) Genre. In P. Cook (ed.) *The Cinema Book* (pp. 58–72). London: British Film Institute.

Gold, J.R. and Ward, S.V. (eds) (1994) *Place Promotion. The use of Publicity and Marketing to sell Towns and Regions*. Chichester: Wiley & Sons.

Gordon, B. (1986) The souvenir: Message of the extraordinary. *Journal of Popular Culture* 20 (3), 135–146.

Grihault, N. (2003) Film tourism – The global picture. *Travel & Tourism Analyst* 5, 1–21.

Gspan, S. (1999) Wirtschaftliche Auswirkungen und Tourismuswirksame Image-Effekte von Film- und TV-Produktionen auf Drehorte und Drehregionen am Beispiel der TV-Serie "Der Bergdoktor". Innsbruck, ETB Edinger Tourismus-beratung Ges.m.b.H.

Guba, E.G. (1990) The alternative paradigm dialog. In E.G. Guba (ed.) *The Paradigm Dialog* (pp. 17–30). Newbury Park, CA: Sage.

Gunn, C. (1988a) *Tourism Planning*. London: Taylor & Francis.

Gunn, C. (1988b) *Vacationscape. Designing Tourist Regions*. New York: Van Nostrand Reinhold Company.

Gunn, C. (1994) *Tourism Planning: Basics, Concepts, Cases*. Washington, DC: Taylor & Francis.

Hall, C.M. (1992) *Hallmark Tourist Events. Impacts, Management & Planning*. Chichester: Wiley & Sons.

Hall, C.M. (1997) Geography, marketing and the selling of places. In M. Oppermann (ed.) *Geography and Tourism Marketing* (pp. 61–84). New York: The Haworth Press.

Hall, C.M. (2002) Travel safety, terrorism and the media: The significance of the issue-attention cycle. *Current Issues in Tourism* 5 (5), 458–466.

Hall, C.M. (2003) *Introduction to Tourism. Dimensions and Issues* (4th edn). Frenchs Forest, Australia: Pearson Education.

Hall, C.M. (2005) *Tourism: Rethinking the Social Science of Mobility*. Harlow: Pearson Education.

Hall, C.M. and Page, S.J. (1999) *The Geography of Tourism and Recreation. Environment, Place and Space*. London: Routledge.

Ham, A. and Hole, A. (2004) *Lonely Planet Tunisia*. Hong Kong: Lonely Planet Publications.

Hanefors, M. and Mossberg, L. (2001) TV travel shows – A pre-taste of the destination. *Journal of Vacation Marketing* 8 (3), 235–246.

Harkin, M. (1995) Modernist anthropology and tourism of the authentic. *Annals of Tourism Research* 22 (3), 650–670.

Harper, L., Mudd, T. and Whitfield, P. (2002) *The Rough Guide to New Zealand*. London: Rough Guides.

Harvey, C.W. and Zibell, C. (2000) Shrinking selves in synthetic sites: On personhood in a Walt Disney World. *Ethics and Information Technology* 2, 19–25.

Harvey, D. (1985) *The Urbanization of Capital*. Oxford: Basil Blackwell.

Harvey, M. (2003) The *Lord of the Rings* Motion Picture Trilogy: The Exhibition. Visitor research findings from exit interviews and observations. Wellington: Te Papa Museum. Received from the author by email.

Harvey, M. (2006) The *Lord of the Rings* Motion Picture Trilogy: The Exhibition (2nd showing): Visitation, awareness and satisfaction. Wellington: Te Papa Museum. Received from the author by email.

Hayes, D. and Slater, A. (2003) The access dilemma: Moving towards a coherent, inclusive and sustainable framework. In R. Snape, E. Thwaites and Ch. Williams (eds) *Access and Inclusion in Leisure and Tourism* (pp. 73–94). Eastbourne: LSA.

Hasson, U., Nir, Y., Levy, I., Fuhrmann, G. and Malach, R. (2004) Intersubject synchronization of cortical activity during natural vision. *Science* 303 (5664), 1634–1640.

Herbert, D. (2001) Literary places, tourism and the heritage experience. *Annals of Tourism Research* 28 (2), 312–333.

Herzl, S. (2000) Where is the gazebo...?. In G. Keul and U. Kammerhofer-Aggermann (eds) *The Sound of Music, zwischen Mythos und Marketing* (pp. 307–311). Salzburg: Salzburger Institut für Landeskunde.

Hester, G. and Gonzenbach, W. (1997) The environment: TV news, real world cues, and public opinion over time. *Mass Communication Review* 22 (1), 5–20.

Hiebert, R.E. and Gibbons, S.J. (2000) *Exploring Mass Media for a Changing World*. Mahwah, NJ: Lawrence Erlbaum Associates.

Higgins-Desbiolles, F. (2001) Battlelines on the beach: Tourism and globalisation. *Policy, Organisation & Society* 20 (2), 116–138.

Hirsch, E. (1995) Landspace: Between place and space. In E. Hirsch and M. O'Hanlon (eds) *The Anthropology of Landscape. Perspectives on Place and Space* (pp. 1–30). New York: Oxford University Press.

Hodge, R. and Kress, G. (1988) *Social Semiotics*. Cambridge: Polity.

Holcomb, B. (1993) Revisioning place: De- and re-constructing the image of the industrial city. In G. Kearns and C. Philo (eds) *Selling Places: The City as Cultural Capital, Past and Present* (pp. 133–143). Oxford: Pergamon Press.

Holmes, D. (2001) Virtual globalization – an introduction. In D. Holmes (ed.) *Virtual Globalization. Virtual Spaces/Tourist Spaces* (pp. 1–22). London and New York: Routledge.

Hopkins, J. (1994) A mapping of cinematic places: Icons, ideology, and the power of (mis)representation. In S.C. Aitken and L.E. Zonn (eds) *Place, Power, Situation, and Spectacle: A Geography of Film* (pp. 47–68). London: Rowman & Littlefield.

Howard, P. (2003) *Heritage. Management, Interpretation, Identity*. London: Continuum.

Hu, Y. and Ritchie, B. (1993) Measuring destination attractiveness: A contextual approach. *Journal of Travel Research* 32 (2), 25–34.

Huber, T. (2000) Wie Julie Andrews Mozart verdrängte. In G. Keul and U. Kammerhofer-Aggermann (eds) *The Sound of Music, zwischen Mythos und Marketing* (pp. 401–419). Salzburg: Salzburger Institut für Landeskunde.

Hudman, L. and Jackson, R. (1999) *Geography of Travel and Tourism*. Albany, NY: Delmar.

Hudson, S. and Ritchie, B. (2006a) Promoting destinations via film tourism: An empirical identification of supporting marketing initiatives. *Journal of Travel Research* 44, 387–396.

Hudson, S. and Ritchie, B. (2006b) Film tourism and destination marketing: The case of *Captain Corelli's Mandolin. Journal of Vacation Marketing* 12, 256–268.

Hyounggon, K. and Richardson, S.L. (2003) Motion picture impacts on destination images. *Annals of Tourism Research* 30 (1), 216–237.

Inglis, D. and Holmes, M. (2003) Highland and other haunts, ghosts in Scottish tourism. *Annals of Tourism Research* 30 (1), 50–63.

Investment New Zealand (2004) *The Lord of the Rings Trilogy – Leveraging 2001–2004 – Final Report*. Wellington, New Zealand: Investment New Zealand.

Investment New Zealand (2007) *Screen Production. Made in New Zealand*. Wellington, New Zealand: Investment New Zealand.

Iso-Ahola, S.E. (1982) Toward a social psychological theory of tourism motivation: A rejoinder. *Annals of Tourism Research* 9 (2), 256–262.

Iwashita, C. (2006) Media representation of the UK as a destination for Japanese tourists: Popular culture and tourism. *Tourist Studies* 6 (59), 59–77.

Jacobsen, J. (1997) The making of an attraction. The case of North Cape. *Annals of Tourism Research* 24 (2), 341–356.

Jamal, T. and Hill, S. (2002) The home and the world: (Post)touristic spaces of (in)authenticity? In G. Dann (ed.) *The Tourist as a Metaphor of the Social World* (pp. 77–107). Wallingford and New York: CABI.

Jamieson, D. and Cook, M. (2003) The ripple effect. *Otago Daily Times Magazine* 6–7 March, pp. 1–3.

Jancovich, M., Reboll, A., Stringer, J. and Willis, A. (2003) Introduction. In M. Jancovich, A. Reboll, J. Stringer and A. Willis (eds) *Defining Cult Movies* (pp. 1–13). Manchester and New York: University of Manchester Press.

Jones, D. and Smith, K. (2005) Middle-earth meets New Zealand: Authenticity and location in the making of the *Lord of the Rings. Journal of Management Studies* 42 (5), 923–945.

Jordan, F. and Gibson, H. (2004) Let your data do the talking. Researching the solo travel experiences of British and American women. In J. Phillimore and L. Goodson (eds) *Qualitative Research in Tourism: Ontologies, Epistemologies and Methodologies* (pp. 215–235). London and New York: Routledge.

Judd, D. (1999) Constructing the tourist bubble. In D. Judd and S. Fainstein (eds) *The Tourist City* (pp. 35–53). New Haven, CT and London: Yale University Press.

Keller, K.L. (2002) Branding and brand equity. In B. Weitz and R. Wensley (eds) *Handbook of Marketing* (pp. 151–178). London: Sage.

Kelly, I. and Nankervis, T. (2001) *Visitor Destinations*. Milton, Australia: Wiley & Sons.

Kennedy, C. and Lukinbeal, C. (1997) Towards a holistic approach to geographic research on film. *Progress in Human Geography* 21 (1), 33–50.

Kim, S., Agrusa, J., Lee, H. and Chon, K. (2007) Effects of Korean television dramas on the flow of Japanese tourists. *Tourism Management* 28, 1340–1353.

King, G. and Krzywinska, T. (2002) *Science Fiction Cinema. From Outerspace to Cyberspace*. London and New York: Wallflower.

Knight, D. (1994) Making sense of genre. On WWW at http://www.hanover.edu/philos/film/vol_02/knight.htm. Accessed 4.11.05.

Konigsberg, I. (1987) *The Complete Film Dictionary* (1st edn). London: Bloomsbury.

Konigsberg, I. (1997) *The Complete Film Dictionary* (2nd edn). New York: Penguin Group.

Kotler, P. and Gertner, D. (2002) Country as brand, product, and beyond: A place marketing and brand management perspective. *Journal of Brand Marketing* 9 (4/5), 249–261.

Krippendorf, J. (1987) *The Holiday Makers: Understanding the Impact of Leisure and Travel.* London: Heinemann.

Künzler, H. (1999) Save Notting Hill. OnWWW at http://www.wahnsinn.com/trend fax/london/07.1999/texte/lifestyle.html. Accessed 18.4.04.

Law, L., Bunnell, T. and Ong, Ch. (2007) The Beach, the gaze and film tourism. *Tourist Studies* 7, 141–164.

Lefebvre, H. (1991) *The Production of Space* (D. Nicholson-Smith, trans.). Oxford: Blackwell.

Le Héron, E. (2004) Placing geographical imagination in film: New Zealand filmmakers' use of landscape. *New Zealand Geographer* 60 (1), 60–66.

Leiper, N. (1990) Tourist attraction systems. *Annals of Tourism Research* 17 (3), 367–384.

Leiper, N. (1997) Big success, big mistake, at big banana: Marketing strategies in road-side attractions and theme parks. *Journal of Travel and Tourism Marketing* 6 (3/4), 103–121.

Lennon, J. and Foley, M. (2000) *Dark Tourism. The Attraction of Death and Disaster.* London and New York: Continuum.

Lew, A. (1988) A framework of tourist attraction research. *Annals of Tourism Research* 15 (3), 553–575.

Lewis, J. (2001) *The End of Cinema as we Know it. American Film in the Nineties.* New York: New York University Press.

Lopez, D. (1993) *Films by Genre.* Jefferson, NC and London: McFarland & Company.

Lugosi, P. (2002) Walk on the wild side: Cultural encounters, organisational tensions and tourism potentials of the entrepreneurial tour company. In K. Wöber (ed.) *City Tourism 2002: Proceedings of European Cities Tourism's International Conference in Vienna* (pp. 335–344). Vienna: Springer Verlag.

MacCannell, D. (1973) Staged authenticity: Arrangements of social space in tourist settings. *American Journal of Sociology* 79 (3), 589–603.

MacCannell, D. (1976) *The Tourist. A New Theory of the Leisure Class.* London: University of California Press (1999 reprint).

MacCannell, D. (2001) The tourist agency. *Tourist Studies* 1 (1), 23–27.

Macionis, N. (2004) Understanding the film-induced tourist. In W. Frost, W. Croy and S. Beeton (eds) *Proceedings of the International Tourism and Media Conference* (pp. 86–97). Melbourne: Tourism Research Unit, Monash University.

Massey, D. (1994) *Space, Place and Gender.* Cambridge: University Press.

Massey, D. (1995) The conceptualization of place. In D. Massey and P. Jess (eds) *A Place in the World?* (pp. 45–85). New York: Oxford University Press.

McClung, G.W. (2000) Theme park selection: Factors influencing attendance. In C. Ryan and S. Page (eds) *Tourism Management: Towards the New Millennium* (pp. 232–245). Oxford: Pergamon.

McCombs, M.E. and Shaw, D.L. (1972) The agenda-setting function of mass media. *Public Opinion Quarterly* 36 (2), 176–187.

McFarlane, B. (1996) *Novel to Film: An Introduction to the Theory of Adaptation.* Oxford: Clarendon.

McHale, B. (1987) *Postmodernist Fiction.* New York: Methuen.

McIntosh, A. (1998) Mixing methods: Putting the tourist at the forefront of tourism research. *Tourism Analysis* 3 (2), 121–127.

McKercher, B. and du Cros, H. (2002) *Cultural Tourism. The Partnership Between Tourism and Cultural Heritage Management.* Binghamton, NY: The Haworth Hospitality Press.

McQuail, D., Blumer, J.G. and Brown, J.R. (1972) The television audience: A revised perspective. In D. McQuail (ed.) *Sociology of Mass Communications* (pp. 135–165). Hammondsworth: Penguin.

McWilliams, E. and Crompton, J. (1997) An expanded framework for measuring the effectiveness of destination advertising. *Tourism Management* 18 (3), 127–137.

Meethan, K. (2001) *Tourism in Global Society. Place, Culture, Consumption.* Houndmills and New York: Palgrave.

Mercille, J. (2005) Media effects on image: The case of Tibet. *Annals of Tourism Research* 32 (4), 1039–1055.

Merriam, S. (2002) Introduction to qualitative research. In S. Merriam (ed.) *Qualitative Research in Practice* (pp. 3–17). San Francisco, CA: Wiley & Sons.

Metz, C. (1977) *The Imaginary Signifier. Psychoanalysis and the Cinema* (C. Britton, A. Williams, B. Brewster and A. Guzzetti, trans.). Bloomington, IN: Indiana University Press.

Miller, J. (2003) The hero and the Other. Alternative masculinities and the "dominion of men" in the *Lord of the Rings*. In S. Fendler and U. Horstmann (eds) *Images of Masculinity in Fantasy Fiction* (pp. 183–203). Lewiston, Queenston and Lampeter: The Edwin Mellen Press.

Milman, A. (2001) The future of the theme park and attraction industry: A management perspective. *Journal of Travel Research* 40 (2), 139–147.

Mordue, T. (1999) Heartbeat country: Conflicting values, coinciding visions. *Environment and Planning A* 31 (4), 629–646.

Mordue, T. (2001) Performing and directing residents/tourist cultures in Heartbeat country. *Tourist Studies* 1 (3), 233–252.

Morgan, N. and Pritchard, A. (1998) *Tourism Promotion & Power. Creating Images, Creating Identities.* Chichester: Wiley & Sons.

Morgan, N., Pritchard, A. and Piggott, R. (2002) New Zealand, 100% Pure. The creation of a powerful niche destination brand. *Journal of Brand Management* 9 (4/5), 335–354.

Morkham, B. and Staiff, R. (2002) The cinematic tourist: Perception and subjectivity. In G. Dann (ed.) *The Tourist as a Metaphor of the Social World* (pp. 297–316). Oxon: CABI.

Morley, D. (2000) *Home Territories. Media, Mobility, and Identity.* London and New York: Routledge.

Morley, D. and Robins, K. (1995) *Spaces of Identity. Global Media, Electronic Landscapes and Cultural Boundaries.* New York: Routledge.

Moser, M. (2003) *United We Brand.* Boston, MA: Harvard Business School Press.

Moutinho, L. (1988) Amusement park visitor behaviour – Scottish attitudes. *Tourism Management* 9 (4), 291–300.

Muresan, A. and Smith, K. (1998) Dracula's Castle in Transylvania: Conflicting heritage marketing strategies. *International Journal of Heritage Studies* 4 (2), 73–85.

Murphy, P., Pritchard, M. and Smith, B. (2000) The destination product and its impact on traveller perceptions. *Tourism Management* 21 (1), 43–52.

Neale, S. (1980) *Genre.* London: British Film Institute.

Neale, S. (1994) Tom Kershaw: Everybody knows his name. *Boston Business Journal* 14 (18), page 18.

Neale, S. (1995) Questions of genre. In O. Boyd-Barrett and C. Newbold (eds) *Approaches to Media: A Reader* (pp. 460–472). London: Arnold.

New Zealand Herald (2004) Power of the Ring lures thousands. On WWW at http://www.nzherald.co.nz/storydisplay.cfm?storyID = 3576476&thesection = news&thesubsection = general. Accessed 15.7.04.

Neumann, W.R. (1990) The threshold of public attention. *Public Opinion Quarterly* 54 (2), 159–176.

O'Connor, N. (2002) The effect of television induced tourism on the village of Avoca, County Wicklow. In N. Andrews, S. Flanagan and J. Ruddy (eds) *Tourism Destination Planning* (pp. 145–159). Dublin: Dublin Institute of Technology.

Olsberg/SPI (2007) *Stately Attraction. How Film and Television Programmes Promote Tourism in the UK*. London: Olsberg/SPI.

Ousby, I. (1990) *The Englishman's England. Taste, Travel and the Rise of Tourism*. London: Cambridge University Press.

Oxford Economics (2007) *The Economic Impact of the UK Film Industry*. Oxford: Oxford Economics.

Palmer, C. (2001) Ethnography: A research method in practice. *International Journal of Tourism Research* 3 (4), 301–312.

Papadimitriou, L. (2000) Travelling on screen: Tourism and the Greek film musical. *Journal of Modern Greek Studies* 18 (1), 95–104.

Pearce, D. (1999) Tourism in Paris. Studies at the microscale. *Annals of Tourism Research* 26 (1), 77–97.

Pearce, P.L. (1982) *The Social Psychology of Tourist Behaviour*. Oxford: Pergamon Press.

Pearce, P.L. (1991) Analysing tourist attractions. *The Journal of Tourism Studies* 2 (1), 46–55.

Peckham, R.S. (2004) Landscape in film. In J. Duncan, N. Johnson and R. Schein (eds) *A Companion to Cultural Geography* (pp. 420–429). Malden, Oxford and Carlton: Blackwell.

Peet, R. (1998) *Modern Geographic Thought*. Oxford: Blackwell.

Pennsylvania Dutch Convention & Visitors Bureau (2005) Witness Movie Experience Tours with special press trips to Pennsylvania Dutch Country. On WWW at http://www.airhighways.com/penn2005.htm. Accessed 1.4.05.

Peters, B.G. and Hogwood, B.W. (1985) In search of the issue-attention cycle. *Journal of Politics* 47 (1), 238–253.

Peters, M. and Weiermair, K. (2000) Tourist attractions and attracted tourists: How to satisfy today's 'fickle' tourist clientele? *The Journal of Tourism Studies* 11 (1), 22–29.

Piggott, R., Morgan, N. and Pritchard, A. (2004) New Zealand and The Lord of the Rings: Leveraging public and media relations. In N. Morgan, A. Pritchard and R. Pride (eds) *Destination Branding* (2nd edn.; pp. 207–225). Oxford and Burlington, MA: Elsevier Butterworth- Heinemann.

Pine, B.J. and Gilmore, J.H. (1999) *The Experience Economy*. Harvard, MA: Harvard University Press.

Preston, J. (2000) The touristic implications of film. An examination of the intersection of film and place promotion. MAppSc thesis, University of Lincoln.

Puttnam, D. (1997) *The Undeclared War. The Struggle for Control of the World's Film Industry*. London: Harper Collins.

Pye, M. and Miles, L. (1999) George Lucas. In S. Kline (ed.) *George Lucas Interviews* (pp. 64–86). Jackson, MS: University Press of Mississippi.

Reeves, T. (2001) *The Worldwide Guide to Movie Locations*. Chicago, IL: A Capella Books.

Relph, E. (1976) *Place and Placelessness*. London: Pion Limited.

Richards, G. (2002) Tourism attractions systems. Exploring cultural behaviour. *Annals of Tourism Research* 29 (4), 1048–1064.

Riley, R. and Van Doren, S. (1992) Movies as tourism promotion. *Tourism Management* 13 (3), 267–275.

Riley, R. (1994) Movie-induced tourism. In A.V. Seaton *et al.* (eds) *Tourism – the State of the Art* (pp. 453–458). Chichester: Wiley & Sons.

Riley, R., Baker, D. and Van Doren, C. (1998) Movie induced tourism. *Annals of Tourism Research* 25 (4), 919–935.

Ritchie, B. (1984) Assessing the impact of hallmark events: Conceptual and research issues. *Journal of Travel Research* 23 (1), 2–11.

Ritchie, B. and Goeldner, C. (1994) *Travel, Tourism, and Hospitality Research. A Handbook for Managers and Researchers*. New York: Wiley & Sons.

Robinson, M. (2002) Between and beyond the pages: Literature–tourism relationships. In H-C. Andersen and M. Robinson (eds) *Literature and Tourism. Reading and Writing Tourism Texts* (pp. 39–79). New York: Continuum.

Robinson, M. and Andersen, H-C. (2002) Reading between the lines: Literature and the creation of touristic spaces. In H-C. Andersen and M. Robinson (eds) *Literature and Tourism. Reading and Writing Tourism Texts* (pp. 1–38). New York: Continuum.

Roest, H., Pieters, R. and Koelemeijer, K. (1997) Satisfaction with amusement parks. *Annals of Tourism Research* 24 (4), 1001–1005.

Rojek, C. (1993) *Ways of Escape. Modern Transformations in Leisure and Travel*. Lanham, MD: Rowman & Littlefield.

Rose, G. (1994) The cultural politics of place: Local representation and oppositional discourse in two films. *Transactions: Institute of British Geographers* 19 (1), 46–60.

Rose, G. (1995) Place and identity: A sense of place. In D. Massey and P. Jess (eds) *A Place in the World?* (pp. 87–132). New York: Oxford University Press.

Rushmore Tours (no date) Fort Hays Dances with Wolves Film Set. On WWW at http://www.rushmoretours.com. Accessed 6.10.05.

Ryglova, K. and Turcinkova, J. (2004) Image as an Important Factor of Destination Management. Working Papers of the Finnish Forest Research Institute 2. On WWW at http://www.metla.fi/julkaisut/workingpapers/2004/mwp002.htm. Accessed 20.10.05.

Salzburg Panorama Tours (2005) Tour participant survey data 2004 and 2005. Received from the company by fax.

San Francisco Film Commission (2008) San Francisco and the movies. On WWW at http://www.sfgov/site/filmcomm_page.asp?id = 33671. Accessed 6.10.08.

Schatz, T. (2003) The new Hollywood. In J. Stringer (ed.) *Movie Blockbusters* (pp. 15–44). London: Routledge.

Schindlmayr, T. (2001) The media, public opinion and population assistance: Establishing the link. *Family Planning Perspectives* 33 (3), 128–132.

Schofield, P. (1996) Cinematographic images of a city. Alternative heritage tourism in Manchester. *Tourism Management* 17 (5), 333–340.

Schramm, W. and Roberts, D. (eds) (1974) *The Process and Effects of Mass Communication*. Urbana, Chicago, IL and London: University of Illinois Press.

Sciolino, E. (2003) Cinematography meets Geography in Montmartre. *New York Times*, 10 August, pp. 5–8.

Scottish Tourist Board (1997) *Film Tourism: Business Guidelines for the Tourist Industry*. Edinburgh: Scottish Tourist Board.

Seibert, T. (2004) Troja hofft auf Touristen. *Nürnberger Nachrichten*, 7 June, p. 6.

Seidman, I. (1998) *Interviewing as Qualitative Research*. New York and London: Teachers College Press.

Selby, M. and Morgan, N.J. (1996) Reconstruing place image. A case study of its role in destination market research. *Tourism Management* 17 (4), 287–294.

Shenk, D. (1997) *Data Smog. Surviving the Information Glut*. San Francisco, CA: Harper Edge.

Silver, I. (1993) Marketing authenticity in Third World countries. *Annals of Tourism Research* 20 (4), 302–318.

Singh, K. (2003) Film-induced tourism: Motivations to the Hobbiton movie set as featured in The Lord of the Rings. BB (Hons) thesis, La Trobe University.

Sirgy, J.M. and Su, C. (2000) Destination image, self-congruity, and travel behaviour: Toward an integrative model. *Journal of Travel Research* 38 (4), 340–352.

Skillings, P. (2009) The Empire State Building. Trivia and fun facts about New York's tallest skyscraper. On WWW at http://www.manhattan.about.com/od/historylandmark/a/empirestate.htm. Accessed 6.10.05.

Smith, M. (2003) *Issues in Cultural Tourism Studies*. New York: Routledge.

Sonder, M. (2004) *Event, Entertainment and Production*. Hoboken, NJ: Wiley & Sons.

Stafford, B. (1997) *Good Looking. Essays on the Virtue of Images* (2nd edn). Cambridge and London: MIT Press.

Stam, R. (1992) Beyond fidelity: The dialogics of adaptation. In J. Orr and C. Nickolson (eds) *Cinema and Fiction: New Modes of Adapting, 1950–1990* (pp. 54–76). Edinburgh: Edinburgh University Press.

Sterry, P. (1998) Serial soap addiction. From screen viewing to pilgrimage. In J.M. Fladmark (ed.) *In Search of Heritage as Pilgrim or Tourists?* (pp. 363–373). Shaftsbury: Downhead Publishing Limited.

Stoddart, V.G. (2003) Under a Tuscan spell; Cortona, Italy, basks in the twin suns of Frances Mayes' best seller and film. *USA Today*, 26 September, p. D.01.

Strasser, C. (2000) *The Sound of Music* – Ein unbekannter Welterfolg. In G. Keul and U. Kammerhofer-Aggermann (eds) *The Sound of Music, zwischen Mythos und Marketing* (pp. 267–293). Salzburger Beiträge zur Volkskunde, Band 11. Salzburg: Salzburger Institut für Landeskunde.

STUFF (2004) Jackson's fantasy to bring NZ real gold. On WWW at http://www.stuff.co.nz/stuff/0,2106,2833180a2202,00.html. Accessed 8.3.04.

Swales, J. (1990) *Genre Analysis*. Cambridge: Cambridge University Press.

Swanson, G.E. (1978) Travels through inner space: Family structure and openness to absorbing experience. *American Journal of Sociology* 83 (4), 890–919.

Tatara, P. (1998) An ode to joy. The ten best films of the Top 100. On WWW at http://www.cnn.com/SHOWBIZ/Movies/9806/20/tatara.top.100. Accessed 11.10.05.

Tenbrock, N. (2005) Film und Tourismus. Zusammenhänge zwischen Film und Tourismus unter besonderer Berücksichtigung der Auswirkungen der Herr der Ringe-Filme auf den Tourismus in Neuseeland. PGDipEcon thesis, Fachhochschule Gelsenkirchen.

The Economist (1999) Movie tourism in the USA Midwest. On WWW at http://www.uwec.edu/geography/Ivogeler/w188/articles/movies.htm. Accessed 4.5.05.

Thrift, N. (1996) *Spatial Formations*. London: Sage.
Thrift, N. (2003) Space: The fundamental stuff of human geography. In S. Holloway, S. Rice and G. Valentine (eds) *Key Concepts in Geography* (pp. 95–108). London: Sage.
Tooke, N. and Baker, M. (1996) Seeing is believing: The effect of film on visitor numbers to screened locations. *Tourism Management* 17 (2), 87–94.
Torchin, L. (2002) Location, location, location. The destination of the Manhattan TV Tour. *Tourist Studies* 2 (3), 247–266.
Tourism New Zealand (2003a) *Lord of the Rings Market Research Summary Report*. Wellington: Tourism New Zealand.
Tourism New Zealand (2003b) Impact of the *Lord of the Rings* film trilogy. Unpublished document, received from Tourism New Zealand by email.
Tourism New Zealand (2004) Brits send tourists Potty. *Tourism News*, May, p. 4.
Turan, K. (2002) *Sundance to Sarajevo. Film Festivals and the World they made*. Los Angeles, CA and London: University of California Press.
Tzanelli, R. (2001) Casting the Neohellenic Other: Tourism, the culture industry, and contemporary Orientalism in *Captain Corelli's Mandolin*. *Journal of Consumer Culture* 3 (2), 217–244.
Urry, J. (1990) *The Tourist Gaze*. London: Sage.
Urry, J. (1995) *Consuming Places*. London: Routledge.
Venture Taranaki (2004a) The Last Samurai. The Articles. On WWW at http://www.venture.org.nz/searchnews/samurai.php?subaction = showfull&id = 1050961621. Accessed 7.10.05.
Venture Taranaki (2004b) *Economic Impact Assessment for the Filming of The Last Samurai in Taranaki*. Taranaki: Venture Taranaki.
Vialkowitsch, A. (2005) Vom Location Placement zum Filmtourismus. Neue Perspektiven für das Destinationsmarketing. In J. Maschke (ed.) *Jahrbuch für Fremdenverkehr* (pp. 7–54). München: DWIF.
Villa Trapp GmbH (2008) Press release on the opening of the Trapp Villa.
VisitBritain (2008) Excerpt from the 2005 National Brand Index. Received via email.
Waggoner, M. (2005) Fans flock to North Carolina's movie sites. On WWW at http://www.suntimes.com/output/travel/tra-news-northcaro20.html. Accessed 4.5.05.
Walmsley, D.J. and Young, M. (1998) Evaluative images and tourism: The use of personal constructs to describe the structure of destination images. *Journal of Travel Research* 36 (3), 65–69.
Wang, N. (1999) Rethinking authenticity in tourism experience. *Annals of Tourism Research* 26 (2), 349–370.
Warren, S. and Thompson, W. (2000) New Zealand 100% Pure. *Locum Destination Review* 1, 22–26.
Weta Workshop (2009) Weta Cast Episode IX, podcast, May 2009.
Winter, T. (2002) Angkor Meets Tomb Raider: Setting the scene. *International Journal of Heritage Studies* 8 (4), 323–336.
Wright, R. (2004) Tourism in Rural Rohan: An investigative and comparative study into the impacts of the *Lord of the Rings* tourism in two rural New Zealand communities. PGDipTour thesis, University of Otago.
Yeabsley, J. and Duncan, I. (2002) *Scoping the Lasting Effects of the Lord of the Rings*. Wellington and Auckland: New Zealand Institute of Economic Research.
Yin, R. (2003) *Case Study Research. Designs and Methods*. London: Sage.
Young, I.M. (1990) The ideal of community and the politics of difference. In L. Nicholson (ed.) *Feminism/Postmodernism*. London: Routledge.
Zukin, S. (1995) *The Cultures of Cities*. Oxford: Blackwell.

Personal Interviews/Personal Communication

Avery, P. (2005) 15 February. Manager Film Venture Taranaki.

Heath, M. (2005) 3 March. Owner of Southern Lakes Sightseeing.

Herzl, S. (2005) 10 September. Owner of Salzburg Panorama Tours.

Radcliffe, S. (2005) 14 February. Owner of Last Samurai Village Tours.

Tennent, P. (2005) 14 February. Mayor of the city of New Plymouth.

Welch, S. (2008) 20 September. Head of 2012 and Partnerships, Visit Britain.

LOTR tour guide I (2005) Southern Lakes Sightseeing, 5 March.

LOTR tour guide II (2005) Southern Lakes Sightseeing, 10 March.